CONTENTS

Foreword by John McEuen ix

Introduction: How This Book Was Born xi
   Is This Book for You? xii
   How This Book Is Organized xii
   How to Get the Most from This Book xiii

Overview: Music, Business, and Integrity Go Hand in Hand xv
   The Band Story xv
   Why the Media Doesn't Help Matters xvi
   Real-World Success Stories xvii

Section One: The Art of Making Good Decisions 1

Chapter One: Why Are You in the Music Business? 3
   The Five Motivations 3
   Key Concepts and Definitions 4
   The Profit Motive: A Basic Issue for Music People 7
   How to Write a Mission Statement 7
   Writing it Down Is Liberating 9

Chapter Two: How Do You Start a Music Business? 13
   The Two Strategic Questions 13
   Risk vs. Reward 14
   Why the Concept of Risk Is So Important 15
   Three Key Elements in Any Music Business 15
   Three Things to Do Before Going into Business 17

Chapter Three: The Bird's-Eye View of the Music Marketplace 19
   How Big Is the Music Industry? 19
   How Businesses Are Organized for Tax and Legal Purposes 20
   Corporate vs. Independent Music Businesses: Myths and Realities 21

Changing Business Models: Record Company vs. Music Company 22
Who Is the Customer in the Music Business? 22
The Two Kinds of Competition 23
The Threat of Indirect Competition 23

Chapter Four: Risk Analysis—When to Quit Your Day Job 27
How Do You Feel About Risk? 27
Is Anyone Buying What I'm Selling? 28
Where Will I Get the Money? 29
Where You *Won't* Get the Money 30
Who Will Handle the Five Key Aspects of the Business? 31
When to Quit Your Day Job 32

Section Two: Creating Your Essential Business Plan 35

Chapter Five: Why Have a Business Plan? 37
Eight Benefits of Writing down Your Plan 38
"It Seems Like a Lot of Work . . ." 41

Chapter Six: What's in a Business Plan? 43
The Memory System Doesn't Work 43
The Five "Chapters" of Your Business Plan 44
A Note About Assumptions 45
What Do Those Percentages Represent? 45
Why Marketing Is Number One 46
How Long and Detailed Is a Business Plan? 47
Your Plan's "Sixth Chapter": The Appendix or Reference Section 47

Chapter Seven: The Planning Flow—From Intention to Action 51
The Right Planning Sequence Makes a Difference 51
Plan Element 1: The Mission Statement 51
Plan Element 2: The Brand Positioning Statement 52
Plan Element 3: The Three-Year Product Plan 55
Plan Element 4: The Operating Plan 56
Plan Element 5: The Daily Action List 57

Section Three: Building Your Brand 61

Chapter Eight: Marketing and Sales Are the Keys to Your Success 63
Competing for Attention 64
What Is Marketing and How Is It Different from Sales? 65

SUCCEEDING in MUSIC
SECOND EDITION

Business Chops For Performers & Songwriters

BY JOHN STIERNBERG

HAL•LEONARD®

Hal Leonard Books
An Imprint of Hal Leonard Corporation
New York

Published in 2008 by Hal Leonard Books
An Imprint of Hal Leonard Corporation
7777 West Bluemound Road
Milwaukee, WI 53213

Trade Book Division Editorial Offices
19 West 21st Street, New York, NY 10010

Printed in the United States of America

Book design by Stephen Ramirez

Library of Congress Cataloging-in-Publication Data is available upon request.

ISBN 978-1-4234-5699-5

www.halleonard.com

The Four Functions of Marketing 65
A Note on Branding. 66
The Four Functions of Sales 67
The Seven Links in the Marketing Chain 68

Chapter Nine: Developing Your Product Strategy 71
Music Industry Products: Examples of Goods and Services 71
Jack of All Trades, Master of Some 72
Your Product Mix Changes Over Time 73
Understanding Product Life Cycles—The Six Phases 74
How Long Does Each Phase Last? 76

Chapter Ten: Your Pricing Strategy 79
An Agent's Tale 79
Charging What the Market Will Bear—Three Factors 79
The Three Basic Pricing Strategies 81
Changing Prices and Revenue Planning 83
What Typically Happens in the Music Industry 84
How to Avoid Pricing Problems and Optimize Revenue 85

Chapter Eleven: Promotion, Branding,and Advertising 87
A Word About Branding. 87
The Promotional Toolbox—Ten Types of Tools. 88
Three Key Questions About Your Promotional Strategy 95

Chapter Twelve: Your Place of Business 99
Why Place Is a Marketing Strategy 99
The Pros and Cons of Home Offices. 102
Your Evolving Place Strategy 103

Chapter Thirteen: Portrait of a Salesforce 105
Everyone Plays a Sales Role. 105
What if I Don't Like the Idea of Sales? 106
A Word About Integrity 106
Characteristics of a Great Salesperson—The "Three C's". 107
The Ideal Sales Rep. 107
What Great Salespeople Look for in a Music "Product" 109

Chapter Fourteen: The Who, What, When, Where, Why,
and How of Your Customers 113
Understanding Buyer Characteristics. 113
A Word About Style: The Blues Brothers Example 114
Buying Habits and Preferences. 115

Individual vs. Institutional Customers 116
What About Non-Viable Customers? 116
How to Slice the Pie 117
Developing Your Target Customer Profile 118
Don't Let Your "Deal-Breakers" Put You Out of Business 119

Chapter Fifteen: Understanding Your Competition 121
The Competitive Environment 121
Identifying Your Direct Competitors 122
Understanding Indirect Competition 122
Exercise: Identify Your Top Five Direct and Indirect Competitors 123
Why Indirect Competition Is Scarier than Direct Competition 124
Competitive Strengths, Weaknesses, Opportunities, and Threats 125
Your Competitive Intelligence System 125
Your Competitive Database 126
Using the Seven Links 127

**Section Four: Applying the Fundamentals in Your
Music Business** 131

**Chapter Sixteen: Doing the Numbers—Setting Realistic Goals
and Objectives** 133
The Importance of Goals and Objectives 133
Quick Review: How Are Goals Different from Objectives? 133
Setting Goals in Three Categories 134
Exercise 1: Your Three-Year Goals 136
Turning Goals into Objectives: When in Doubt, Quantify 138
Three Key Questions About Setting Objectives 138
What's Actually Achievable? 139
The Schoolteacher Paradigm 139
How to Forecast Sales Revenue 140
Using the Five-Year Window™ to Forecast Revenue 141
Exercise 2: Your Three-Year Objectives 142
The Lure of the Entertainment Industry—Are My Goals Realistic? 143
Sharing Your Goals with Others 143
A Word of Caution 144

**Chapter Seventeen: Common Sense Business Lessons
for the Uncommon World of Music** 147
Lesson 1: "When in doubt, quantify." 147
Lesson 2: "The chain is only as strong as the weakest link." 148

Lesson 3: "The business stuff—especially sales—
    is a full-time job." 149
Lesson 4: "Build on strengths and delegate the weaknesses." 150
Lesson 5: "Understand your customers and give them
    what they want, plus a little more." 151
Lesson 6: "Understand your competitors and
    differentiate yourself from them." 152

Chapter Eighteen: Putting It All Together 155
Section One: The Art of Making Good Decisions 155
Section Two: Creating Your Essential Business Plan 155
Section Three: Building Your Brand 155
Section Four: Applying the Business Fundamentals
    in Your Music Business 156
Your Business Planning Checklist 156
Where Can I Get the Cash I Need to Build My Business? 157
Frequently Asked Questions About Business Plans 157

**Chapter Nineteen: Words of Encouragement—
More Common Sense Lessons** 163
Lesson 1: "Planning is your first and best business investment." 163
Lesson 2: "No product sells itself." 164
Lesson 3: "Artistic integrity and commercial viability
    are intrinsically compatible." 165
Lesson 4: "The biggest marketing challenge is
    standing out from the competition." 166
Lesson 5: "It's okay to be risk-averse." 166
Applying What You've Learned 167

**Chapter Twenty: A Look to the Future:
Perspectives on Our Evolving Industry** 169
Records vs. Music 169
Digital vs. Analog 170
The Value of a Song 170
Multiple Revenue Streams 170
Record Company vs. Music Company 171
Diversity Is Good 171
Is It Just Me? 172
Where Is It All Headed? 172

Epilogue: Two Key Questions Revisited 175
Three Final Points 175

Section Five: Reference, Worksheets, and Resources 177

Reference Section. 179
    Sample Business Plan 179
    Worksheets 179
    Resources 180

Sample Business Plan 181
    "Our Band" Business Plan. 181

Worksheets and Checklists 195
    Risk Analysis Checklist 195
    Goals and Objectives: Using The Five-Year Window Tool 200

Resources 211
    Glossary of Key Terms, Concepts, and Buzzwords. 211
    For Further Study: Twelve Classic (or Soon-to-Be Classic)
        Business Books 218
    Music Industry Reference Books. 219
    Web Resources 219
    CD-ROM Contents 220
    Index 221

FOREWORD
BY JOHN MCEUEN

I wish I had access to a book like this in 1966 when I signed my first major-label contract (Liberty Records, a four-album cross-collateralized deal). Had *Succeeding in Music* been around—and had I taken what I was doing with my life seriously—in the following ten years I would have made *and collected* about $150,000 more than I did.

When someone asks me, "How can I make it as a singer?" I always advise vocal coaching. And to those who want to enter the music business, I say, "Either study all you can about it, or make enough money to hire a great lawyer to keep you from losing what you make. However, most musicians (songwriters and performers) I know spend more money on health clubs and skiing lessons than on vocal coaching or business consulting. But have you ever seen a great athlete without at least one coach?

You are the business, like a farmer looking for a grocery outlet for his produce. You create things that you hope others will love, but it is *your* responsibility to get those creations to market. It is also your responsibility to make sure that the money earned goes to you. Rest assured the companies you get involved with will be looking out for their best interests, not yours.

The music business has taken me from the Northern Lights to Japan to Georgia (both U.S.A. and Soviet Union) and to more than 5,000 shows. You can make your own rules, as I and many others have, but the sooner you know *their* rules, the better off you will be. It is not easy; it's almost always challenging. It's usually fun—and it can be quite profitable. But as the salesman in *The Music Man* says, "You gotta know the territory!" *Succeeding in Music* is the map of that territory. This book will give you many more hours to devote to your music and your success in it while helping you avoid countless hours of mistakes.

A founding member of the Nitty Gritty Dirt Band, John McEuen is an award-winning musician, producer, performer, and composer whose work graces movies and television scores, as well as dozens of CDs. His latest recording is Round Trip [Rural Rhythm Records]. You can find out more about John at ***www.johnmceuen.com***.

HOW THIS BOOK WAS BORN

In 1998, I was invited to present a seminar on business planning at the annual convention of the International Bluegrass Music Association. Nancy Cardwell, my contact at IBMA, explained that the audience represented the whole range of music people: bandleaders, musicians, agents, managers, record label personnel, concert and festival promoters, broadcasters, songwriters, publishers, and journalists.

"Do they *want* to learn about business planning?" I asked, recalling how most of my music friends and colleagues over the years had avoided learning business fundamentals.

"We don't know. We've never offered this type of seminar," was Nancy's answer.

There were courses and panel discussions on getting bookings, understanding music publishing and royalties, recording and producing your own record, signing with a record label, being a better broadcaster, increasing ticket sales at festivals, and using e-mail as a promotional tool. All good stuff, but all assuming that the audience already had an understanding of the business fundamentals of planning, marketing, finance, and management.

Wanting to contribute to the business education of music people, I rose to the challenge and accepted the invitation. I prepared worksheets, reference materials, and slides for the overhead projector. I rehearsed. I mentally prepared for no one to show up, or for the audience response to be lukewarm. I was delighted when the room filled up and participants became eagerly engaged in the topic: "Constructing a Business Plan: Adapting Common Business Sense to the Uncommon Art of Bluegrass." I got a standing ovation at the end.

"Wow," I thought, "I've struck a nerve here." In fact, several of those original seminar attendees asked if I had written a book on the topic. Over the next year, I developed and presented additional live seminars and did a lot of research. I began to see that the *fundamentals of business* are relevant to *all music people*, regardless of industry role or music genre. That realization is what led to the book you are reading now. I continue to be inspired by music seminar audiences, and am driven to bridge the gap between musical creativity and commerce.

I did Internet searches on keywords like "music business" and "business planning." Hundreds of listings turned up. They fell into two main categories:

Category 1: The general business books, which cover the business fundamentals we will present here. The content of these books is relevant, but they do not cite *music* business examples, and consequently can be boring, intimidating, or even insulting to music people.

Category 2: The music industry books, which cover topics ranging from negotiating a recording contract to eating healthy while on the road. *Succeeding in Music* provides the business foundation you need to get more out of this type of material.

In fact, this book bridges the gap between the two categories. It presents the fundamentals of business planning and marketing, which are essential for business success, but emphasizes the unique challenges facing music people in the twenty-first century.

IS THIS BOOK FOR YOU?

If you are involved in the music industry—or just thinking about becoming involved, this book is for you. The primary focus is on two types of music people:

- Musicians of all kinds active in all styles of music
- Performing and non-performing songwriters and composers

The anecdotes, business lessons, examples, and worksheets provided in this book are geared to the groups listed above. However, the fundamentals of business covered here are relevant to *all* music people, including:

- Booking agents, managers, and artist representatives
- Promoters and presenters of events, ranging from church coffeehouses to major festivals
- Record producers and record label personnel
- Music teachers and coaches
- Amateur musicians considering turning pro
- Music business students
- Music technicians including roadies, recording engineers, and gearheads
- Partners, spouses, friends, and parents of the above.

HOW THIS BOOK IS ORGANIZED

Succeeding in Music includes four main sections plus a Reference Section and a companion CD-ROM. It flows from the general to the specific, with key business terms and concepts defined and illustrated along the way.

- Section One: The Art of Making Good Decisions
- Section Two: Creating Your Essential Business Plan

- Section Three: Building Your Brand
- Section Four: Practicing the Fundamentals in Your Music Business

The Reference Section at the end of the book and the CD-ROM provide worksheets, exercises, planning templates, a glossary, and resources for more information.

What you *won't* find here are gimmicks, "diet pills," and get-rich-quick schemes, or material that is readily available elsewhere (like the many excellent books on music publishing, performing, songwriting, concert promotion, etc.).

Succeeding in Music is designed to be read relatively quickly and easily. This leaves you with more time to apply your new knowledge without struggling through arcane references and hyper-academic language.

HOW TO GET THE MOST FROM THIS BOOK

Everyone learns differently, so there is no single best way to enjoy this book. That said, here are suggestions for getting optimum results:

Review the table of contents. See how the book is put together and where it's going. That will help you decide which sections to focus on (and hopefully inspire you to read the whole book).

Think about what you most want to get out of this book. Do you want to clarify basic business terms and concepts? Do you want to start writing a business plan or marketing plan? Trying to decide if you should go into or stay in the music business? Need to get inspired to advance to the next level? The opportunity for each of these is here.

Quickly read the whole book once before digging into individual exercises (risk analysis, mission statement, business plan, etc.). This puts everything into perspective before you start making decisions and getting specific.

Focus on the sections that mean the most for your specific situation. For example, if you are already in the music business full-time, the "When to Quit Your Day Job" section may be irrelevant—although many have said, "I wish I knew that before I got into the business." If you are one of the fortunate few who already have a written business plan, focus on the practical applications and compare the concepts and templates provided here to the ones you know.

For a quick preview—and review—of the book, turn to the "Key Points in This Chapter" section at the end of each chapter. These are designed for concept reinforcement and ready reference.

Plan to have a little fun. Many music people are initially put off by the business side of the business. But once they get into it, they realize that business is rewarding beyond making a living—it's a different way to be creative. I've tried to capture that spirit here without sounding too corny or idealistic. In any case, keep a sense of humor and perspective throughout.

Now, on with the show, and good luck!

MUSIC, BUSINESS, AND INTEGRITY GO HAND IN HAND

Music is a vital part of world culture. Music is everywhere we turn, from the ubiquitous mobile media players to the background music we hear in restaurants and office buildings, to live stadium shows featuring major stars. Whether music is performed live, recorded for sale as records or digital downloads, broadcast on radio or television, or streamed on the Internet, a team—people other than the original composer or performer—is needed to make it happen. Without the business teams of the music industry, music would not reach the ears of its global audience.

Why mention this? Because so many music people, including performers and songwriters, think that they can do it all themselves, and that they need to "sell out" or sacrifice artistic integrity to be financially successful. This unfortunate scenario seems to happen all too frequently, and with negative consequences. Can you relate to the following scenario?

THE BAND STORY

Four musicians start a band, buy stage equipment with their life savings (and their spouse's credit cards), and soon quit their day jobs to rehearse and look for bookings. While the music sounds great, at first they have a hard time getting paid gigs. After a year or so, they are performing regularly, but still using performance revenue primarily to make equipment payments.

Another year goes by. Traveling a little bit now, the band sleeps in their van or stays with friends, unable to afford better accommodations on the road. One band member quits due to "family pressure" (spouse wants more quality time and a "real life"). The remaining members decide to go three-piece for a while.

Even though the band has invested in making a self-produced record and is working pretty regularly, they are only able to pay themselves a small amount of money once in a while. Relationships start to wear thin, both in the group and with family, friends, and fans. The shows aren't fun any more, and the audience can feel it. Attendance and record sales decline. After three years of ups and downs, the band calls it quits.

You can read in all you want about the rest of the negative stuff: divorce, substance abuse, bad credit, bitterness, and disillusionment. As we shall discuss later, this all-too-common scenario does not have to end this way.

Here are other brief examples, relating to the same band story:

- Booking agent/manager. After a few months of finding their own bookings, the band decided it needed an agent and manager to "handle the business stuff" so the band could focus on performing and recording. They got the wife of one of the band members to "handle the money" and a friend to "look for gigs." While these people were dedicated at first, they quickly became overwhelmed with their duties—in addition to their other jobs and family responsibilities—but kept at it out of loyalty to the band.

- Record producer. Unable to attract the interest of a professional record company, the band decided to produce its own CD. With little recording experience and less business sense, they found another former musician who had a recording studio in his basement. "Let's start our own record company. We can sell CDs at gigs and downloads on the Internet." When the band broke up, the producer still had half of the original shipment of discs from the manufacturer and never recouped his investment in the band.

If you are a performer, songwriter, or play any other role in the music industry, I'm sure you can think of your own horror stories. The basic problem is this: Music people leap into the business with little or no business knowledge or experience. They believe that their musical chops, sweat, and sincerity are all they need to draw a crowd, book lots of show dates, sell records, get rich, and be famous. Sorry, it doesn't work that way.

WHY THE MEDIA DOESN'T HELP MATTERS

The general public (including you and me) gets most of its music industry information from popular media, ranging from *USA Today* to *Rolling Stone* magazine to VH1's *Celebrity Rehab* series. Television shows like *American Idol* and *Making the Band* send the message that virtually anyone can become rich and famous in the music business. We hear primarily about the *exceptions* and the fringes of the industry, not the mainstream. For example:

- Opera singer Luciano Pavarotti (1935–2007) was reportedly paid $1 million per performance.
- The Rolling Stones grossed over $550 million in two years (2006-07) during their "Bigger Bang" tour, setting an all-time record and performing for three generations of fans worldwide. The band had been together over forty years at the time.
- Garth Brooks sells 100 million albums in ten years and retires.

- Beyoncé Knowles, originally a member of the all-time best-selling female group, Destiny's Child, continues to build a solo career as singer, recording artist, actress, producer, and fashion designer.
- U2 sells out tours worldwide after twenty-five years with the same band lineup, all while campaigning valiantly for humanitarian causes.
- Bob Marley's estate accounts for a high percentage of Jamaica's gross national product years after his premature death.
- B.B. King wins a Grammy award and performs over 200 show dates per year at age eighty.

And on and on. We also hear about the negative extremes. Famous musicians die of substance abuse. Personal managers and accountants are sued for taking advantage of superstars' fortunes. Record label people go to jail for bribery and conspiracy related to radio airplay. Pop stars' personal lives are chronicled in the media daily, from stints in rehab to custody battles to tax fraud. It's tabloid journalism and it's everywhere.

Why mention all this? Because most people get their first exposure to the music industry through television, radio, the Internet, and stories like those cited above. We have to wade through the exceptions to find examples of mainstream music business activity—the stuff that really happens day in and day out to good people who make a living and enjoy a fine career in music.

I bring this up now to assure you this book is about business fundamentals for all music people, and not about how to be one of the exceptions.

REAL-WORLD SUCCESS STORIES

There are an estimated three million people working in the music industry worldwide. The vast majority deal with music day in and day out and succeed commercially and artistically; they are not among the "exceptions." This does not include the literally millions (!) of performers, songwriters, and bands with MySpace pages, doing music for fun or to see where it takes them. Don't get me wrong. Anyone can potentially become a superstar, as has been proven so many times. The point is that you can enjoy your part of the music business without enduring that constant "do or die" pressure inflicted upon us by the media. Measure your success using your own set of criteria, rather than anyone else's.

Here are a few examples of successful music industry professionals:

- Working musicians. Whether you are a symphony member, society band leader, performing songwriter, touring sideman, session pro, military band member, or part of a house band at a theme park or casino, there are plenty of opportunities for full-time career players.
- Agents and managers. Someone needs to get the bookings and handle the business affairs, especially people who represent full-time performers.

- Record labels. Despite the troubles of the so-called "majors," hundreds of independent record labels have proven that they do not need million-selling hit records to stay in business and make a living. Consider the many labels that have extensive catalogs that never go out of print and keep music people employed year after year.
- Music teachers. In addition to those who work in public and private schools, colleges, and conservatories with music programs, there are thousands of private music teachers who work in music stores and home studios.
- Music publishers, songwriters, composers, concert and event promoters, publicists, recording engineers, producers, music video directors, stage and instrument technicians—the list goes on.

There are hybrid situations too. Many music people combine activity in several of the areas mentioned above, patch it all together, and do just fine. Consider the following:

- The performing songwriter who records and earns money from royalties, record sales, and show dates.
- The studio musician who tours occasionally as a sideman and teaches privately.
- The managers who own record labels and handle the publishing and merchandising of the artists they represent.
- The event promoters who have record labels, syndicated radio, television, and Webcasting operations tied to their events.
- The online merchants who sell records, tour merchandise, memorabilia, and collectibles via eBay or their own sites.

What unifies these people and the industry is a love of music and the desire to make a good living by doing what they love. Exceptions notwithstanding, music people have high integrity, positive values, and generally want to succeed. Sound corny? No, it's just like any other creative or technical field. People get into art, film, dance, theater, graphic design, photography, videography, creative writing, or scientific research for the same set of creative, financial, and personal reasons.

Here's the point. Music, business, and integrity go hand-in-hand. They are not mutually exclusive. Business skills are learned skills just like reading music, singing, or recording. You develop business "chops" with practice, just as you do musical skills. While some people think that you have to be born with either musical talent or an aptitude for business, both can be learned at any age.

To bring this point home, here is Stiernberg's "Business Chops Philosophy."

1. Musical integrity and commercial viability are intrinsically compatible. You can have both. This means you can make great music and a great living at the same time without fear of compromising one for the other.

2. Business chops are learned skills just like musical or technical chops. You had to practice to become a great singer, instrumentalist, engineer, conductor, or songwriter. You can learn the technique (chops) of business just like you learned to play an instrument or operate studio gear.

3. In order to understand the music business, you first need to understand business. In the last century, too many music people left the business stuff to other people and learned to regret it. In the twenty-first century every professional music person needs a basic understanding of business fundamentals, just like you need to know how to use a computer or drive a car.

Learning and applying the fundamentals of business to your specific situation is what this book is all about.

KEY POINTS IN THIS CHAPTER

1. Music is everywhere; it is a vital part of world culture.

2. Many music people leap into the industry without training or experience in the business aspects of music. The problems revealed in The Band Story scenario can be prevented.

3. Most people get their music business news from the popular media: magazines, television, radio, and the Internet. We hear mainly about the exceptions, not the mainstream. There are far more music business opportunities than the media report.

4. The music industry is a global business involving over three-million professionals, not including millions of aspiring musicians, songwriters, and bands. There are plenty of success stories beyond the superstars and behind-the-scenes moguls, and there are many possible career paths, including hybrids.

5. Music people are unified by their love of music and their desire to make a good living by doing what they love.

6. There is no need to fear "selling out" in order to enjoy a successful career in music. Great music and great business go hand-in-hand.

7. Business chops are learned skills just like musical or technical chops.

8. Business problems in the music industry can be prevented. By first understanding the fundamentals of business, you will gain a better understanding of the music business. A little knowledge goes a long way.

THE ART OF MAKING GOOD DECISIONS

CHAPTER ONE

WHY ARE YOU IN THE MUSIC BUSINESS?

E veryone in the music business has different aspirations and motivations. Consequently, each of us is likely to answer the "why" question a little differently. Still, motivations fall into five primary categories:

THE FIVE MOTIVATIONS

1. **Make a living.** This ranges from "pay the bills" to "get rich." Some people are motivated primarily by money or financial need, but everyone needs some source of income. For those of us who are not independently wealthy, the prospect of making a living by doing something we love, like working in music, is a positive motivator.

2. **Fulfill a dream.** "I've always wanted to do something in music," or "If only I could be in the industry doing music full-time . . ." Some of us want to see our name on the marquee, on records, or in the *Billboard* charts. Others aspire to business or technical support roles, but still want to be involved in music as a career.

3. **Create a legacy.** "When I'm gone I want people to remember my music (or influence on the music industry)." Looking a little further into the future, some of us are motivated by the idea of creating a company or a body of work that takes on an identity or a "life of its own."

4. **Benefit other people.** This ranges from "Take care of my family financially" to "Inspire others." Some of us focus on our immediate family and friends while others are driven to benefit the broader music community or society as a whole.

5. **Adrenaline rush.** "There's no other feeling like the energy coming from a crowd during a show." This applies whether you are on stage, backstage, or in the audience, and it can also be a positive motivator.

A possible sixth category is "all of the above." See how this sounds to you.

- "I've always wanted to do something with music that will benefit mankind—the big audience out there. If I'm successful, I'll make a good living along the way and be remembered as a positive influence on the world. When I hear the applause after one of my performances (or that of someone I'm supporting), I remember what it's all about—the music."

Sound idealistic? Maybe so, but a whole lot better than, "Oh well, I might as well get a job in the music factory because it's better than working the counter at McDonald's for minimum wage all my life."

KEY CONCEPTS AND DEFINITIONS

Before we get into the first fundamental business planning exercise (writing a mission statement), let's establish a common vocabulary. The following words and concepts will recur throughout this book. You'll also hear them on the street or in business situations. Note: Key words and concepts are included in the glossary in the Reference Section and on the CD-ROM that accompanies this book.

Hobby vs. Career

Is music your hobby, or do you want to pursue it as a career? "That depends on what you mean." Here's what I mean:

- Hobby: leisure activity; something done for fun
- Career: business activity or occupation; something done to make a living

Can you have fun while you make a living? Sure—they are not mutually exclusive, but they are different enough that it is important to make a distinction. Some music people turn a hobby into a career while others do just the opposite.

Full-time vs. Part-time

As in virtually every other field of endeavor, music people can work at their respective roles to varying degrees in terms of time spent. While many devote all of their professional energy to music in some way, others do something else as a primary source of income (your "day job") and supplement that with music. Working definitions:

- Full-time: geared to making 100 percent of financial income; implies focus and dedication.
- Part-time: dividing time and focus among various pursuits or sources of income.

Amateur vs. Professional

Just as the time factor does not refer to the quality of the results, nor does the "amateur versus professional" concept—to a degree. In competitive sports, for example, the top amateurs can compete effectively with the top professionals. Everyone plays by the same rules and is judged according to the same performance standard. A primary difference is that amateur athletes have not "declared professional status."

How does this relate to music? Consider the definitions:

- Amateur: no compensation; a labor of love
- Professional: declared intent to work for pay; may require special training or certification by a third party

Here's the rub. Whether sports, music, astrophysics, or any other avocation or occupation, "amateur" connotes a *different and lower* set of performance standards than "professional." Would you hire an amateur heart surgeon? While music and entertainment are not life or death issues, the connotation carries over into music business culture.

Goals vs. Objectives

These words frequently get confused. Goals and objectives are related to one another, yet they are different in an important way.

- Goal: a desired result, often long-term; something good that you aspire to over a long period of time.
- Objective: an aspect or subset of a goal that is specific, measurable, and achievable.

Here's an example. A common goal: "I'd like to get rich and retire young." Getting rich and retiring young are desirable long-term results, but are not objectives.

How you get there and how you measure success flows from the objectives related to the goal. Consider the following objective:

"I plan to have $2,000,000 in the bank by the time I am sixty years old, so I can live on the interest. That will put me in a position to retire without sacrificing quality of life, and still have lots of years left to enjoy it."

This is a well-stated objective. It is specific ($2,000,000 by age sixty), measurable (you can track progress from now until the objective is reached), and for the sake of illustration, achievable.

Strategy vs. Tactics

This is another pair of frequently confused words. It's also important to make a distinction between these two, so here are the definitions:

- Strategy: a *decision* made now that affects future activities. In other words, a strategy is a thought process leading to a decision and commitment, not necessarily the behavior or work itself.

- Tactic: an *activity* designed to achieve a desired result. Tactics are the things you do to implement a strategy. Where strategy describes "what," tactics describe "how to."

Also, note the connection to goals and objectives. Decisions are made (strategies) and activities are undertaken (tactics) in pursuit of desired results, both long-term (goals) and short-term (objectives).

Sound a little dry? Don't worry—I'll relate this to the music world in a moment.

Art vs. Commerce

Music is an art form. Commerce implies doing something for money. The two—art for its own sake versus making money for its own sake—seem to conflict with one another. Before leaping to a conclusion, consider the following definitions:

- Art: human expression in sensuous form, often "for its own sake." The word "expression" is very important, because it implies that the motivation comes from within the artist rather than somewhere else. More to come on this.
- Commerce: buying and selling of goods and services. This implies financial transactions, which further implies a profit motive.

Entertainment vs. Self-Expression

If art is human expression in sensuous form, what is entertainment? Are they related? Consider the following:

- Entertainment: amusement or diversion including public performances or shows. Entertainment, including music, is usually created with the needs of the audience in mind, first and foremost.
- Self-expression: conveyance of personal feeling, as in art. This implies that the feelings, emotions, and personal needs of the artist (composer, songwriter, performer, producer) take the highest priority. If a wide audience responds positively, that's good, but is not essential to the definition of art.

Why mention this in a business book? Because so many music people confuse the issue in their own minds and get stuck. I am not advocating one over the other, just pointing out the difference. When you write your mission statement (just ahead), you'll come back to this concept in your thinking.

THE PROFIT MOTIVE:
A BASIC ISSUE FOR MUSIC PEOPLE

Here's a simple financial rule and formula that drives all businesses:

Revenue Minus Expenses = Profit

Profit is simply the money left over after a business pays the costs of doing business. If you are a one-person music business, profit also represents the money that is available to live your life: food, housing, clothing, recreation, education, etc.

Some music people are put off by the concept of profit, feeling that the idea of having something left over after "working hard for the money" is evil, tacky, lowlife, non-artistic, anti-art, or whatever pejorative word comes to mind. Here are my observations on this situation, gathered over a thirty-year period:

- Unless you are independently wealthy (relatively few people are), the need to make money is a motivator for music people.
- The general public buys concert tickets, records, merchandise, and related material created by musicians and promoted by the industry. Fans "vote with their pocketbooks," meaning they buy what they like and come back to the music that they enjoy on a repeated basis.
- To judge whether a specific song, record, or performance is "good or bad" from an artistic standpoint is largely subjective. What appeals to me may or may not appeal to you, and that's okay. Diversity keeps things interesting.

Again, the business point is: Business Chops Philosophy Element #1: Musical integrity and commercial viability are intrinsically compatible. Musical integrity, business integrity, and commercial success go hand in hand. You don't need to compromise musical or artistic values to make money in music. Also, simply being commercially successful does not assure positive reviews by the critics or other measures of artistic success. Remember, I'm talking about the mainstream here, not the exceptions publicized by the media.

HOW TO WRITE A MISSION STATEMENT

A mission statement answers the question, "Why are you in business?" Whether you are a self-employed individual, owner of a small music business, or in a management position in a larger firm, articulating the answer to this question is the foundation for strategic planning. Here are some guidelines:

1. Strong mission statements are usually one or two sentences long. I've seen mission statements that have gone on up to three pages of cryptic single-spaced text. Longer ones are flawed. They will not be remembered and may not emphasize the right areas when it comes to planning and taking action.

2. Short mission statements are often supplemented by clarifying comments. These most frequently take the form of "vision statements" and "values statements." This is a good way to deal with the temptation to make your mission statement too long.

3. Mission statements do not change much over the long haul. If you find yourself tempted to change your mission statement, you may be talking about a new business.

4. Vision statements describe your view of the future of the industry or market. They are part prediction, part trend analysis, and part context information. They also assert your personal forecast of things to come, and are therefore unique. Vision statements can change periodically as market conditions and your perspectives change.

5. Values statements are your code of ethics and the operating principles that are fundamental to your business. They are unlikely to change over a long period of time. If you work alone or own the company, you can assert your own values in your music business. If you work for someone else, it is important to make sure that your personal values are reasonably aligned with those of the organization. This helps prevent problems and more importantly, it drives the business in a positive way.

For illustration, here are excerpts from the mission, vision, and values statements in my consulting company's business plan.

Mission:

- Our mission is to help our clients meet or exceed their business goals and objectives. To do this, we help our clients bridge the gap between creativity and commerce through applied strategic planning and market intelligence.

Vision (excerpts):

- Individuals (the general public) will enjoy a gradually increasing amount of discretionary time, both on and off the job. This is an irony, as most will perceive that they have less time to do the things they want. This is due to a variety of factors, including information overload and the increased rate of technological and cultural change.

- There is no single best way to reach a market, as there has not been a mass market for some years now. This opens the door to music, entertainment, and communications-based businesses that did not exist or could not flourish before.

- The relationship between creativity and commerce, while somewhat murky in the early twenty-first century, will stabilize eventually. Creative people (artists, musicians, engineers, entrepreneurs) will embrace the business aspects of their work in order to reach wider audiences and enjoy increased commercial success.

- As governments streamline and decentralize, businesses will increasingly support the arts with money and other resources. The two can peacefully co-exist.
- To that end, we have coined a phrase: "Artistic integrity and commercial viability are intrinsically compatible." In other words, a creative or technical person does not need to "sell out" (compromise quality) in order to be financially successful.

Values (excerpts):
- Double the planning time and cut the implementation time in half. This time management "rule of thumb" is essential to our approach to problem solving, personal growth, and business system design. Planning is a critical success factor.
- In any system, the chain is only as strong as the weakest link. Artistry or a great product alone cannot make up for a lack of expertise in sales, marketing, production, management, or finance. This is why it is so important to take a comprehensive view.
- Information overload can be managed and conquered. Too much information can create as many problems as not enough information.
- Every business is a people business. It is important to understand and deal with the human factors on all levels, from staff to customers to suppliers.
- Change is a pre-requisite for growth. To be better implies being different; being different points to the need for both change and adaptability.
- Honesty and integrity are essential to success in business. This fundamental principle often goes without saying, but we think it is important to emphasize.

Mission, vision, and values represent the foundation elements of your business. They are critically important because they inform every decision that you make in the music business. We'll re-visit this in Chapter Seven. Also, the Reference Section and CD-ROM includes a sample mission statement that can be adapted to your music business.

WRITING IT DOWN IS LIBERATING

A recurring theme in this book is: "If it's not written down, it's not a plan." Sure, you have to think through the issues, and yes, you may have a good memory. Yet, there is something about the act of writing that is both clarifying and liberating.

If you are a songwriter or composer, you know what I mean. You write down sketches, notes, or fragments and put them together later. The words or notes jump off the page and make more sense the second or third time around. It's the same idea with your mission statement and the rest of your business plan, for that matter.

The other real benefit of writing everything down is that the material can then be shared with others: your co-workers, employees, family, investors, vendors, or other stakeholders. We'll come back to this later. For now, I suggest that you take a stab at drafting your mission statement, or revising the one you currently have. Start by completing the following sentence:

We are in business to _____.

Congratulations! You've taken the first step in understanding the fundamentals of business and in advancing your music business to the next level.

KEY POINTS IN THIS CHAPTER

1. Everyone has their own motivations for going into the music business. These may combine the desires to make a living, fulfill a dream, create a legacy, and benefit other people.

2. It's essential to understand the difference between (a) hobby versus career, (b) full-time versus part-time, (c) amateur versus professional, (d) goals versus objectives, (e) strategy versus tactics, (f) art versus commerce, and (g) entertainment versus self-expression.

3. The profit motive drives all businesses. The simple formula is "Revenue Minus Expenses = Profit." Profit is the money left over to run your life, or to reinvest in your business.

4. While some music people are uncomfortable with the ideas of money and profit, it is important to understand that they are essential to business success. The first element of the Business Chops Philosophy is "Artistic integrity and commercial viability are intrinsically compatible." Musical integrity, business integrity, and commercial success do go hand-in-hand.

5. Your mission statement answers the question, "Why are we in business?" and drives all other business decisions. Strong mission statements are brief—usually one or two sentences—and can be supported by additional clarification in the form of vision and values statements. Mission statements generally do not change over time.

6. Vision statements describe your unique view of the future of the industry or market. Values statements are your code of ethics and the operating principles that are fundamental to your business and unlikely to change over a long period of time.

7. Your mission, vision, and values statements represent the foundation elements of your business plan. Starting with a clear written statement of mission, vision, and values drives the rest of the planning process. "If it's not written down, it's not a plan."

8. If you work for or with someone else, be sure your vision and values are aligned with those of the company. This is especially important in a band or small music business situation.

CHAPTER TWO

HOW DO YOU START A MUSIC BUSINESS?

In this chapter we will outline the steps for starting a new music business. If you are already in business, I encourage you to read this section as if you were just starting out. There are likely to be references to things you've already done and done well. Consider those as positive reinforcement. There are also likely to be some new items or different approaches. See how these fit with your thinking and be open to going back and filling in the gaps.

THE TWO STRATEGIC QUESTIONS

Whether starting a new business from scratch or taking your current business to the next level, there are two key questions to ask yourself.

Question 1. What do I want to accomplish?

The answers to this question tie to your motivations, goals, and objectives. Are you primarily in it for the money? Want to be around music and music people full-time? Want an outlet for your creativity?

Write down everything that comes to mind, without editing. By "without editing," I mean try to resist the temptation to say, "I'll never be able to do that . . ." before you write down what you want to accomplish. You can always change it later.

Remember that at this stage, what you are envisioning and writing is just for you and there are no right or wrong answers. Also keep in mind that your goals and objectives change over time, so you'll need to ask this question on a regular basis. We'll come back to this in more detail in Chapter Sixteen. For now, we are laying the foundation for your business plan.

Question 2: How much am I willing to risk?

Any business involves risk. Risk is the possibility of danger, loss, or some other negative consequence. In any business, whether you work for yourself or someone else, your time, money, reputation, and self-esteem are at risk. Let's look at each of these briefly.

- Time. You may spend a lot of time learning new skills (musical chops, technical chops, business chops), establishing relationships, and working at the music business before you achieve your financial or creative goals. How much time do you have? Can you afford to take time away from other things? Are you patient or impatient by nature?
- Money. Starting and operating a business requires cash. Do you have enough? Are you willing to put your own money at risk? If yes, how much? If no, where are you going to get the money?
- Reputation. When you operate a business, whatever you do both in your business and in your personal life is subject to public scrutiny. This is significant for performers and songwriters. Your life is an open book, especially as you build your brand and become more successful. How do you feel about that? Are you open to praise and criticism on a regular basis, or are you more private? If you already have a string of positive accomplishments, are you willing to risk others' opinions of your work if you or your company makes a mistake?
- Self-esteem. Your confidence is an asset that must be protected. I'm not referring to vanity, arrogance, or exaggerated self-importance. I am referring to the need to have a positive feeling about yourself and what you do. In any business, especially a subjective and creative field like music, your self-esteem is always at risk.

Self-esteem relates to reputation, but is really a separate concept. I've known many music people who have great reputations but are constantly criticizing themselves for what they perceive to be weaknesses or faults. They lack confidence and end up frustrating themselves and those around them as a result. Without confidence, you will never achieve your full potential.

RISK VS. REWARD

A key business fundamental is the concept of risk versus reward. In business, you are unlikely to get rewarded without taking some kind of risk. While it is true that the more you risk, the greater the potential reward, it is also true that the more you risk, the more you stand to lose.

Consider a lottery or raffle. You buy one lottery ticket for a dollar. As more people buy tickets, the pool (potential reward) gets bigger, but your chances of winning decrease.

As you buy more tickets, your chances of winning increase, but you also have more to lose if you do not win. As the expression goes, "The stakes get higher."

A similar "risk/reward ratio" exists in business. A key difference in business versus lotteries or other forms of gambling is in the amount of control that you have. In business, you control much more of what happens; the risk is more calculated. Yet, unlike the lottery, the odds of winning in business are not purely mathematical.

The point is this: *Be willing to take risks or don't go into the music business (or any other business for that matter).*

WHY THE CONCEPT OF RISK IS SO IMPORTANT

Why dwell on risk right up front? Why not get right into the rest of music business strategy? The answer comes from my own experience in the music industry. Early in my own career, I did not understand that I was taking a risk by not having business skills when I started as a musician, and later as a booking agent. I "learned the hard way" and lost more time and money than I wanted to.

I also have known too many people who entered the music business without considering the risk factor. They ended up frustrated, broke, and quitting the business because they did not know what they were getting into. Some have even told me that if they *had* known, they would have gone into another field and kept music as a hobby.

Still, my motivation in this book is to inform and inspire you, not scare you off. That's why I will stress repeatedly that risk can be calculated and controlled. More on this in Chapter Four.

THREE KEY ELEMENTS IN ANY MUSIC BUSINESS

As you start or develop your business, anticipate questions that other people will ask you about what you are doing. "Other people" may be your family or friends, or they may be prospective employees, partners, investors, or vendors. Here are three simple questions that define three key elements in your music business.

1. What's the business or what is the product? The answer to this question is a brief description of what you do and how you add value.

   - Performer: entertain audiences via live shows or records.
   - Songwriter or composer: create original works of music to be performed live or recorded by others.
   - Agent or manager: provide business services for artists.
   - Promoter: stage concerts, festivals, or other events where music is featured to entertain target audiences.

2. What's the market or target customer for what you do? Who buys the product? A customer is "the one who pays for your product." Products (see #1 above) can be goods like records and T-shirts, or services like live performances, composing, or songwriting.

- Performer: customers include event promoters, record labels, and the general public or target audience.
- Songwriter or composer: customers include performing and recording artists, record labels, publishing companies, and record producers.
- Agent or manager: customers include performing artists, songwriters, composers, event promoters, record labels, and production companies.
- Promoter and event producers: customers include venue owners, the corporate world, entertainment conglomerates, or in the case of most independent promoters, the ticket-buying public.

3. How does everyone get paid? What is the "revenue stream?" The answer here includes but goes beyond the concept of "cash, check, PayPal, or credit card." You need to understand the basis for payment and earning a profit margin.

- Performer: soloists and group leaders are paid fees by event promoters. Sidemen are paid by the leader or business manager. Fees are negotiated in advance and widely variable. Record royalties are paid by the record company or publisher.
- Songwriter or composer: paid by publishing companies or performance rights organizations (BMI, ASCAP, SESAC, etc.). Royalty rates in most countries are standardized and regulated. Payment is based on number of records or downloads sold and number of "public performances for profit" via radio, television, film, Webcasts, and other media.
- Agent or manager: paid by the artist, usually on a commission basis. This is a predetermined percentage of the artist's revenue from performances, royalties, and merchandising.
- Promoter: paid fees by corporate clients (as in producing a meeting or private party) or paid on a per-ticket basis by the general public. For large events, third-party ticket agents (Ticketmaster, Live Nation, etc.) may be involved.

These are basic business concepts that we will build upon later. Here are some additional fundamentals:

- Many music people do more than one thing. In this case, there can be multiple products, customer bases, and revenue streams.
- Agents, managers, and producers are increasingly paid fees or commissions based on all of the artist's revenue streams. More on this in Chapter Twenty.
- If you can't describe your product, you'll have a hard time selling it. More on this in Chapter Nine.
- If you don't know where the money is coming from, you'll have a hard time getting paid. This is part of the reason that so many music people have been

"burned" in the past. You can prevent this problem by understanding the concept of revenue stream and how your share is determined.

THREE THINGS TO DO BEFORE GOING INTO BUSINESS

Too many music people have followed the popular "just do it" motto and gone into business without business knowledge or a business plan. While some get lucky and succeed, others suffer and fail. Success is not just a matter of musical talent or raw determination. The single most critical success factor is understanding what you are getting into—in a word, *planning*.

Much of the rest of this book focuses on three critically important things to do before going into the music business:

1. **The market overview.** Understand what's going on in the music industry and how business is conducted. This is covered in Chapter Three.
2. **The feasibility study, or risk analysis.** Understand what's at risk for you and how that may have an impact on what you do in the music business. Chapter Four addresses the question, "When to quit your day job."
3. **The business plan.** Having a written business plan is essential for long-term success, and is much simpler to complete than most music people think. Section Two (Chapters Five, Six, and Seven) covers how to construct a business plan.

Sure, you can go into business without doing any of this—and frankly, most business people (not just *music* business people) do just that. If you are already in the music business and have experienced its ups and downs, you can likely relate to my advice. But if you are contemplating going into business, you can learn *now* how to prevent problems by doing the three things I've just suggested.

KEY POINTS IN THIS CHAPTER

1. Before going into business, ask yourself two key questions: (1) What do I want to accomplish? and (2) How much am I willing to risk? Write down your long-term goals and objectives early on, understanding that you will refine and revise them over time.

2. Understand the "risk versus reward" principle. All business involves risk. The higher your aspirations, the more time, money, reputation, and self-esteem you risk—though it is a *calculated* risk.

3. Knowing what your product is, who your customer is, and where your revenue comes from, varies according to your role in the music industry (performer, songwriter, etc.). Knowing how everyone gets paid is the first step in raising financial consciousness without "selling out."

4. There are three bits of homework to do before starting a business: 1) the market overview; 2) the risk analysis; and 3) the business plan. These are covered in great detail in the rest of this book.

5. "Just doing it" will often get you into situations you can't control or places you don't really want to be. The most critical factor for success in any business is doing the planning work up front.

THE BIRD'S-EYE VIEW OF THE MUSIC MARKETPLACE

HOW BIG IS THE MUSIC INDUSTRY?

Music is big business all over the world. While the industry is fragmented and diverse, the various facets of the music industry add up quickly. Here, I'm referring to the number of people employed and the resulting sales and profits, not just the cultural and entertainment value of music. While sales statistics are available for some parts of the industry (e.g. SoundScan record sales numbers, BMI/ASCAP publishing statistics, or Pollstar touring revenue figures), no one knows exactly how many people work in the industry or how much revenue is generated annually. When concerts, record sales, publishing royalties, and music business service revenues are added together, they total in the tens of billions of dollars.

Your music business is one of tens of thousands. No one has completed a global music business census. My consulting firm estimates that over one million people are employed in the industry (part-time and full–time, in various capacities) in North America alone. Consider the following statistics:

- The American Federation of Musicians (AFM, the Musicians' Union) has over 90,000 members in the United States and Canada. The AFM estimates that it represents 20 percent of active musicians. That means that there are over 450,000 performers in North America.
- There are over 660,000 songwriters and publishers registered with ASCAP, BMI, and SESAC. In addition there are an estimated 180,000 songwriters who are registered with non-US PRO's, plus countless non-registered songwriters and composers.
- There are over 800,000 acts (solo, duo, and bands of all kinds) that have posted songs on music networking Websites including MySpace, Broadjam, PureVolume, Facebook, and others. Assuming an average of three persons for each act, that's 2.4 million musicians. While relatively few of these acts are professional, the number of North American performing and recording musicians could be as high as 3 million.
- There are over 550 companies listed in directories of agents, managers, and promoters. Firms vary widely in size, from a single person to over 100 people

on staff. Even with an average of three people, this means that over 1,500 people are employed, just in those businesses that are listed.

- Songwriter and musician associations such as the Nashville Songwriters Association International, Circle of Songs, and Just Plain Folks have combined membership estimated at over 100,000.

As in any industry, some of the businesses in the music industry are large and complex while most are small and simple. Many music businesses consist of a single individual or "owner/operator" who does it all, sometimes with temporary help, on a project basis. Any way you look at it, the music industry is large and dynamic. It is loaded with both opportunities and competitive challenges.

HOW BUSINESSES ARE ORGANIZED FOR TAX AND LEGAL PURPOSES

We hear a lot today about the differences between the "corporate" music and entertainment world and its relationship to the "indies" or independent music businesses. What does this mean? Why is it relevant? Here's a quick overview.

In any industry, music or otherwise, there are several ways to organize a business from a legal and tax standpoint. Note: While the examples below relate to United States tax and legal codes, businesses in most countries have a similar range of structures.

- Sole proprietorship. In this type of business, one person owns the company. There may be employees, but the sole proprietor owns the assets and is responsible for the liabilities of the company. The owner is taxed on "ordinary income," business revenue minus deductible business expenses. There is no "stock" as in corporations, so the stock cannot be traded and no shares can be sold or given in return for in-kind services.
- Partnership. In this type of business, more than one person owns the company, and the various owners are frequently active in the business. As with a sole proprietorship, the partners share the assets and liabilities and are taxed on their share of net company income.
- Corporation. In this type of business, there can be any number of owners (as few as one), but the company is organized according to a set of laws and tax codes which are designed to regulate larger firms. The various owners own shares of stock in the company, and that stock can be bought and sold periodically with little or no disruption to the business.
- Limited Liability Company (LLC) and Limited Liability Partnership (LLP). These are hybrid business structures in which the owners' liability for the financial and legal obligations of the company are protected by the partnership agreement, without some of the administrative detail involved in a full corporation. The concept of limited liability is attractive to investors who do not want to risk more than their individual cash investment in a given

company. Basically, the partners get the liability protection of a corporation with the tax advantages and simplicity of a partnership.

- Public vs. Private. Virtually all companies listed on the various world stock exchanges (New York, London, Vancouver, Tokyo, Hong Kong, etc.) are corporations. In order to be listed (and for stock to be traded on the open market), the corporation needs to "go public," meaning that it offers shares of stock to anyone who is financially qualified to buy them. Private corporations can sell stock, but are usually closely held (relatively few shareholders) and the transactions are open to public scrutiny or regulated by the government as with public companies.

Note: Recommending one business structure or format over the other is beyond the scope of this book. Seek advice from your lawyer or accountant regarding the best structure for your specific situation.

CORPORATE VS. INDEPENDENT MUSIC BUSINESSES: MYTHS AND REALITIES

How does this all relate to music? First, it is valuable to understand that you have a choice of business structures when you set up your music business. Second, know that you can change the structure from time to time. Third, this may help you understand all the news and hype about the stock market.

For music people, "Corporate versus Independent" is more about the structure, size, and scope of the business (as discussed above), than about the quality of the music or the integrity of the people involved. Yet, the popular media often depicts the corporate music world and the "Majors" (including EMI Music, Sony BMG, Universal Music Group, Warner Music Group and various entertainment conglomerates) as the "bad guys," "suits," or "sellouts," and the independent world, the "indies," as the good-guy underdogs who "live for the music."

Let's clear up the myths.

Myth 1. Big is bad—they're just after the money.

Reality: Big corporate music businesses can be just as committed to their artists and to the music as small independent music businesses. The risk is higher because the cash investment is usually greater. As a result, the corporate world generally focuses on "safer" mainstream music instead of fringe or niche music with smaller audience appeal.

Myth 2. Smaller means more artist-focused and therefore better.

Reality: Small independent music businesses can be just as profit-motivated or (regrettably) insensitive to the artistic side of music as a larger business. This has more to do with the experience, skill, or personalities of the people involved than the size or scale of the company.

In simple terms, there is no inherent connection between company size and the quality of the people or the music. Business Chops Philosophy, especially the idea that "artistic integrity and commercial viability are intrinsically compatible," applies equally to the corporate and the indie worlds of music. I'll talk more about the dynamics of the global music industry in later chapters.

CHANGING BUSINESS MODELS: RECORD COMPANY VS. MUSIC COMPANY

The year 2007 marked the beginning of a shift in business models in the global music industry. Declining sales of traditional formats, like CDs, created a frustrating and volatile market for recorded music. Responding to market dynamics, music businesses were driven to adapt their business models. Here are three business examples:

- Record companies are becoming music companies (again). Much like independent artists today, and Motown Records in the 1960s, record companies today are looking for *multiple* revenue streams. To accomplish this, they are redefining themselves as music companies, positioned to earn a share of song royalties, merchandising revenue, and live performance revenue from signed artists.
- Concert production companies are becoming music companies. While concert promoter Live Nation's core business is live entertainment, their well-publicized "360 deals" with Madonna and other artists generate revenue from records, merchandise, and publishing, thus making them a "music company."
- Artist management companies are becoming music companies. While artists' managers have been paid on multiple revenue streams in the past, many are now developing their own record labels and concert production divisions— still another version of a "music company."

This may be a bit ironic for many self-managed performers and songwriters. Can you relate to this example?

"I write, record, and publish my own songs. I perform at shows that I book myself and sell CDs and downloads. Guess I got myself a 360-deal!"

WHO IS THE CUSTOMER IN THE MUSIC BUSINESS?

Part of understanding the market is identifying your target customer base. As you begin to draft a market overview document for your business plan, this is a critical step. In Chapter Two we talked about the business, the market, and how everyone gets paid. In Section Three, we'll get into detail on marketing. For now, please understand two key points:

- Your customer is whoever pays you directly. This is the buyer you are responsible to in terms of adding value on a consistent basis. It's where the cash changes hands.
- The "buying public," or the general music audience at large, is the ultimate customer for our whole industry. If the public did not buy records and concert tickets, listen to the radio, visit music sites on the Internet, or watch television and films, there would be no need for performers, songwriters, agents, managers, promoters . . .you get the picture.

Isn't this obvious? Why mention it? This is relevant because so many music people forget where the money comes from, and that the customer relationship is critical. Which leads us to . . .

THE TWO KINDS OF COMPETITION

Any market overview and subsequent marketing plan includes a description of the competitive environment. Who are the competitors and how do they behave? Chapter Fifteen shows how to prepare a detailed competitive analysis. For now, understand that there are two basic types of competition:

- Direct Competition. Similar businesses in the same product category. Examples include other performers, songwriters, booking agents, managers, event promoters, etc.
- Indirect Competition. Any product, goods, or service that pursues the same target customer's attention ("mindshare") and money. Examples include not only the obvious entertainment specialists (games, cinema, sports, etc.), but alternative purchases like furniture, clothing, home improvements, computers, cars, and/or activities like vacations, hobbies, and education.

For example, if your business is a band that performs reggae music, other reggae bands are your direct competitors. So are any other acts, regardless of style of music. Why? Because any act (single, duo, band) wants to perform as many show dates as possible to an increasing, but finite, audience. If promoters already enjoy and program reggae, it may be relatively easy to get their attention. Still, artists and agents representing other music genres—from Appalachian to Zydeco—are also trying to sell their wares to as many promoters and fans as possible. General interest in music (as opposed to other entertainment forms) is the common thread.

THE THREAT OF INDIRECT COMPETITION

Music fans are also likely to enjoy and consume other types of entertainment. Bowling, baseball, books, magazines, movies, Guitar Hero, Scrabble, dancing, theater, museums, skateboarding—all of these activities take attention and cash away from music. These are examples of indirect competition from other forms of entertainment.

Put yourself in the fan's position. In addition to the multitude of music and entertainment options available, you have lots of other things to do with your discretionary time and money.

"Should I buy a new dining room set or a new home theater system? A European vacation or a new motorcycle? Send my kid to private school, or buy investment property?" Or on a smaller scale, "Should I go shopping for some new clothes, go out for a nice dinner, or go to a concert?"

In Chapter Fifteen, we'll discuss how to understand and deal with both types of competition. For now, understand that there are two kinds of competition. The indirect competitors generally pose a larger threat than the direct competitors.

Now that we have a perspective on the music industry, let's move on to putting your personal situation into the industry context.

KEY POINTS IN THIS CHAPTER

1. The global music industry is vast, diverse, and complex. There are an estimated three million people employed (at least part-time) in the North American music industry alone, which takes in tens of billions of dollars of revenue each year.

2. You have choices for organizing your business from a legal and tax standpoint: sole proprietorship, partnership, corporation, or limited liability company. Get advice from your lawyer or accountant on which one is right for you.

3. "Corporate versus Independent" is more about the structure, size, and scope of the business than about the quality of the music or integrity of the people involved.

4. Both "corporate" and "indie" music businesses can be motivated by musical integrity as well as profit. Although the media often portrays the corporate world negatively, there are more business similarities than differences between "corporate" and "indie" companies.

5. Music business models are changing and adapting in the twenty-first century. Record companies, concert promoters, and management firms that used to focus on one element of the industry, are now diversifying into "music companies." This enables them to tap into multiples streams of revenue. Ironically, many bands and performing songwriters have used this music company business model for years.

6. If you want to get paid in the music business, understand who your customer is and where the money (your cash flow) comes from.

7. The buying public is the ultimate customer for your industry. They buy the records, merchandise, and concert tickets, and provide the revenue basis for all commercial music businesses.

8. Be aware of your competition. Direct competitors offer similar products to your target customer base. Indirect competitors offer products from outside your category, but also target your customers.

9. Understanding the market is the prerequisite for your risk analysis. Once you've assessed the size and scope of the music industry, you can better determine where you want to fit in and what you are willing to risk in order to get what you want.

RISK ANALYSIS— WHEN TO QUIT YOUR DAY JOB

In Chapter Two we introduced the concept of risk by asking two key questions:
1. What do I want to accomplish?
2. How much am I willing to risk?

We also identified the four things that are at risk in any business: time, money, reputation, and self-esteem. Now we will begin applying your answers to the risk questions in practical terms and equip you to answer the ultimate question: "When should I quit my day job?"

HOW DO YOU FEEL ABOUT RISK?

There are both objective and subjective aspects to answering the business questions about risk. If you are independently wealthy and have time on your hands, your perspective on what is at risk is different from the person who works a "day job." Are you, or do you know anyone who is working as a retail clerk, restaurant server, cab driver, stock broker, hotel concierge, or other occupation, but really aspires to be in the music business full-time? It's a common scenario. See if you can relate to these comments.

- "I'm working to support my music habit. When I have enough money, I'll quit to do what I really love."
- "I'm hoping to meet someone in my straight job who can invest in my music career."
- "I tried music full-time but could not make a living. I'm doing other work to pay the bills so I can still be involved in music part-time."
- "I know that the music business is risky. I owe it to my family to provide security."
- "I love the performing and songwriting but I hate the business stuff. I guess I'm not ready to take that kind of risk."
- "I love music, but I'm not willing to give up my lifestyle."

Some people are comfortable with risk. Others are "risk–averse;" they consciously avoid risk and are willing to accept lower returns as a result. Refer to the risk versus reward concept in the previous chapter. Where do you fall on the risk spectrum? Let's do a brief exercise to find out.

In the table below, simply check the boxes in each category that make the most sense to you. Remember there are no right or wrong answers. Also keep in mind that you can change your mind over time as conditions change. Here we go.

What's at Risk	Hate to Risk Much	Willing to Risk Some	Would Risk Lots
Time			
Money			
Reputation			
Self-esteem			

Now look at where you placed the check marks. I've presented many music business seminars where I take the audience through this exercise. I always ask: "Did anyone check all four boxes in the first column, (hate to risk much)?"

In the typical audience, one or two hands go up. My advice to those people: Look for a job in the music business where you work for someone else. Don't go into business for yourself. If you are uncomfortable taking at least a moderate risk, being an entrepreneur would be a frustrating and scary experience.

IS ANYONE BUYING WHAT I'M SELLING?

Ever wonder why a record label, agent, or manager would not sign your act? Or if you are a songwriter, ever wonder why a publisher, producer, or artist was not interested in the song you were pitching? The subjective willingness to take risk is a bigger factor than many music people acknowledge. Also, there are countless objective and practical reasons to buy or not buy what you are selling. Every customer has a unique set of buying criteria, including their risk tolerance. This underscores the value of establishing target customer profiles as part of your overall marketing plan. We'll write a detailed target customer profile in Chapter Fourteen.

As you do your risk analysis, ask yourself, "Is anyone buying what I'm selling?" and consider these points:

- "Is the market for what I want to do big enough to support my music business?"
- "Is there anyone else who is doing what I want to do successfully? Can I learn from them?"

- "Can I get enough facts about the size of the market to satisfy my risk tolerance?"

This last question is important because if you have a high risk tolerance, you may be willing to leap ahead without understanding exactly how many records you need to sell or gigs you need to book to make a profit. Whatever your risk tolerance is, I suggest that you get more information on market size before quitting your day job.

WHERE WILL I GET THE MONEY?

Whether you are starting a new music business or developing your existing business, you need cash for operating capital in order to grow. It is simply unrealistic to think that you will be paid in advance. It is idealistic and too risky to think:

"I'll book some gigs and use the money to buy
recording equipment. Then I'll record and pre-sell
enough records to pay for the manufacturing of the CD.
Websites are virtually free, so I'll use the Internet to
sell my music (CDs and downloads) and promote my act.
The music is so good, it will sell itself . . ."

As most of you know, the system does not work this way. You will need cash to start the business and to operate it over time. This money is called "working capital." Sources of cash you can access include:

- Savings. You may have a "nest egg" in the form of a savings account (your "piggy bank"), which you are willing to invest in your own business.
- Sale of assets. You may have real estate, stocks, bonds, collectible instruments, or other securities, which can be sold and turned into cash to invest in your business. Further, cars, furniture, electronic gear, or other unused household items can be potential sources of cash.
- IRA or 401k retirement accounts from your day job. You may be able to liquidate or borrow against the retirement fund money you have accumulated by working in a non-music occupation.
- Second mortgage. If you own your own home or other real estate, you may be able to get a home equity loan or secured line of credit to free up additional cash.
- Credit card debt. Have you heard about movies that were financed by filmmakers taking cash advances on their credit cards? The interest rates are high, but it is a source of ready cash.
- Friends and relatives. You may have the proverbial "rich uncle" who is willing to take a financial risk on your music career.

- Private investors. You may find individuals, other than family and friends, who are willing to invest or loan money. These people are often called "angels" or "backers." Be prepared to show, in financial terms, (dividends or interest), how and when you are going to make their investment pay off. More on this later.

- Reinvested profits. Once your business, (music business or another business activity) is generating a profit, you can choose to reinvest some or all of that cash profit as working capital.

- Banks and finance companies. Ironically, banks will only loan money if you can prove that you do *not* need it. The reason is that banks, while in the business of loaning money, have collateral and payback capacity requirements. This level of accountability makes it more difficult to borrow from banks and finance companies than from other sources. Bankers often take a dim view of music people from bad publicity surrounding the music industry or prior experience because of unpaid loans from failed music businesses. Don't take it personally if your bank is not interested in lending you money.

WHERE YOU *WON'T* GET THE MONEY

The following are *not* viable sources of business funding:

- Spouse or family income. Many music people ask their spouse or other family members to share the risk and invest in their music business. This is generally not a good idea. You may ask, "Why not? My family is really supportive." It may be a tough call, but there are two primary reasons to avoid tapping into the family livelihood. First, there may not be enough cash available to make a difference, even if their spirits are willing. Second, relating to your tolerance for risk of reputation and self-esteem, if anything goes wrong, you probably *don't* want to sacrifice family relationships for a few bucks.

- Part-time jobs. "But I already have a part-time job just so I can be in the music industry. Why tell me it's not a viable source of working capital?" This is another judgment call on your part. Consider this: A person attending one of my seminars said, "I work full-time at a non-music job to pay my bills and part-time at another non-music job to support my music. I use the side money for equipment, business cards, and buying books and records." This is fine if music is your hobby. If you plan to make music your *career*, you simply won't have time to work one or two other jobs.

- "Bake sales and car washes." These are fund-raising activities, often associated with schools, churches, and charities. Other examples may include selling magazine subscriptions, household cleaning products, or cosmetics. Like part-time jobs, these activities are unlikely to raise enough money fast enough to make a difference.

- Illegal activities. There are plenty of other ways to raise the money, so avoid stealing, selling controlled substances, gambling, and other nefarious methods.

WHO WILL HANDLE THE FIVE KEY ASPECTS OF THE BUSINESS?

Any business, music or otherwise, has five key elements:

1. **Product development.** This involves getting your goods or services ready to offer to your target customer base. An obvious music example is the need to rehearse before performing on stage or in the studio. Getting your musical chops together is an example of product development. That part of the process, before anything is sold, represents product development.
2. **Product delivery.** Using the performer example, once you have rehearsed and your performance dates are booked, you need to show up and do the work. If you are a songwriter, once you've written a song, you need to deliver it to your publisher or the artist you are pitching.
3. **Sales and marketing.** Someone needs to handle the sales and marketing of any product. We'll devote quite a bit of this book to this subject in Section Three.
4. **Accounting and finance.** Someone needs to keep track of the money, pay the bills, raise extra working capital when needed, file the tax returns, and keep an eye on the eventual profits of your business.
5. **Management.** Even a one-person business needs to be managed. Beyond handling administration and operations (information systems, workplace facilities, human resources), management has four key responsibilities. They are (1) planning, (2) organizing, (3) motivating, and (4) controlling. The larger your business, the more these four essential management functions are likely to take up 100 percent of someone's time.

Many music people try to do it all. Some are content and successful, others become frustrated. Does this sound familiar? "I'm a songwriter and performer. I handle my own bookings and promotion. I record in my home studio and make discs to order on my CD recorder. When I get a record order, I pack it up, enclose a personal thank you note, and take the package to the post office. I'm my own Webmaster, have a MySpace page, and send an occasional e-mail blast to my fan list. I balance my own checkbook, and troubleshoot my computer when it goes down."

I admire these people. In fact I've known quite a few over the years. I've also known many music people who want to focus on what they love to do and what they do best. There is no right or best way. As a practical matter, no single person can do everything effectively, especially as the business grows. You simply won't have enough time, even if you have the skill.

Think about the music people that you admire or emulate. Do they do everything themselves? Relatively few career performers, songwriters, or recording artists handle their own bookings, management, and accounting. Conversely, agents and managers are seldom performers. Excellence requires full-time focus on what you do best.

Here's the point. Someone needs to take care of each of the five essential elements of your music business. Is it you for all five, or can you focus on one or two? What are you best suited for? What feels right? Where do you have the best business chops? How can you make the best contribution? How can you have the most fun along the way?

Addressing these questions is part of your risk analysis. It is human nature to be willing to take more risk in the areas where you are more skilled and confident. You may also be more comfortable sharing the risk with others who understand these concepts and are willing to contribute their part to complement yours. Now, how to answer the important question.

WHEN TO QUIT YOUR DAY JOB

If you are doing something other than music to make a living but would like to focus on music full-time, this is *the* important question. If you are already doing music full-time, the following conditions are still valuable to put into perspective.

There are three conditions to be met before you can "quit your day job" with confidence:

1. You have a written business plan ready to share with others. This is the subject of Section Two of this book (you're almost there!)
2. You have funding to cover both business and personal expenses for at least one year. Once you have drafted your business plan, you'll know how much money you will need. Why one year? Because you will need at least a year to work through your plan in most cases. You are likely to generate *some* revenue in much less than a year, but having the financial support up-front provides the confidence to move ahead and the cash reserve in case a problem or opportunity arises.
3. You are comfortable taking the risk. We've spent a lot of time talking about the various kinds of risk. Some people handle risk easily, others don't. There is no rule on how much risk to take, so don't feel that one or the other is the best way. Just determine how much risk *you* are willing to take, and proceed from there.

It also helps a lot to have family and friends who are comfortable with your music business idea. Having that emotional support is likely to make things go a lot easier, especially on the home front.

If any of the three conditions are not met, you are probably not ready to quit your day job. You may say, "I'm comfortable with the risk and I have some money, so I don't need a business plan." Or, "I've got a business plan, so I'll use it to raise the money." Or, "I'm already in the business, I'll finance it from cash flow, and I'll just get used to this sick empty feeling in my stomach, wondering how I'm going to pay rent and phone bills."

These are what I call "eager rationalizations." The "eager" part is very positive. You want to do it because music is so important to you. Beware of idealistic over-rationalization, however. I've talked to dozens of music people who still believe that "getting discovered and signed to a music company" is the fast track to wealth and fame and the best way to deal with the vagaries of the music industry. While I acknowledge that there will always be a few exceptions, I believe that careful planning drives the better, less risky approach.

Why did you buy this book? How did you get to this point? It is probably because you want to get ahead by some means other than trial and error. I'll say it again: Don't quit your day job until you have 1) drafted a solid business plan, 2) secured twelve months' worth of cash reserves, and 3) dealt with the risk factor.

KEY POINTS IN THIS CHAPTER

1. Be comfortable with risk, or don't take risks. There is no best way or single right answer to the question of how much risk to take.

2. Understanding what's involved in going into business is essential to understanding the risk factor. Many music people, unaware of what it takes to operate a music business, leap in prematurely.

3. Understand the market for your music product before developing your business further. Ask the question, "Is anyone buying what I'm selling?"

4. Any music business requires working capital and cash in order to operate and grow. There are many sources of cash other than the revenue generated by the business. Some sources are better than others when it comes to dealing with both financial and emotional risk.

5. Savings, retirement accounts, sale of assets, second mortgages, credit card advances, and private investors are among the *viable* sources of working capital. Examples of *non-viable* sources of cash include spouse or family income, part-time jobs, and "fundraisers," like bake sales and car washes.

6. The process of creating your business plan will help you determine how much money you need. Be prepared to show your business plan to investors or funding sources, even your "rich uncle."

7. Any music business has five key elements: (1) product development, (2) product delivery, (3) sales and marketing, (4) accounting and finance, and (5) management. Be assured that you do not necessarily need expertise in all five areas. Focus on the idea of building your team.

8. Don't quit your day job prematurely. To focus on your music business full-time, you must: (1) have a written business plan, (2) have enough cash to cover business and personal expenses for a minimum of one year, and (3) be comfortable taking risks. If one of these three conditions is not met, you are not ready to go into music full-time.

9. Beware of "eager rationalizations" or the tendency to be idealistic. Having a written business plan is the first step toward quitting your day job, and it is the topic of the next section of this book.

CREATING YOUR ESSENTIAL BUSINESS PLAN

"Fail to plan, plan to fail."—Business truism

CHAPTER FIVE

WHY HAVE A BUSINESS PLAN?

A business plan is a document which guides any business toward its future goals and objectives. Two key words there: document and future. The word "document" implies that the contents of the plan are written down. The word "future" implies that the business is moving in a forward direction, eager to make progress over time.

Sound simple? It is. Then why do so few businesses in any field, music or otherwise, have written business plans? While most businesses have some sort of record keeping system and a financial budget, only about five percent have a comprehensive plan. Many of my consulting firm's clients over the years have initially said, "Sure I have a business plan. It's all right up here," pointing to their head, indicating that the plan was etched in their memory.

Yikes! How do you share such a plan with staff, customers, vendors, or investors? By telepathy? What if the boss, which could be you, ends up unable to share the information? Even the most creative ideas and "best laid plans" need to be written down. Consider the following scenarios:

- The business founder or leader loses interest and goes on to another job or project.
- The lead person dies or becomes unable to talk or write, let alone work.
- The ideas upon which the business is based are wrong, outdated, or incomplete.
- A dispute arises over who had an idea first.
- Key people like employees or partners (which could be band members, support staff, managers, or investors) lose interest and move on.

I've seen all of these happen at one time or another and the results are not pretty. People end up losing time, money, reputation, and self-esteem. Problems could have been anticipated and prevented, but they weren't. Further, lost opportunities could have been seized.

EIGHT BENEFITS OF WRITING DOWN YOUR PLAN

Key point: A business plan is the single most valuable tool that any business has. Here are eight reasons or benefits for not only having a business plan, but writing it down.

Benefit 1: Road Map

Your business plan is your road map to a successful future. There are multiple routes to that future. Consider this analogy:

You want to visit a city you've never been to before, and you plan to drive there in your car. You look at a road map, and discover that there are several routes to your destination. One is the most direct and the fastest, via interstate highway, but a little boring. Another is the scenic route. It takes a little longer but there are interesting sights along the way. A third route goes along county highways most of the way and is pretty fast, but allows you to get a feel for the local culture as you travel.

In business, there are also multiple routes to your business goals and objectives. Some are faster, but more costly. Others leave open the possibility for "sight seeing," or experimenting as new ideas or opportunities crop up. The map (your plan) shows you the options and provides a reference to fall back on if you get lost or encounter unexpected "road construction" along the way.

Benefit 2: Measuring Stick

There's a business axiom that states:

"What gets measured, gets done." Remember the definition of an objective? "An aspect of a goal which is specific, measurable, and achievable."

Your business plan includes goals and objectives, financial and otherwise. Those objectives are plotted on a time line or list of milestones (another road map reference). The plan allows you to see how you are doing relative to your objectives at any point in time. Chapter Sixteen deals with how to set realistic financial and professional goals and objectives. For now, understand the value of having a written reference to use for measuring your success.

Benefit 3: Opportunity Management Tool

Most music businesses have more opportunities than they can handle. There are more possible show dates to play or promote, and songs to write and record than any one business has the capacity or expertise to accommodate. This applies to the big corporate companies as well as the small independent ones. The business buzzword here is "capacity." You may have ambition and opportunity, but if the capacity, rationale, or capability is not there, the results may be less than desirable.

Your business plan is an opportunity management tool. If the next hot creative idea is within the scope of your plan, you can address it with energy and confidence. If not, you can pass or refer the opportunity to someone else, also with confidence. By thinking of your plan in this way, you'll be less likely to take bookings or hire team members who present themselves as available, but don't make sense or "feel right." You also have a polite way to turn down the marginal opportunities. It's better to say, "Sounds good, but it's outside the scope of our business," than to get involved in the wrong project and regret it later.

Benefit 4: Stress Management Tool

Everyone in business is under stress to some degree. Stress is a demand on your mental and physical energy. There are two types of stress: distress and eustress. Distress is the negative kind, which results from too many things to do in too short a period of time with too few resources. Sound familiar? You've probably encountered the uneasy feelings that come from information overload, financial concerns, deadlines, or uncertainties inherent in your job or family situation.

Eustress is the good feeling that comes from having a creative idea that energizes you. Think about when you were a kid and looked forward to a birthday party, family vacation, a favorite sport or music that you loved doing. You stayed up all night, thoughts of the positive activity spinning in your head. Have you ever had that type of feeling about your music career? I hope so. Songwriters and composers can relate to this easily, but so can any other music person who has a good idea and opportunities for success.

Consider the stress on yourself and your employees as the business grows. Much energy, time, and money are wasted in the business world because the people doing the work simply don't know what to do at any given time. Your business plan helps everyone answer the question:

"Am I doing the right thing for my business, right now?"

***When you know the answer is yes, you proceed with
higher confidence and lower stress.***

Your business plan is a terrific stress management tool. It helps you anticipate and prevent problems. It provides the context information and contingencies for dealing with unanticipated challenges. It helps you focus your creative energy on your goals and objectives. All of these activities help you lower or manage the normal stress that comes with being in the music business.

Benefit 5: Catalyst for Your Best Work

"But I want to be open to anything. I don't want to feel encumbered by a business plan. That's why I'm in a creative field like music."

Consider the great graphic artists. I enjoy visiting art museums, and am particularly fascinated by the artists' sketches and notes that led to great paintings and sculpture. Michelangelo and da Vinci, Rembrandt and Van Gogh, Picasso and Hopper, are all fine artists who created their own "business plans" for their major works in the form of sketches and studies.

Songwriters can easily relate to this. Virtually all of the songwriters that I know keep extensive notebooks with lyrics, titles, chord progressions, and fragments of thematic ideas that later develop into finished songs. Was the first set of lyrics the one that eventually got recorded and performed? Rarely.

When you have an idea of what you want the finished work to look like and have written it down, you can channel your creative energy toward achieving the best possible results. It's likely that your creativity will be unlocked rather than stifled!

Benefit 6: Competitive Weapon

Your business plan helps you deal with both your direct and indirect competitors. As I've noted, only about five percent of businesses in all fields have written plans. In the music industry and other creative and technical fields, that number is probably less, although no hard statistics exist. You may ask, "If that's the case, why bother? My competitors are no better off than I am."

Consider two key points. First, a higher percentage of your *indirect* competitors (the big, scary ones from outside the music industry) are likely to have business plans. That puts them at an advantage over you. Second, 95 percent or more of your *direct* competitors are unlikely to have a business plan. That puts you at an advantage over them.

In either scenario, your business plan is a competitive weapon. It helps you defend your business from competitive threats at the same time that you seize competitive opportunities that are consistent with your long-term goals and objectives.

Benefit 7: Fund-raising Tool

A written plan is essential for fund-raising. Have you ever tried to borrow money for anything? Whether you are asking a friend for some spot cash until payday or seeking a mortgage on a new home from a bank, you can anticipate two questions:

- What are you going to do with the money?
- When and how are you going to pay it back?

When you have a plan, you don't have to hem and haw or avoid these questions. You can proudly say, "Thank you for the question. Here's the answer." Even if you are using your own savings or a credit card cash advance to finance your next stage of growth, you will need to ask yourself these same questions. Your business plan points to the answers.

While some angel investors or banks will provide small amounts of money having received minimal details, the process gets tougher as the stakes get higher. Anticipating this, your business plan is an essential fund-raising tool.

Benefit 8: Team-Building Tool

How do you find people with complementary skills, including musicians, writing partners, agents, managers, publishers, publicists, etc., to round out your team? What are they going to ask you when you find them? What's the pay and benefit package? What does the future look like? Where is this all going? Your business plan includes the answers to these questions and more.

Once your team is put together, the plan serves as a guide, measuring stick, or road map, if you will, for everyone involved, not just the owners and investors. Employees, from band members to accounting clerks, feel like they are "on board" when they have access to the company's mission, vision, values, operating policies and procedures, goals, and objectives. Your business plan is your best team-building tool.

"IT SEEMS LIKE A LOT OF WORK . . ."

You may be thinking, "Okay, you've presented a logical argument for constructing a written business plan, but it still seems like a lot of work. Is it really *worth* it?"

Once again, I'll go back to the concept of risk versus reward. If you are comfortable putting everything on the line and rolling the dice with minimal planning, that's your decision. Your family, staff, partners, investors, and customers are probably more risk-averse than you are. In that case, do it for them, and enjoy the extra benefits yourself.

Another way to think of it is to ask yourself the question "What if I don't write down my plans? What if my competitors do?" The downside risks can be significant, even alarming.

You'll probably also find out that the planning process can be creative, fun, and invigorating. Once your plan is written, you'll look back and wonder what you did without it. But don't just take my word for it—get started.

KEY POINTS IN THIS CHAPTER

1. "Fail to plan, plan to fail." This business truism points to the need to have a plan for any business, large or small.

2. A business plan is a document that guides your business toward its future goals and objectives. Your plan keeps you in control, helping you anticipate, rather than react to opportunities and threats.

3. Many businesses think they already have a plan when the owner or key executives have the best interests of the company in mind. That's nice, but if it's not written down, it's not a plan.

4. There are eight compelling benefits to having a written business plan: (1) road map; (2) measuring stick; (3) opportunity management tool; (4) stress management tool; (5) catalyst for your best work; (6) competitive weapon; (7) fund-raising tool; and (8) team-building tool. Any one of these is reason enough to create a business plan, but a combination of factors support the value of planning.

5. Staff, vendors, partners, investors, family, and customers respond positively when you have a business plan. The benefits more than justify the effort required to create the plan.

6. The planning process is creative, invigorating, and can be fun. Get started now!

CHAPTER SIX

WHAT'S IN A BUSINESS PLAN?

In this chapter we'll provide the details on the various elements of a business plan. To get started, here's our working definition:

A business plan is a written system of documents that puts your business and its market environment in context over the course of the next several years. It describes (1) what you are going to do, (2) how you are going to do it, and (3) the consequences or results.

You may be thinking, "I know the answers to those questions already." Good! Now is the time to write them down.

Note: This chapter gives a brief overview of what's in a business plan, so you can see how the parts fit together in a systematic way. We'll break down each part in more detail in subsequent chapters. See the Reference Section of this book or the CD-ROM for definitions of any business terms that may be new to you and for a sample business plan illustrating the concepts presented here. Remember that even if you work alone, think of yourself as a "company" for planning purposes.

THE MEMORY SYSTEM DOESN'T WORK

A recurring theme in this book is: "If it's not written down, it's not a plan." Here's why the "memory system" of business planning doesn't work.

- No one person has all the answers, let alone the ability to remember every detail of the plan.
- Your memory can't always be consulted on demand, like when you are on vacation and a staff person, manager, or agent back home needs to make an operating decision.
- Even if you are a single-person business, it's inefficient to communicate all the details verbally to family, friends, vendors, coworkers, bankers, investors, or anyone else who needs to know. *They* want it written down.

THE FIVE "CHAPTERS" OF YOUR BUSINESS PLAN

Before we talk about length and format, let's first understand the content of a business plan.

A comprehensive plan has five sections or "chapters." I'll explain the relevance of the percentages after each chapter a bit later.

Chapter 1: Description of your company, business, and place in the industry (15%)

Briefly describe what business you are in, who your customers are (by category versus individual names), a summary history of your activities up to this point, and what role you play in the global music and entertainment industry.

Chapter 2: Description of products (goods and services) (15%)

Go into more detail here about the specific things you do, merchandise you sell, or services you provide. Discuss key features and customer benefits, along with your competitive advantages. Remember that your "product" is what you get paid for.

Chapter 3: Market overview and marketing strategy (35%)

Describe the size and growth of your specific market. Keep in mind the big picture, as we discussed in Chapter Three of this book. Talk about target market segments, the competitive environment, your promotion strategy, geographical territory and place of doing business, channels of distribution, and salesforce. Include profiles of target buyers and examples of key current customers. Tie the promotion strategy to your three-year goals and objectives.

Chapter 4: Management team and organizational overview (25%)

Here's your chance to relate your professional experience and why you are qualified to do what you are doing. If the business includes more than one person, include brief biographies of the current management team and a description of staff, consultants, and vendors. Show the reporting structure and how the organization will change over time as the company grows. If the company is just you for now, that's okay. Include brief descriptions of positions on your team that have not been filled yet, but are planned.

Chapter 5: Financial summary (10%)

Provide details on sales revenue, expenses by category, capitalization, cash flow, and income forecast. Just show the financial highlights and key financial assumptions. You should include budgets and pro forma income statements in the appendix to the plan.

A NOTE ABOUT ASSUMPTIONS

The word "assumption" comes up regularly in business. You may have heard the old expression, "Never assume anything." This is generally good wisdom, but the slogan is an abbreviation of something with a slightly different meaning: "Never assume that anything is 100 percent committed and unchangeable."

In a business context, here is the definition of the word *assumption* that we use:

- Assumption: the answer to the question, "How did you get the numbers?"

In business, you need to make plans based on a set of assumptions. There are market assumptions, financial assumptions, staffing assumptions, creative assumptions, and scheduling assumptions. How well you plan and how well you succeed are both entirely dependent on the reasonableness and accuracy of your business assumptions.

Some business people, including music people, have a hard time writing down assumptions. "I won't write it down if I don't know for sure. I don't want to make a commitment I can't keep." A noble philosophy, but it *just doesn't work* most of the time. Here are examples of potentially faulty assumptions that might *not* have been made if they had been written down.

- "I'll move to the city, get discovered, get a record contract, tour, and get rich."
- "All I have to do to get more bookings is hire a manager."
- "All I need to do to make more money is play more gigs." (Or sell more records, write more songs, sell more tickets, etc.)
- "There's no way I can make a living in music, so I'll just keep working these three part-time jobs to support my music habit."
- "No one is interested in my style of music."

The list can go on and on. Here's the point. Making assumptions and then backing them up with answers to the questions posed in this book are essential to both the business planning process and to long-term success in music.

WHAT DO THOSE PERCENTAGES REPRESENT?

Back to the contents of your business plan. Did you notice those percentages shown above after each chapter description? What do they signify? Where do they come from?

Chapter 1: Company, business, and industry overview (15%)
Chapter 2: Products overview (15%)
Chapter 3: Market overview and marketing strategy (35%)

Chapter 4: Management team and organizational overview (25%)
Chapter 5: Financial summary (10%)

The percentages indicate the relative *weight or importance* of each section. They add up to 100 percent, and all are essential to your plan. Here they are again, ranked in order of importance:

Chapter 3: Market overview and marketing strategy (35%)
Chapter 4: Management team and organizational overview (25%)
Chapter 1: Company, business, and industry overview (15%)
Chapter 2: Products overview (15%)
Chapter 5: Financial summary (10%)

The ranking system has its roots in the investment world; it was developed by hard-core business people. In this case, the guidelines are those provided by the Los Angeles Economic Development Council (LAEDC), a city office that assists inventors or entrepreneurs who are seeking financing or investment capital. The LAEDC screens hundreds of business plans each year, and provides this weighting scale to help small businesses make their presentations to investment bankers, venture capitalists, private angel investors, and other financial organizations or sources of cash.

WHY MARKETING IS NUMBER ONE

When I first came across this set of planning guidelines years ago, I thought to myself, "Wow! I would think that financial people would rank the financial component of my business plan as the highest in importance." Seems logical, but here is the reality.

You can make the "financials," sales revenue, expenses, profits, etc., look any way you want on paper. Financial people are wise to that. While the numbers are important, ten percent significance in terms of your overall strategy, the other aspects of the plan are more important! In other words, being able to answer questions such as . . .

> *"How did you get the numbers?" or "What are you going to do to achieve your sales targets?" is actually more important than the numbers themselves.*

This is a key point. Look at the percentages noted above one more time. What's number one in ranking? Market overview and marketing strategy. Other than creating an excellent product, competing for attention—marketing—is the biggest business challenge facing any music endeavor. Savvy business people, including financial experts, know this. That's why we devote Section Three of this book to marketing and sales.

HOW LONG AND DETAILED IS A BUSINESS PLAN?

Back to your own business plan. I encourage you to write one, whether you are going to show it to financial people or not. The first inclination for most people drafting a business plan is to think, "More is better. Let's gather all the facts and impress our staff or financial backers with lots of details." This is part right and part wrong.

The correct part is to do your homework and have facts available. The incorrect part is to assume that anyone other than you will actually read a novel-length business plan, with reams of text, graphs, charts, "circles and arrows," clippings, and other support materials. Ironically, this mistaken assumption is a big reason why such a high percentage of all businesses don't complete a written plan.

My reality-based suggestion is to first, remember that the plan is primarily for you, so you decide how much detail you need. If you are developing an organization or seeking financing, you may need more than one version of the plan. This is analogous to songs that are recorded multiple ways depending on how they are going to be used, like radio mix, club mix, album mix, live mix, or ringtone. The core content is the same, but the packaging is different depending on the target audience.

Remember, that while your prospective investors and stakeholders are likely serious and well meaning, they will not read a plan that is too long. They'll say something like "Wow this looks great. Lots of good stuff here. I'll dig into it this weekend (or on the plane, or after the kids are in bed)." Good intentions notwithstanding, they may never pick it up again. It's better to be concise and (like a good live show) leave them wanting more.

"So, where do I start?" A solid business plan includes the following:

1. Fifteen to twenty pages of text, following the five-chapter outline above.
2. Financial schedules, including detailed monthly budgets, for the next year and summary budgets for two more years.
3. Reference material that supports the text and the financials. We'll go into more detail on how to put the plan document together in Chapter Eighteen.

YOUR PLAN'S "SIXTH CHAPTER": THE APPENDIX OR REFERENCE SECTION

It's human nature to procrastinate reading or writing long, copiously detailed documents. You can help everyone by breaking your plan down into bite-size chunks. To keep the text portion of the plan brief and concise, put the backup information in an Appendix or Reference Section. Note: The details *are* important, but it's the essence of those details that comprise the core of your plan.

Here are examples of items that can be included in the Reference Section:

- Detailed biographical information and history
- Organizational chart

- Job descriptions
- Information policy
- Master client or product history spreadsheet ranked by total sales
- Product plan spreadsheet
- Historical financial data
- Customer profiles and target customer criteria
- Sample promotion materials, press clippings, awards, Website content
- Employee handbook including company policies and benefits
- Market research reports and statistics
- Detailed profiles of competitors.

Seem like a lot? It is, but don't worry. You're about to learn how to gather the information for your business plan and assemble it in an organized way.

KEY POINTS IN THIS CHAPTER

1. A business plan is a written system of documents that describes (1) what you are going to do, (2) how you are going to do it, and (3) the consequences or results.

2. "If it's not written down, it's not a plan." Having the plan organized and relatable to others is a powerful and essential tool for business success.

3. A business plan has five key "chapters":

    Chapter 1: Company, business, and industry overview (15%)

    Chapter 2: Products overview (15%)

    Chapter 3: Market overview and marketing strategy (35%)

    Chapter 4: Management team and organizational overview (25%)

    Chapter 5: Financial summary (10%)

4. The market overview and marketing strategy section carries the most weight, especially with financial people or investors.

5. Assumptions answer the question, "How did you get the numbers?" There are market assumptions, financial assumptions, staffing assumptions, creative assumptions, and scheduling assumptions. All need to be written into the business plan.

6. Less is more. Be brief, concise, and accurate. Good, readable business plans consist of about 15–20 pages of text, plus detailed financial schedules and reference information. If your plan is too long, even willing stakeholders will not read it all the way through.

7. Put the back-up details in the Appendix or Reference Section or the "sixth chapter" of your plan. Examples of elements in this section include organizational charts, sample promotion materials, and market research information.

CHAPTER SEVEN

THE PLANNING FLOW–FROM INTENTION TO ACTION

THE RIGHT PLANNING SEQUENCE MAKES A DIFFERENCE

We've discussed the contents of your business plan. Now we'll help you create a "planning flow" for taking steps in the right sequence to optimize results. We'll present the "perfect world" scenario first, and then provide tips on dealing with the reality that it's not a perfect world. Many music businesses are already up and running, with or without a business plan.

Planning in the right sequence can prevent problems and help preserve artistic integrity. That's a strong statement. Consider a scenario in which you are starting your business from scratch and you have time to plan before leaping into the market. Here is the recommended planning flowchart.

Plan Element	How Long	Level of Precision
Mission statement	Indefinite	Values
Brand positioning statement	Indefinite	Goals; long-term objectives
Product plan	2–5 years	Strategy
Detailed operating plan	1–2 years	Tactics; short-term objectives
Daily action list	Daily	Implementation

PLAN ELEMENT 1: THE MISSION STATEMENT

The best business planning flows from concise statements of mission, vision, and values. We touched on this in Chapter One. Remember the exercise where you answered the "why are we in business" question, your vision of the future music market, and your personal and company values?

As the chart above indicates, mission statements are designed to last indefinitely. When you are tempted to change your mission statement (this will happen periodically), take a step back and see whether you are reacting to an unforeseen opportunity or problem, or actually considering a separate business with a separate mission. Once you pinch yourself and see what's really going on, you are likely to keep your mission intact and adapt other elements of the plan, rather than changing things to reflect your feelings in the moment.

Here's the key point again. Your business "foundation elements"—mission, vision, and values—are unlikely to change over time. You can add clarity from time to time as things evolve, but remember that if your mission changes, you are probably talking about a different business.

PLAN ELEMENT 2:
THE BRAND POSITIONING STATEMENT

Once you've articulated your mission statement, the next element in the planning flow is the "brand positioning statement." Like the mission, the position that you plan to develop for your brand (even if the "brand" is you) is likely to last a long time unless business or personal conditions change substantially. Many music businesses get into trouble by changing strategic direction whimsically and frequently. Your brand positioning statement is a key tool in preventing that problem and in focusing your business efforts.

Your brand positioning statement is a one-page document that answers the following four questions:

1. What business are we in? (What you do.)
2. Who are our customers? (Where the money changes hands.)
3. What makes us special? (Relative to our competitors.)
4. What's in it for everybody? (Including you, your customers, employees, vendors, and the community.)

Here's a sample brand positioning statement for "Our Band," a performing group. Note: This is repeated in the Reference Section in the context of Our Band's full business plan. You can adapt this example for yourself (including other types of music businesses) by using the templates included in the Reference Section of this book and on the CD-ROM.

Our Band is in the business of providing music and entertainment services on a contract basis. Our Band's clients include promoters, record labels, and fans worldwide. We focus on those customers (promoters and fans) who share our love of dance and pop music of the 1980s and 1990s.

Our fans are motivated by a combination of needs, including:

1. The need for entertainment with positive messages.
2. The need to dance, as well as listen to music.
3. The need to identify with artists who consistently present a positive image.

We provide our fans with a special blend of cover and original material in both live and recorded performances. We can entertain virtually any audience—young or old, hip or square. We consistently exceed fan and promoter expectations and are uniquely competitive in the following areas:

- *Quality of the music. We are expert songwriters, arrangers, and performers. We are well-rehearsed and cohesive entertainers.*
- *Adaptability and flexibility. We integrate easily within each promoter's unique environment. We are versatile and work comfortably in most performance situations.*
- *Marketing and promotion. We provide high quality promotional materials and participate willingly in interviews and showcases. Our representatives maintain the highest standards of creativity and cooperation in making events successful for promoters and fans alike.*
- *Attention to detail. We know that the little things count. We take pride in our thoroughness and accuracy in communication, professional image, and follow-up.*
- *Timeliness and accountability. We show up on time and work within schedules. We understand the time value of money and the monetary value of time, and work closely with our clients to optimize resources.*

Promoters and fans regard Our Band as a friend and musical resource. We write, record, and/or perform, depending on the situation. While project and engagement lengths vary, relationships are long-term.

We are acknowledged by clients and competitors in the music industry as a leading band. Our success is measured in terms of our promoters' ability to make money and our fans' ability to be entertained. We also provide steady income and a creative work environment to Our Band team members.

See how all four questions were answered? If Our Band was your business, how would you feel? What have we accomplished? Once again, you may be thinking, "I know all that. Why should I write it down?" For the answer to the "why write it down" question, see Chapter Five. It's more likely that you may be thinking, "I've never really answered these questions in a concise way. It looks good on paper—almost *too good to be true.*" That's the more typical response. When you have a written brand positioning statement, you have a tool which can be used in the following ways:

- Foundation for your marketing plan. By thinking through the four questions early in the planning process, your marketing plan will be easier to construct.
- Basis for evaluating opportunities. As opportunities arise, including booking possibilities, recording offers, publishing deals, or whatever is relevant to your business, you can check them against your brand positioning statement as well as your mission. If they fit, keep going, if not, you can respectfully decline with a clear conscience and no hard feelings.
- Elements of company promotion materials. As you develop sales literature, publicity, advertising, Website content, podcasts, album liner notes, and other sales materials, you can use the brand positioning statement to be sure that your public message is consistent with your plan. It helps keep you in control of the marketing process.
- An intended target. Since you are drafting the positioning statement early in the planning process, it sets the tone and provides a foundation for your long-term goals and objectives. It's okay if it sounds a little idealistic or motivational.

To elaborate on the last point above, I often hear the following from music people who have just written their first brand positioning statement: *"It sounds good but it doesn't really describe us. We have a lot of problems and challenges to work out. Why not tell it like it really is?*

You are going to identify all the negatives of your business when you do the risk analysis and identify weaknesses and threats. The brand positioning statement informs this on a relative basis. Besides, who would want to work for or invest in a business that aspires to anything less than success?

The "Elevator Test"

One of the ways to be sure that your brand positioning statement does not ramble is to apply the "elevator test." Imagine that you get on an elevator in a tall building with someone you have never met. That person asks the question, "What do you do?" You only have the time that it takes go up or down about ten floors in the elevator, but you want to make a good first impression.

Rather than fumble or respond with "It's a long story," or the "Well you gotta understand, I wear many hats," type of answer, mentally prepare to answer with your brand positioning statement which answers the first two points:

- "I'm in the music business as a (fill in your role here)."
- "My customers are (fill in your target customer profile here)."

This clarifying experience helps you answer the key questions concisely and in language that does not presuppose music industry knowledge on the part of the person asking the question. While you may never have a stranger ask you for this information in an elevator, the following types of people are likely to ask at some point.

- Prospective customers, employees, and vendors
- Your banker, accountant, or lawyer
- Your parents, friends, and family
- People you meet at parties, weddings, or other events (like your class reunion)

Remember, you never know how someone might be able to help you. It's better to give a concise and accurate answer to the "What do you do?" question than to leave a weak impression and miss an opportunity.

Here's the business point. A properly articulated brand positioning statement is a key element in your business plan and a tool that has multiple applications. You are better off thinking through the answers to the four questions *early* in the planning flow rather than later or not at all.

PLAN ELEMENT 3:
THE THREE-YEAR PRODUCT PLAN

Understanding your product and where it is going three years into the future is the next element in planning. First, a quick definition of product: *Your product is the result of your labor and what your customers pay for.*

There are two broad categories of products: goods and services. Goods are tangible, services are intangible. Much of the music industry is based on *services as products.* Consider the examples below.

Your Industry Role	Product Example	Goods	Services
Performing musician	Live performances		×
Songwriter	Original compositions		×
Booking agent	Secure bookings		×
Manager	Provide management services		×
Record label	Recorded music (CDs, etc.)	×	
Event promoter	Entertainment experiences		×
Producer/engineer	Recording and production services		×
Music teacher	Learning experiences		×
Merchandiser	T-shirts, jackets, identity items	×	
Publisher	Song promotion and royalty administration		×

We'll expand on this theme in Chapter Nine when we discuss product strategy in the context of your comprehensive marketing plan. For now, the point is to understand that your long-term product strategy drives the tactical aspects of the business plan. For example, you simply can't set sales revenue objectives or plan staffing and promotional techniques if you do not know what products you plan to offer.

PLAN ELEMENT 4: THE OPERATING PLAN

Once you've got the first three elements—mission, brand positioning statement, and product strategy, you are in a position to create an operating plan. This is the part of the plan that most people think of when they think of a business plan. Let's make a distinction here. Remember the definition of strategy versus tactics? A strategy is a decision; a tactic is a method. A business plan articulates both strategies and tactics.

Most businesses have a sales forecast and expense budget, both key elements of a tactical operating plan. Relatively few businesses frame the numbers with the strategies and operating assumptions that really make a good plan come to life. Here are the key elements of the tactical operating plan:

1. **Detailed revenue forecast.** Revenue equals units sold times average selling price. If you are selling records on a wholesale basis or calculating song royalties, the process is pretty simple. If you perform live in multiple types of venues at different prices, it's a little more complicated, but manageable. If you do more than one thing, like perform, write songs, and sell your own records, you will need a line item in your revenue forecast for each item. We'll come back to this in Chapter Sixteen.
2. **Marketing plan.** The Seven Links in the Marketing Chain™ (seven elements of the marketing plan) will be covered in detail in Section Three.
3. **Budgets and pro forma financials.** These are the hard-core financial schedules, related to both income (see the revenue forecast) and expenses in all areas. The words "pro forma" come from Latin and imply that portions of the material are hypothetical (future) as opposed to actual (real history). Examples of financial materials include departmental or project expense budgets, profit and loss (P&L) or income statements, and balance sheets. See definitions in the glossary.
4. **Organization plan.** This includes a listing of each staff position, the reporting structure (best illustrated in a graphic organizational chart), job descriptions for each position, and a description of employee benefits provided by the company. Benefits include: (1) health, life, disability, and liability insurances, (2) paid holiday, vacation, and personal day policies, (3) retirement, profit-sharing, or stock options, and (4) any extras not covered elsewhere, like day care, fitness counseling, on-the-job training, or tuition reimbursement.

5. **Capital purchase schedule.** Capital purchases are those items the company buys that have a useful life of longer than one year. In most cases, the Internal Revenue Service requires that capital purchases be "depreciated," meaning deducted on a pro rata basis from taxable revenue over the useful life of the item (several years) rather than all at once. Examples include vehicles, equipment (such as instruments, stage rigs, recording gear, or computers), and real estate. Other countries may have different tax codes and accounting requirements.

Taxes notwithstanding, understanding the concept of depreciation will help you plan for replacing that worn out van or mixing console. Besides the tax obligations and benefits, capital purchases usually require that you have an advance idea of where you're going to get the money to pay for each item. Can you pay from cash on hand, or will you need to finance the item? Once again, doing the planning up front helps you anticipate financial needs and prepare accordingly.

Note: Each of the key elements of an operating plan can potentially be the subject of a book of its own. We've provided an overview here to show how the pieces fit together. We'll expand on the marketing plan element in Section Three. Also see the Reference Section for additional information and samples of other elements.

PLAN ELEMENT 5: THE DAILY ACTION LIST

Once you've got an operating plan for the current year, you are ready to go to work. While you don't necessarily have to consult your operating plan every day, you are likely to do so more frequently once you have perspective on the activity flow as it is presented here.

Relating Business Planning Theory to Your Music Business

Most businesses already have parts of the plan but not the whole plan. Little, if any is written down. In many cases, the planning flow goes like this:

> Element 1: Product plan
> Element 2: "Budget" (rough revenue plan and estimate of expenses)
> Element 3: Daily action list

While this is better than nothing, it leaves a lot to chance. When the foundation elements (mission, vision, values, and brand positioning statement) are missing, it is virtually impossible to make consistently good business decisions.

You may be thinking, "But I'm already in business! This whole thing sounds overly complicated and unrealistic. I just want to make a decent living in music, not necessarily own a business. I can balance my checkbook but I'm not good at bragging about my future accomplishments."

Remember that we are still presenting the "perfect world" scenario, offered here as a set of reference tools and definitions. If you are already in business, I encourage you to keep going and take time to fill in the missing plan elements. If you are not yet in business, you are getting a head start by understanding the fundamentals. Chapter Seventeen deals with practical ways to integrate these concepts into your particular situation.

How Often Does the Plan Change?

We've already mentioned that the mission, vision, values, and brand positioning statements are designed to last indefinitely. What about the other plan elements? Here are guidelines for revising your business plan.

- Product plan. Revise the product plan once every year and include details that paint a picture of your business two-to-five years in the future. That way you are always looking several years ahead, with the added benefit of learning from the year that just passed. Your strategic vision may extend many more years into the future, but three years is generally enough for a committed product plan.
- Operating plan. The operating plan is short-term in focus. Plan your monthly revenue and expense budgets twelve months in advance. Then make a quarterly plan (three-month increments) for the next twelve months. Add the third year as a 12-month summary, not broken down by month or quarter. As with the product plan, this should be revised each year, adding a year each time so you are always looking three years ahead.

The Five-Year Window™

In our consulting practice, we encourage our clients to revise their operating plan every year, looking at a rolling five-year window every year. The five years include last year, this year, plus three years into the future. This approach keeps you focused on the future but is grounded by actual recent business activity. We'll come back to this and elaborate in Chapter Sixteen.

KEY POINTS IN THIS CHAPTER

1. Your strategic business plan helps guide your daily action and is key to preserving your integrity, sanity, and cash flow.

2. The planning flow starts with the foundation elements: your mission, vision, values, and brand positioning statements. The other planning flow elements include the three-year product plan and detailed operating plan.

3. Whether you are already in business or just starting, be sure that you have articulated these items so that everything you do is consistent with your long-term goals.

4. The brand positioning statement answers four key questions:

   a. What business are we in?
   b. Who are our customers?
   c. What makes us special?
   d. What's the payoff for everybody involved?

5. Understanding what business you are in and who your customers are equips you to pass the "elevator test" with flying colors. Beware of telling people that what you do is "a long story" or that you "wear many hats."

6. Your product plan maps out what you plan to sell over the next three years. "Products" are the results of your labor and what your customers buy, from "services" like live performances or original songs, to "goods" like records or other merchandise.

7. The operating plan includes a detailed revenue forecast, marketing plan, budgets and pro forma financial schedules, organization plan, and capital purchase schedule.

8. Practical reality: Things don't always go according to the plan, "by the book," or according to a "perfect world" scenario. That is why it is important to revise your plan yearly and monitor your progress monthly.

9. The tactical marketing plan is so important that we will cover it in detail in Section Three.

BUILDING
YOUR BRAND

MARKETING AND SALES ARE THE KEYS TO YOUR SUCCESS

Here we will explore the difference between marketing and sales and how the two work together in the music business. In addition, we'll briefly define the Seven Links in the Marketing Chain—seven essential elements of any marketing plan. This will set the stage for Chapters Nine through Fifteen in which we'll examine each of those links in more detail.

Let's look at music industry statistics. As of 2008, there are over three million people active in the music industry in North America. Here are related numbers to help put this in perspective:

- There are an estimated 450,000 performing musicians. Of those, over 90,000 are members of the American Federation of Musicians, the union representing musicians in the United States and Canada.
- Apple's iTunes music store offers over six million registered songs from over 150,000 artists (solo performers and bands).
- Over 220,000 artists sell music via the CD Baby online store. Thousands of artists also use amazon.com and other online merchants for fulfillment of record sales.
- There are an estimated 660,000 songwriters who have written millions of songs that are registered with BMI, ASCAP, and SESAC.
- There are hundreds, perhaps thousands, of record labels releasing over 75,000 record albums per year. In addition, there are countless artists who self-produce records and sell them direct to the public, "under the radar screen" of the music industry. The number of new releases has increased dramatically in the past ten years.
- SoundScan tracked the sales of 75,774 new album releases in the year 2006, up 33 percent from 56,831 in 2005. Records released in the past eighteen months are considered current, over eighteen months are considered "catalog," and those released over three years ago are considered "deep catalog."
- Also according to SoundScan, in 2006, about one percent of new titles accounted for over eighty percent of new album sales. About seventy-four percent of all releases sold less than 100 units in 2006, and eighty-nine percent sold less than 1,000 units. This means that frightfully few records

sell enough to pay back their recording and marketing expenses, let alone provide income for the artists and songwriters involved.

Other numbers are more difficult to determine, because so much of what happens in the music industry is not formally tracked or reported. What about:

- All those wedding and private party gigs?
- Show dates booked directly by the artist, with no agent or manager involved?
- Songs that are written and performed but never published?
- Concerts and festivals put on by private and civic groups who do not consider themselves professional promoters?

Here's the point. The music industry is vast, fragmented, and only partially organized. This has advantages and disadvantages.

COMPETING FOR ATTENTION

Here's the point of presenting industry statistics. The biggest business challenge facing any music person or music business is competing for attention at all levels. There are so many competitors in all categories that the customer's challenge of simply wading through the possible choices can be overwhelming. Consider the following questions:

- How do performers choose what material to perform and record?
- How do agents choose which artists to represent? Which venues are viable for the artists they represent?
- How do record labels or producers decide which artists to sign and produce?

And of course, the ultimate challenge:

- How do music fans decide which shows to attend and records to buy? Will they pay for your products when there are so many free alternatives available?

Here's why I bring this up now. *Your marketing plan represents the single most important tool for addressing these issues.* It prompts you to not only ask these questions, but determine answers that guide the operation of your music business. Further, when you understand what you're up against, and you've done your homework, you have a huge competitive advantage.

Remember the earlier comment about how so few music businesses have solid business plans? The need for "attention management" (keeping your customers focused on you and your product) intensifies the need for planning, especially as the market becomes even more cluttered with the choices mentioned above.

WHAT IS MARKETING AND HOW IS IT DIFFERENT FROM SALES?

Let's make a distinction right up front. Marketing and sales are different but intimately related functions in any music business.

Even the dictionary has a hard time differentiating between marketing and sales. The definitions are cross-referenced to the extent that a casual reader could conclude that they mean essentially the same thing. However, they are as different as art and science, yet willing partners in the world of business. Here is a composite dictionary definition:

Marketing: the act of developing products (goods or services) and exposing them for sale to a specified customer base.

Sales: the act of causing and expediting a purchase at a specified price, or within a price range.

The key word is "specified." It implies that the activities are deliberate, as opposed to accidental or random. In less formal language, here are several ways to say the same thing:

- Marketing opens the door. Sales close the deal.
- Marketing prepares a sales environment. Sales operate within that environment.
- Marketing defines the product and prepares targeted customers to buy. Sales finish the job by completing the transfer of goods or services at a set price.
- Marketing is the art of communicating with potential customers. Sales is the science of converting potential customers into real paying customers.
- Marketing "hooks 'em." Sales "reels 'em in."

THE FOUR FUNCTIONS OF MARKETING

Let's turn the definitions into examples of functional activities in each of the two areas, starting with marketing. When I've asked clients and seminar audiences, "What comes to mind when I say the word marketing?" the most frequent answer is "advertising." While advertising and related promotional activities are indeed part of marketing, they are only one small aspect among many others.

Here are examples of marketing functions, organized in four key areas:

Marketing Function 1. Planning and Positioning the Product
- Develop product definitions and product strategy.
- Monitor business conditions and competitive activity; conduct market research.

- Perform market tests, such as dress rehearsals, focus groups, and regional record rollouts.
- Model comprehensive marketing plans.
- Forecast and control inventory, ranging from tour schedules to CDs in stock.

Marketing Function 2. Communicating with Your Target Market

- Tell your company story; build your image through publicity and related efforts.
- Provide newsletters, press releases, Website content, e-mail blasts, and other communications to your target customers and the general public.
- Handle press relations, including editorial placement of reviews, interviews, and articles.
- Maintain industry relations; participate in professional organizations; attend conferences, trade shows, and other music business events.

Marketing Function 3. Managing Customer Relationships

- Advise and assist customers on a continual basis.
- Qualify customer requests and refer them to the proper follow-up person.
- Handle charity or sponsorship requests; participate in benefit concerts; make donations to nonprofit organizations.
- Follow-up on complaints and suggestions.

Marketing Function 4. Advertising and Promotion

- Plan, produce, and schedule media advertising.
- Plan and produce promotion materials, including photos, biographies, press kits, Web content, and merchandising materials.
- Plan and coordinate trade shows, showcases, conferences, and special events.
- Plan and locate sources for premiums, incentives, and identity items, such as T-shirts, jackets, fly swatters, refrigerator magnets, and key rings.
- Fulfill and track prospective customer inquiries.

Once again, notice that while advertising and promotion are important, they are among many other marketing functions.

A NOTE ON BRANDING

A brand is a *symbol* that causes the audience or your customers to connect with you in a positive way. The stronger your brand, the stronger your competitive position—and your sales and profits.

- Your brand brings to mind your unique characteristics.

- Your brand highlights differences rather than similarities.
- Your brand message should be short and easy to remember.
- Branding relates to visual, as well as verbal identity.

More on branding later . . .

THE FOUR FUNCTIONS OF SALES

Let's take a look at sales functions in a similar fashion. Many people think of sales only in terms of negotiating and processing contract paperwork or orders for records and merchandise. There's more to sales than just asking for the order.

Here are examples of sales functions, organized in four key areas:

Sales Function 1. Achieving Sales Objectives, or "Hitting the Numbers"

- Negotiate and develop relationships with target customers.
- Train and support sales representatives, such as agents, managers, or dealer salespersons, including distributors or record store personnel.
- Secure and expedite sales orders, including all contract paperwork.
- Track sales and expense results; monitor sales revenue versus quota, and expenses versus budget.

Sales Function 2. Participating in Events

- Get involved in promotions or special sales activities, like artists showcases, clinics, or in-store events with record merchants.
- Lead or participate in sales meetings, key client negotiations, and sales presentations.
- Attend trade shows, conferences, and seminars.

Sales Function 3. Managing the Sales Territory

- Plan and develop product distribution or client relations within an assigned territory.
- Control use of free product samples, including unpaid auditions, promotion-only records, or complimentary show tickets.
- Develop relationships with staff and influencers of key customers, such as event promoters' crew members or booking agency assistants, who do not necessarily buy, but can influence a purchase.
- Implement sales and marketing programs in the field, like promoting a song or record at a retail store, online event, or radio station.
- Balance office and field travel. Sell face-to-face, as well as on the phone and via e-mail.
- Monitor business conditions and the competitive environment; regularly report details to the company.

Sales Function 4. Handling General Administrative Tasks

- Maintain equipment and supplies as required, from office phones to personal digital assistants, from paper clips to promotion materials.
- Interface with internal departments such as sales, marketing, and accounting, and contract service providers such as agents, business managers, recording studios, or tour crew.
- Do the paperwork, including expense reports, sales forecasts, travel itineraries, special correspondence, and maintenance of contact databases.

Note: *Contract* paperwork and collection of payment comes under Key Sales Function Number 1, "Achieving Sales Objectives." Why? Because (and here is one of the greatest pieces of business wisdom I've learned): *"A sale is not a sale until it is paid."*

THE SEVEN LINKS IN THE MARKETING CHAIN

Textbook marketing (a term referring to the basic fundamentals of marketing taught in most business schools) talks about the "Four P's" of your marketing plan: Product, Pricing, Promotion, and Place. In our consulting practice, we expand these four elements to seven, and call them the "Seven Links in the Marketing Chain." Here are brief descriptions of the seven links:

- Link 1: Product strategy. Identify the goods and services you currently offer and plan to offer over time.
- Link 2: Pricing strategy. Understand how much things sell for or "what the market will bear," then set your prices and pricing objectives accordingly.
- Link 3: Promotional strategy. Create media advertising (print and broadcast), publicity, sales literature, Web presence, trade shows, showcase performances, and direct marketing materials.
- Link 4: Sales channel strategy and place of business. A sales channel is an intermediary who purchases your product for resale. A place of business has two dimensions: geographical territory, and your personal workspace, whether a home office or a corporate facility. For performers and promoters, place of business also includes target performance venues.
- Link 5: Salesforce strategy. Decide who does the selling, what skills your salespeople need, and how much it costs to employ good salespeople.
- Link 6: End-user or audience and buyer profiles. Identify key characteristics of target customers and understand their buying habits and preferences.
- Link 7: Competitive environment. Identify your competitors' strengths and weaknesses, and anticipate their activities over time.

Note: Each of the above links is covered in detail in Chapters Nine through Fifteen.

Now you can easily see that marketing is much more than advertising and promotion. As the old saying goes, "The chain is only as strong as the weakest link."

For example, you could have the greatest act in the world (link 1), but if you do not understand your audience (link 6) and competitors (link 7), you may accidentally price (link 2) or promote (link 3) your act the wrong way, use the wrong salespeople (link 5), or sell through the wrong channels (link 4).

All combinations work the same way. You could have a great agent and beautiful promotional materials, but if the act (the product) is weak or the audience is too fragmented to target, the results are compromised. The chain is only as strong as the weakest link.

At this point, it may sound more complicated than it actually is—don't worry. We're about to explore how to develop your product strategy, and examine each of the seven links in detail.

KEY POINTS IN THIS CHAPTER

1. There's lots of competition out there. Your music business is one among tens of thousands vying for attention and market share.

2. Lots of competition indicates lots of market opportunities. This is good. The sheer number of music businesses means that your buyers have many positive product choices.

3. Your biggest challenge is competing for the buyer's attention. This points to the absolute necessity of a marketing plan and strong marketing and sales functions.

4. Marketing and sales are different from each other, but intimately related. Marketing "hooks 'em." Sales "reels 'em in."

5. The four marketing functions are: (1) planning and positioning the product, (2) communicating with your target market, (3) managing customer relationships, and (4) advertising and promotion.

6. Your brand is a symbol of the good things about you and your business. Promote the differences rather than the similarities.

7. The four sales functions are: (1) achieving sales objectives, or "hitting the numbers," (2) participating in events, (3) managing sales territory, and (4) handling general administrative tasks.

8. Any marketing plan has Seven Links in the Marketing Chain. The seven links are: (1) product strategy, (2) pricing strategy, (3) promotional strategy, (4) sales channel strategy and place of business, (5) sales force strategy, (6) end-user or audience and buyer profiles, and (7) competitive environment.

9. As the old saying goes, "The chain is only as strong as the weakest link." If one of the seven links is weak or missing, your business potential and results are compromised.

CHAPTER NINE

DEVELOPING YOUR PRODUCT STRATEGY

L et's examine the first link in your marketing chain—product strategy. At the strategic level, you decide what product category or categories you will offer over time. At the tactical level, it's time to get specific and go into more detail.

MUSIC INDUSTRY PRODUCTS: EXAMPLES OF GOODS AND SERVICES

Let's look at the music goods and services matrix one more time.

Your Industry Role	Product Example	Goods	Services
Performing musician	Live performances		×
Songwriter	Original compositions		×
Booking agent	Secure bookings		×
Manager	Provide management services		×
Record label	Recorded music (CDs, etc.)	×	
Event promoter	Entertainment experiences		×
Producer/engineer	Recording and production services		×
Music teacher	Learning experiences		×
Merchandiser	T-shirts, jackets, identity items	×	
Publisher	Song promotion and royalty administration		×

Now let's go a little deeper. Following are examples of music business products that are likely to be familiar to most readers:

1. Live performances—concerts, festivals, club dates, and private events such as weddings, parties, corporate meetings, etc. If you are a performer, you are involved in live performances as a product category by definition.
2. Record sales—any delivery medium for music: audio, video, or multimedia via compact disc, vinyl, DVD, or digital download. Records are sold through distribution (retailers, mail order, or Websites) or direct from the artist. Virtually all music people get involved with record sales on some level.
3. Music publishing—royalties from broadcast airplay (radio, television, films) and record sales (downloads, ringtones). While songwriters, publishers, and recording artists are most involved with publishing, agents and managers also play a role in many cases. Songs are also published in sheet music or songbook form. This gives the songwriters and performers another product opportunity.
4. Business services—booking, management, accounting, publicity, promotion, and tour management. This is primarily the domain of agents, managers, lawyers, accountants, and other specialists who also provide business services as products.
5. Technical services—recording, mastering, graphic design, Web content production, sound reinforcement, instrument repair and maintenance, and even tour bus maintenance. (While somewhat outside the scope of this book, be aware that technical services are "products" and essential elements of the product plans of those service providers.)

JACK OF ALL TRADES, MASTER OF SOME . . .

At most levels of the music industry, individuals and firms offer a variety of music business products, crossing over the basic product categories. Here are some examples. Can you relate to any of them?

- Performing songwriters sell live performances, songs to other artists, songbooks, and records.
- Non-performing songwriters sell songs, songbooks, and records. Many establish their own publishing or record production companies.
- Booking agents sell consulting services to promoters, and management services to artists, in addition to securing performance bookings for artists.
- Managers provide advice and business service to artists, and may also operate record labels, performance venues, or publishing companies.
- Promoters may operate record labels, management firms, or publishing companies in addition to presenting concerts and festivals.
- Many performers do it all: write and record the songs, book and perform show dates, and operate record labels, booking agencies, and publishing companies. While no one has hard statistics, it is likely that self-managed performing songwriters represent the largest single category of music people.

YOUR PRODUCT MIX CHANGES OVER TIME

Few music businesses start by doing everything at once. Consider our original band story from the Overview. The group started as performers, then booked themselves, and later recorded and sold records. Songwriters get into publishing and record label work. Agencies start promotion and business services divisions.

The reverse is also common. Multi-category businesses may occasionally delete products or spin them off into separate companies.

Here's the point. You don't have to do everything yourself, or everything at once. This is a key business planning principle, and one which music people often overlook. Further, it is valuable to plan your product strategy several years into the future. Try this brief exercise. Fill in the chart below by checking the boxes that are relevant. (This planning matrix is also in the Reference Section and on the CD-ROM.

Product Category	This Year	Next Year	Year Two	Year Three
Live performances	_____	_____	_____	_____
Secure bookings	_____	_____	_____	_____
Provide management services	_____	_____	_____	_____
Recorded music (CDs, downloads, etc.)	_____	_____	_____	_____
Entertainment experiences—tickets	_____	_____	_____	_____
Original compositions	_____	_____	_____	_____
T-shirts, jackets, identity items	_____	_____	_____	_____
Song promotion and royalty administration	_____	_____	_____	_____
Other (specify):	_____	_____	_____	_____

UNDERSTANDING PRODUCT LIFE CYCLES—
THE SIX PHASES

Each product has a "life cycle" roughly analogous to that of human life: conception, birth, childhood, adolescence, adulthood, maturity, seniority, and death. The business world uses slightly different terms and organizes the product life cycle into six phases.

- Phase 0: Research and development. This phase occurs *before* the product is ready to sell. For all music people, this is when you do market research, analysis, and planning. As a performer or songwriter, it is when you are rehearsing an act, writing original material, or recording.

Note: Research and development is called phase 0 (as opposed to phase 1) because business schools and textbooks refer to the first phase as "introduction," presuming that development work has been done before the product is launched. Thus, you get six phases, though it looks like five.

- Phase 1: Introduction. As a performer, this phase represents your first gigs, often performed for little or no money and to small audiences. As a songwriter, the introductory phase may focus on self-produced demo records or covers of your compositions by artists that you know personally.
- Phase 2: Early growth. In this phase, the business starts to take off. As your business gains more customers and revenue, the audience profile begins to change. Performers advance to higher paying and more prestigious gigs. Songwriters begin to place material with established artists. Airplay creeps into the picture for recording acts.
- Phase 3: Late growth or shake-out. In music industry terms, this phase is when acts "break nationally." It is also the phase that most music people and businesses aspire to. Artists perform consistently in larger venues, command higher fees, and tour over wider geographic areas. Songwriters earn increasing royalties from record sales, broadcast airplay, and from sales of sheet music and songbooks.

Note: The term "shake-out" refers to the fact that many businesses merge, sell to another company, or go out of business during this phase. There are (relatively) fewer competitors in the market in phase 3 (and subsequent phases) than in phases 1 and 2.

- Phase 4: Maturity or saturation. After a while, an artist's record sales, airplay, and concert attendance reach a plateau. They stop growing. While the numbers may be large, the audiences and the performance fees are not getting bigger. The market is saturated. Fans have had enough, and newer artists (particularly those in phase 2 and 3 of their careers) have captured the imagination of the audience. Note to performers: This has a ripple effect on agents, managers, and promoters. There is plenty of business done, but a little less "buzz" than in the late growth phase.

- Phase 5: Decline. This is the phase that everyone wants to avoid, as it signifies a loss of popularity, marketability, and earning power. This is when former "name" artists perform on package shows or festivals, cruise ships, corporate events, and private parties. While the fee per performance may be enough to make a living, the average fee and number of dates is less than in earlier phases. Record companies drop declining artists whose products have become cutouts or "midline" releases. Acts may tour on the strength of a "greatest hits" release versus a record with all-new material. As in the saturation phase, the performers' ability to draw an audience and sell records has a direct impact on agents, managers, songwriters, and promoters. They are usually already looking elsewhere for new artists—fresh blood at earlier career stages, or early phases in the product life cycle.

Six Phases of the Product Life Cycle

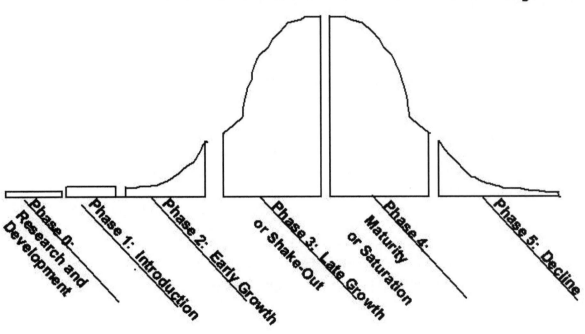

All products go through life from conception to birth, childhood, adolescence, adulthood, maturity, seniority, and death. The business world refers to six phases as shown above: Research and Development, Introduction, Early Growth, Late Growth or Shake-out, Maturity or Saturation, and Decline.

On first glance, it is easy to conclude that decline and death are inevitable. You may ask yourself, "If that's the case, then why bother?" Or, "How do I get to Phase 3, late growth, and simply stay there?" That's actually the better of the two questions, and one that many music people simply never address. Some music business careers begin and end within one year. Others last for decades.

You've heard the expression, "one-hit wonder," which refers to performers or songwriters who achieve a measure of recognition (and maybe even get rich) based on a single song. I've only met a few music people who aspired to be "one-hit wonders." Most want a sustainable and long career.

Then there's the other end of the spectrum. Consider the work of classic artists past and present who have performed for over fifty years: Louis Armstrong, Bill Monroe, B.B. King, Tony Bennett, Pete Seeger, Ella Fitzgerald, Etta James, and Isaac Stern. Many rock and roll and pop music acts of the early twenty-first century are carrying on in this tradition and are likely to continue performing indefinitely: Madonna, the Rolling Stones, Bruce Springsteen, Billy Joel, and Elton John among others. Lots of people admire these artists and others like them. Outside of having the requisite talent, planning and business skills make the largest difference between the two extremes.

HOW LONG DOES EACH PHASE LAST?

Can you accurately predict how long your product will take to develop, launch, and mature? The short answers are "it varies" and "no." That means that there are no firm rules and certainly no guarantees. That said, you can model each phase as part of your planning process. That's what business planning is all about—getting control of your business.

Back to the "how long" question . . .

The goal is to get through research and development and launch your product relatively quickly. Let's say that takes months, as opposed to years. Then the challenge is to build your business through the introduction and early growth phases and get to the late growth phase as quickly as possible. While that may take a few years, as opposed to months, you can still make a living and enjoy your music business along the way.

Think of examples from music genres that are familiar to you. Do you know any performers or songwriters who fall into each of the phase categories? Where are *you* currently? The relevant point here is to relate your current product phase to your product strategy for the next two years, and then be sure that the rest of your marketing plan is consistent with that strategy. We'll come back to this in the rest of Section Three as we examine the other links in the marketing chain.

KEY POINTS IN THIS CHAPTER

1. "Products" include goods and services. The first step in developing a product strategy is to understand your current products and product mix.

2. Products are what you get paid for. Performers get paid for live performances and recording; songwriters and composers for creating original material. Performing songwriters have multiple products and revenue streams.

3. Don't try to be a musical "jack of all trades." While many artists start out multi-tasking (booking and recording while writing and performing), it is difficult to master (or have time for) all aspects of the music business.

4. Your product mix is likely to change over time. Start by assessing what you are doing now, then look ahead three years and see what products you will add or delete. Strategic planning means deciding now where you want to be in the future.

5. All products go through life from conception to birth, childhood, adolescence, adulthood, maturity, seniority, and death. This is called the "product life cycle."

6. The business world organizes the product life cycle into six phases (0) research and development, (1) introduction, (2) early growth, (3) late growth or shake-out, (4) maturity or saturation, and (5) decline.

7. Every product goes through the six phases consecutively, each taking a different amount of time. Your mission is to get through the introduction and early growth phases as quickly as possible. The volume and long-term profit potential are in the late growth and maturity phases.

8. Successful music people make the late growth phase last as long as possible. It's the phase associated with the largest audiences, financial rewards, and "buzz."

9. Each phase represents a different customer profile and requires a different marketing plan, product configuration, pricing strategy, promotional platform, distribution channel, and sales program.

CHAPTER TEN

YOUR PRICING STRATEGY

The second link in the marketing chain is your pricing strategy. For some music people, setting price can be mysterious, sensitive, and a bit scary. Pricing strategy involves the decisions you make about pricing *before* you go to market. How do you set prices? Do they change over time? How do you know if your prices are market worthy? This chapter explores these issues and provides guidelines for preventing mistakes and optimizing revenue opportunities.

AN AGENT'S TALE

There's an old story that booking agents tell. It is meant to both amuse and inform.

An agent was interviewing an artist to see if they could develop a business relationship. The agent asks, "How much do you charge for a show date?"

Artist: "$150,000 a performance."
Agent: "At that price, you won't get many dates."
Artist: "At that price, I don't *need* many dates!"

It's a fact of business that few artists are paid $150,000 or more per date on a regular basis. The amusing part (at least to experienced agents) is that some naïve artists think they can just "name their price." The practical lesson is that artists can set pricing *goals* and work toward ever increasing per-performance fees, based on pricing *objectives*. This relates to the product life cycle concept. Let's turn this into a set of practical guidelines.

CHARGING WHAT THE MARKET WILL BEAR—THREE FACTORS

You probably have heard the expression, "Charge what the market will bear." This implies (correctly) that the market (*customers or clients*) determines pricing in the long run. Three key factors influence how much customers are willing to pay.

Pricing Factor 1: "Supply and Demand"

This is a fundamental business principle. Prices go up or down based on the balance between *supply*, or product availability, and *demand*, or number of potential customers in the market.

For example, a music store may mark down the prices of instruments or gear in stock if they have too much inventory or if customers are not asking for the product. Conversely, the same store may sell custom guitars at list price because the maker's output is limited and the market is small but willing to pay a higher asking price for a unique instrument.

This principle applies to some, but not all, categories of music people and their products. Two contrasting examples:

- Barbra Streisand, Madonna, U2, Led Zeppelin, or the Rolling Stones (among other big name acts) command large performance fees because they perform relatively rarely and fans are willing to pay higher-than-average ticket prices to see them, creating more demand than supply.
- On the other hand, many performers are often locked into the talent budget of a club or festival and take what the venue or promoter offers. If the act doesn't like the price, the promoter hires someone else, because there is more supply than demand.

Pricing Factor 2: Pricing Conventions and Traditions

"We've always done it that way." I hear this all the time. Every industry, including music, has its time-tested pricing guidelines or methods. Here are some music industry examples:

- Sidemen and technicians are paid flat rates per performance, tour, or season. The amount is negotiated in advance and stays the same over the contract period.
- Booking agents charge a flat percentage of performance revenue, usually in the 10 to 20 percent range.
- Managers also charge a flat percentage, often based on artists' total revenue (performances, royalties, recording advances, merchandising, etc.), usually in the 10 to 25 percent range. When compensated on the high end of the percentage range, the manager may pay outside booking agent commissions from the manager's share.
- Recording artists and songwriters earn royalties at rates that are established by law and administered by the music publishing industry. While the rates change occasionally, the individual artist has little or no control over them.
- The record industry has its own set of pricing conventions. For example, most single-disc CDs with forty to seventy minutes of music sell for approximately ten dollars wholesale and twelve to eighteen dollars retail. The same "album" sells for $9.99 as an iTunes download. Production and marketing

costs or the relative popularity of the artist have little effect on the selling price. As of 2008, record pricing is up for grabs—more on this later.

- Concert, festival, and club ticket prices vary with the notoriety of the act(s), size of the venue, and price of competitive entertainment offerings (sports events, movies, theme park admissions, etc.). As a result, live music ticket prices paid by fans range from zero dollars (free) for subsidized events like community festivals to over $200 for premium seats at major concerts and festivals.

Pricing Factor 3: Your Sales and Marketing Ability

Regardless of musical talent, some acts are marketed and sold more effectively than others. This capability is developed over time and is fundamental to the premise of this book. It's all about branding. Consider the following examples:

- Acts with professional-looking promotion materials often command higher prices. This is not simply based on the materials, but on the idea that the club or promoter can use the materials (photos, bios, press clippings, video clips, etc.) to help charge higher ticket prices and draw a larger crowd.
- Live acts with recorded product can generally charge more than unrecorded acts.
- Recording artists and songwriters with established track records (strong recording and airplay history) can potentially command higher royalty advances than unproven artists.
- Songwriters with "cuts" (songs on released recordings) by significant artists are in greater demand for placing songs on television or in movies.

THE THREE BASIC PRICING STRATEGIES

Every business has a pricing strategy, whether it is conscious of it or not. In the classic or textbook business sense, there are three basic strategic pricing options: 1) low cost producer, 2) differentiation, and 3) hybrid. Below we'll look at two examples of each strategy, the first in each from outside the music business.

1. **Low-cost producer strategy**. In this approach, the supplier prices to the low end of the market and earns acceptable profits by controlling internal costs. Our examples:

- Generic or "store brands" at the grocery. Ever wonder how your local supermarket can afford to charge so much less for its own can of soup compared to the nationally advertised brands? In some cases, the ingredients and quality are essentially the same, but the store brand is cheaper than the name brand. This is because they have learned how to control costs, charge less, and still make an acceptable profit margin. Pricing below the competition is a conscious marketing decision.

- Independent versus major label recording projects. As stated above, records sell for about the same price no matter what label they are on or who the artist is. How can independent record labels afford to compete with the mass-marketed majors? In many cases, the independent label controls recording, production, and marketing costs differently from the major label. This allows the label and artist to make an acceptable margin at lower unit volumes. This is also why so many artists have chosen to produce and sell their own recordings online or using physical media, rather than sign with a label.

Note: Simply watching expenses and looking for ways to undercut competitive prices do not constitute a low cost producer strategy. Any well-run music business pays attention to its production and operating costs. Those adopting this pricing strategy deliberately find ways to turn cost control into higher profits.

2. **Differentiation strategy**. Here the supplier charges the highest price possible, based on the product's features and competitive advantages. Differentiation assumes that there are aspects of each competitor's product that can be distinguished easily. Those features and benefits are promoted to target customers who are willing to pay a higher price for something different (and presumably better). Again, two examples:

- "Designer" clothes versus department store brands. This is the converse of the grocery example above, and one that most people can relate to. Whether you shop at Wal-Mart, Target, Nordstrom, or a designer boutique, you can choose from among brands of blue jeans with slightly different styling and features—and radically different prices. The designer-label clothes have a feature/advantage/benefit story to tell, and sell for more.
- Established acts versus new or unproven acts. It's common in the music world for established acts to draw crowds that are larger and/or willing to pay higher ticket prices. If the music essentially sounds the same, what difference does it make? Entertainment is entertainment, right? From the fan's point of view, the answer is: "Not necessarily." The established act is more likely to have that "story" to tell: recordings, good reviews, fan buzz, or legacy. More on this in later chapters.

Most music businesses are based on the differentiation pricing strategy. The goal is to increase prices over time based on the marketable difference between you and your competitors. While the market will bear only so much (in terms of performance fees, ticket prices, etc.), the range is wide.

3. **Hybrid strategy**. In this approach, the supplier offers more than one product and uses both the low cost producer and differentiation strategies selectively.

Some products may be viewed as "commodities" and are subject to competitive market pressures. Others can be "differentiated" and priced accordingly. The examples:

- In-stock versus special-order motor vehicles. When you shop for a car, you have a choice of buying one "off the lot" or having one made to order. The dealer prices the cars on the lot to be competitive with the market and conducive to quick sales. If you want something special, like the upgraded sound system or custom color upholstery, you pay more and wait longer. The fact that the dealer offers *both* is an example of a hybrid pricing strategy.
- Multiple music "products." As described in Chapter Nine, many music people offer more than one category of product. For example, a performer is likely to price live shows using a differentiation strategy, but price self-produced records and downloads using a low-cost producer strategy.

While product differentiation drives the music industry, many music businesses end up with a hybrid pricing strategy due to their mix of products. Further, those who are reliant on income derived by charging a percentage of some other revenue (such as songwriter royalties or agent commissions), need to be conscious of both cost control and techniques to increase fees on a per-transaction basis.

CHANGING PRICES AND REVENUE PLANNING

A key part of your long-term pricing strategy is to forecast your revenue several years in advance. When you look at your sales plan over a longer period of time, you can apply the fundamentals described in this chapter to your best advantage. We'll cover goals and objectives in detail in Chapter Sixteen. In the meantime, here is a simple formula to start the process of planning revenue: *Revenue equals units sold times average selling price.*

Sounds simple, and it is. This formula applies to all music people, regardless of what you do. There are worksheets in the Reference Section that apply to both performers and songwriters. For now, let's use the example of a performing act.

	Last Year	This Year	Next Year	Year Two	Year Three
Show dates per year	20	30	60	90	120
Average $ per date	$150	$200	$500	$1,000	$2,000
Total performance $	$3,000	$6,000	$30,000	$90,000	$240,000

Remember that this is a simplified example, just to show the fundamentals of revenue planning. When you do this with your own numbers, you will find that it is often a "wake-up call" that you aren't charging enough. How do I know that? Because I've done it myself, and I know many music people who have done it and ended up changing their pricing strategies as a result.

See how the table above corresponds to the product planning matrix in Chapter Nine? This is a recurring theme. When your three-year objectives are staring you in the face, it is much easier to make operational business decisions than if you had written nothing down or had only thought a few months ahead.

WHAT TYPICALLY HAPPENS IN THE MUSIC INDUSTRY

Let's go back to the "$150,000 a date" story. The artist was "naming the price" and the agent knew it was unrealistic. Here are examples of the consequences of *not* having a realistic pricing strategy:

- Never enough revenue to make a living. Too many music people think that price increases either never come or will simply be offered spontaneously by their customers. Here's another ironic expression: "I plan to lose $100 on every date, but make it up on volume." Yikes! It doesn't work that way. If you are losing money on every date, figure out how to either increase fees, lower costs, or both.
- Pricing out of the market. While it's true that, "At $150,000 a date I don't need to work much," it is possible that if your prices are too high, you simply will not get any work.
- Costs get out of control. As discussed in the three pricing strategies above, it is essential to understand your expenses before you determine selling prices. Wake-up calls in this area often result, for example, in six-piece bands becoming four-piece bands.
- Inaccurate or limiting image or reputation. Ask yourself how you would like to be regarded *relative to pricing*. This is a key element in branding. Your price is suitable for what you deliver. While there is no right or wrong answer, see which of the following pricing images best suits you.

"Always plays for the door (or tips)."
"Cheap. I don't know how they stay in business."
"Penny-wise and pound-foolish."
"Willing to work for anything."
"A great value. We all make money."
"Premium quality, premium price."
"Overpriced. You're paying for the name."

People in creative fields, like music, frequently adopt a differentiation pricing strategy, either consciously or unconsciously. Specifically, many music people believe that their product is unique and price it as high as possible. This can apply to show dates, tickets, and recording and publishing advances.

Those with business plans and market awareness will best understand the differentiation approach and work toward it long-term. That's part of an overall plan to make more money, have more fun, and stay in business longer. Even a booking agent paid on a fixed commission schedule, works to drive acts' prices higher whenever possible.

Others look out in the market and set prices at or below what competitors are charging. While this can be a viable approach, I believe that many music people "leave money on the table," unconsciously assuming that they have no influence on customers' budgets or willingness to pay.

Here's the point.

> *Not enough music people actually have a conscious pricing strategy. As a result, they default to charging too much or too little. Sometimes this works, but it frequently leads to problems.*

Some artists charge too little and end up subsidizing the music by working the proverbial day job. Others burn out prematurely, due to overwork at under-market prices. Others charge too much too soon, and can't get enough work to stay in business. You can do better. That's why you are reading this book.

HOW TO AVOID PRICING PROBLEMS AND OPTIMIZE REVENUE

Pricing problems lead to revenue problems. Music people seldom have enough money. Hmmm, there might be a connection here! While you may not be able to "name your price," there are three things you can do to avoid problems.

Pricing Tactic 1. Understand the *range* of prices charged by others who do what you do before you establish or quote prices in the market place.

Pricing Tactic 2. Do your revenue planning using the five-year view (last year, this year, plus the next three years) and formula before making major business decisions, like going on tour, cutting the next record, hiring additional people, or investing in promotion materials.

Pricing Tactic 3. Understand that you have a higher degree of control over how things change over time than you might first imagine. This ties to the importance of doing things consciously versus unconsciously as you develop your brand.

KEY POINTS IN THIS CHAPTER

1. Pricing strategy involves conscious decisions on how you set prices over time.

2. Many music people either think they have to work for whatever is offered, or that they can "name their own price." Both of these extremes are unrealistic. Understand the *range* of prices applicable to your type of product before constructing your own pricing strategy.

3. The market influences pricing as it relates to "supply and demand." If there is more supply than demand (such as opening acts looking for exposure), the average market price is relatively low. If there is more demand than supply (like the one and only Madonna or Rolling Stones) the market price is relatively high.

4. The market sets the price, but only to a point. There are established music industry traditions and conventions that impact agent/manager commissions, publishing and performance royalties, and record sales.

5. You can control and manage your pricing over time, if you are realistic. Work toward increasing prices and revenue as you develop your business and your brand.

6. From a classic business standpoint, there are three basic pricing strategies relevant to the music industry: 1) low-cost producer; 2) differentiation; and 3) hybrid. Most music businesses strive for higher earnings through increased fees over time, applying a long-term differentiation strategy.

7. Revenue equals units sold times average selling price. You need a pricing strategy to forecast revenue and create budgets that look ahead three years in connection with your product strategy.

8. Many music people charge too little, as opposed to charging too much. Using a conscious planning approach, you can often avoid not making enough money, allowing costs to get out of control, or developing the wrong image.

9. Pricing problems can be prevented in many cases with a well-planned, long-term pricing strategy. You have a higher degree of control over how things change over time than you might imagine.

PROMOTION, BRANDING, AND ADVERTISING

Now we turn to the third link in the marketing chain, promotional strategy, which has three distinct elements: promotion, branding, and advertising. It is vitally important to remember that these three elements are just one link in the chain. They do *not* constitute the whole of marketing, a common misconception. That said, let's examine your promotional strategy.

As with marketing and sales, the dictionary cross-references advertising and promotion to the extent that a casual reader would conclude that they are the same thing. For our purposes here, let's use the following definition:

Promotion is the process of delivering *controlled* messages about you and your products to your target customers, audience, and other stakeholders. Stakeholders may include your staff, vendors, community, financial investors or creditors, family, or the general public.

A WORD ABOUT BRANDING

Just like marketing, advertising, and promotion, we hear the word "branding" used in a variety of business contexts. So what is branding, anyway?

Branding is the creation of indelible images of you and your products in the minds of your target customers, audience, and stakeholders. Examples of music business brands include your name or stage name, your company name, names of songs, records, festivals, concert series, clubs, and other venues. Brands can consist of both words and graphic images (logos and trademarks) associated with your business.

Your brand is the *symbol* of what you do and what you stand for. While music fans are unlikely to say, "I really like the Rolling Stones' big lips brand symbol" in casual conversation, they are likely to recognize that brand when they see it and think of what it stands for: the mark of the "world's greatest rock 'n' roll band."

Likewise with jazz fans. All you have to do is say "Duke" or "Bird" or "Wynton" in a jazz context and an image comes to mind. Or, how about country music? Willie, Garth, Reba . . . the list goes on. We could do the same for virtually every genre of music. The name, logo, and other images remind fans and music business people of something special (hopefully something good) about the artist and their music "products."

The business point is that these artists consistently sent controlled messages to their target customers, audience, and stakeholders over a long enough period of time to have become "brands." We'll come back to this concept in Section Four.

THE PROMOTIONAL TOOLBOX— TEN TYPES OF TOOLS

There are many ways to promote. It is beyond the scope of this book to present an exhaustive list of promotional tactics or to suggest how to use them. There are many good books and other educational materials, some geared to the music business, already available on the topic of promotion. For now, we will focus on brief definitions that you can use as a guide as you develop your marketing plan and build your promotional toolbox. Consider the following as a checklist of options.

Tool 1: Advertising

Here's an irony of the world of promotion. Ask ten people this question: "What's the best form of advertising?"

What comes to your mind? Even people who are not marketers are likely to answer, "Word of mouth." This means that the most credible and cost-effective way to get a promotional message into someone's mind is to have it delivered in person by someone with knowledge and authority. Wow! That's easier said than done.

The business term "missionary selling" means meeting face-to-face with prospective customers and sharing your sales message with one person or one small group at a time. Ever have someone try to sell you magazine subscriptions or Girl Scout cookies, or get you to vote for a political candidate through in-person canvassing?

> *Door-to-door or "lead them by the hand" promotion and sales may work for some products, but it is generally impractical for selling concert tickets, records, or music business services. You get the picture.*

Note to songwriters: The exception to the above is pitching songs to artists, producers, and publishing companies. This is classic missionary selling work, best done one-on-one and face-to-face, where possible. Nonetheless, you still need to build your brand in order to get meetings.

Advertising is the act of delivering a paid promotional message to a target audience. A key word here is "paid." You pay someone to deliver your message to a predetermined or target audience.

There are two types of advertising: trade and consumer. Trade ads are sometimes called "business to business" or "B2B" ads. Consumer ads focus on end-users or the general public. Advertising media categories include print (magazines, newspapers, directories), broadcast (radio, television, podcasts, mobile phones), outdoor (billboards and other signage), and online (Websites and e-mail).

For example, if you are releasing a record and want to promote it to record retailers, you might advertise in a trade publication like *Billboard* magazine. If you already have distribution, or sell directly to the public, you might advertise the same record in targeted consumer magazines like *Rolling Stone, Wired, Guitar Player, Utne Reader* or *The New Yorker*. You might also share clips from the record on your MySpace page, CD Baby, or YouTube. These are all examples of advertising.

Songwriters seldom use advertising as a promotional tool, but a music publisher may advertise a song or record in a broadcast industry trade magazine or insider newsletter. The performing rights organizations (BMI, ASCAP, SESAC, etc.) occasionally advertise the work of award-winning songwriters in trade publications.

So what's the irony in this? It's that while word of mouth *is* the most effective form of advertising, it simply is not efficient by itself to get your message across to the wider audience. The relative efficiency of reaching many people simultaneously is the rationale behind using advertising as a promotional tool.

Tool 2: Publicity

Media advertising has a place in many marketing campaigns, but there are alternatives. Publicity (also referred to as public relations or "PR") is another form of media, but is clearly not advertising.

Publicity is the act of delivering an unpaid educational message to a target audience. The key words here are "unpaid" and "educational." While you do pay for advertising space or time, you do not pay for publicity.

The media's rationale is that an educational message (as opposed to a "here's the product and price, come and get it" ad message) is of general interest to their target readers, viewers, and listeners. They need news and other material on a constant basis. You make the editor's job easier by providing newsworthy information on your activities and products.

Note: There are costs associated with generating publicity. It is not "free advertising" as is commonly believed. Professional publicists charge fees for their services and are hired because they already have relationships with the right editors, reviewers, and media outlets. Alternatively, you may pay for the delivery of your own publicity in the form of newsletters, press releases, press conferences, and press tours or interviews. You cover your own production and travel expenses in the hope that the media will pick up your story.

Put yourself in the position of a booking agent or talent buyer, reading trade publications and attending trade shows. If you saw a performer's advertisement in the magazine or show directory, you are likely to skip over it. If you saw an interview, tour itinerary, or record review covering the same artist, you may be more likely to take notice and take some sort of action, like checking out a live show or listening to a record.

Continuing this example, if you read an interview and want to know more about the performer, you may need to consult a directory or some other form of advertising to get complete contact information (address, telephone, e-mail, Website). So, as you can see, advertising and publicity work together. (Unless, of course, someone knocks on your door and hands you the information you are looking for just at that moment—unlikely.)

Tool 3: Sales Literature

Sales literature includes brochures and other items that describe and depict your product. This is tangible print material, which you can deliver to prospective customers by mail, online, or in person. By the way, the word "promo" is an abbreviation for "promotion." Here are examples:

- Performer: Artists can provide their own business cards, biographies, photos, reprints of reviews, interviews and other publicity, testimonials, posters, fliers, and handbills.
- Songwriter: Non-performers can provide the same items, plus lists of publishing and recording credits ("cuts").

While physically printed material is used less in the twenty-first century than in the twentieth century, the content described above still needs to be produced for online or electronic delivery.

Tool 4: Demo Recordings and Other Collateral Materials

Collateral materials (also referred to simply as "collateral") include those promotional items that work with, but do not take the place of, basic print sales literature. As with the other tools in your promotional toolbox, your collateral materials are designed to help promote your product to your target customer.

Examples of collateral materials for performers and songwriters include demo recordings (audio CDs, DVDs, downloadable song clips), souvenir items, songbooks, tour itineraries, or concert programs.

Tool 5: Direct Marketing

Direct marketing is a catch-all term that includes any promotional activity in which direct contact is made with the target customer. While advertising and publicity are *indirect* promotional methods, direct marketing, also called direct response marketing, allows you to get immediate and trackable feedback from your target customers. Examples of direct marketing techniques include:

- Direct mail. From post cards promoting show dates to press kits promoting new record releases, music people use direct mail regularly and often. Virtually all performers and songwriters use the mail in some way (beyond routine one-to-one correspondence). Note: Direct mail includes both postal "snail mail" and e-mail.
- Telemarketing. Ever get a phone call from someone trying to sell you mortgage financing, vacation packages, or newspaper subscriptions? Those are examples of using the telephone to promote a product directly to target customers. Kind of annoying, huh? Still, music people use the telephone, though not in the same fashion. For example, a performer or songwriter without personal referrals looking for an agent may identify prospective agents in one of the industry directories and make initial contact by telephone.
- Cold canvassing or missionary selling. Remember door-to-door sales of vacuum cleaners, magazine subscriptions, or candy for fundraisers? Or those roving photographers at theme parks, clubs, or restaurants, who snap your picture, then offer you a print for sale as a souvenir? Those are examples of direct face-to-face marketing. While not always practical, there are plenty of music industry stories about songwriters approaching artists at concerts with a "hey, please listen to my CD" pitch. Sometimes they work, but the success stories are closer to "urban legends" than to proven promotional methods.
- To repeat a key point, the attractiveness of direct marketing as a promotional method lies in its "track-ability" (results versus cost) and fast feedback.

Tool 6: Trade Events

Quick review: The best kind of advertising is word of mouth, but that's not always practical. Cold canvassing gets immediate feedback and is trackable, but may also be impractical or inappropriate. Music industry trade shows, conferences, and seminars (the all-inclusive term is "trade event") represent hybrid promotional opportunities.

Trade events focus on business, as opposed to concerts, festivals, or other show dates, which are about providing an entertainment experience for the target audience. Depending on 1) your overall promotional strategy and 2) your proximity to the action, trade events may offer a cost-effective medium for reaching a group of target customers, face-to-face, in one location, in a relatively short period of time.

How do trade shows, conferences, and seminars differ? Aren't they essentially the same thing? Here's a quick overview:

- *Trade Shows* usually last two to four days and include an exhibit hall, networking activities, and educational workshops or seminars. Many music trade associations present trade shows on a regular basis.
- *Conferences* generally last one to three days and include the educational activities along with social or networking opportunities. Conferences offer multiple activities simultaneously, organized around themes or "tracks."

The lack of an exhibit hall usually means that the price of admission and quality of education is higher than at trade shows.

- *Seminars and workshops* generally last one to twelve hours and focus on a single topic. The class size is often limited to allow the attendee individual access to the instructor.

Conferences and seminars often share location with trade shows. For example, a conference promoter partners with a trade show promoter to stage a series of educational workshops in the same city, in the same convention facility or hotel, and on the same dates. Why? Because the events are relevant to the same target audience.

Why mention trade events in a chapter on promotion?

Trade event promoters look for advertising or sponsorship revenue based on the buying power and promotional value of the audience they attract.

Promoters are also eager to enrich the value of the conference, seminar, or workshop for the attendees so they are more likely to return in future years. Your target customers may be the ones attending the event.

At trade events, you have the opportunity to do the following:

- One-on-one, face-to-face promotion. You've heard the terms "networking" or "schmoozing." These are prime activities at trade events.
- Advertising. Most trade event promoters sell space in show directories, conference programs, or special event-related publications.
- Exhibit booth. If the event is a trade show with an exhibit hall, you can "set up shop" and conduct business right on the show floor. Your booth is a place to hold meetings, present your products, and take the pulse of the event.
- Sales literature and collateral material distribution. From business cards and bios to sample CDs or DVDs, you have the opportunity to get your materials into the hands of multiple target customers over a short period of time.
- Special event sponsorship. Special events like showcase concerts, keynote speeches, or private receptions are also promotional opportunities at most trade events. You may have the opportunity to fly a banner, distribute literature, or even speak to an assembled audience.

Tool 7: Key Influencer Relations

Influencers are people who do not buy from you, but who can influence your target customers. Here are examples of influencers, arranged by industry role:

- Performers can influence who gets booked as their opening act, who gets signed to their record labels, whose songs they record, and what other performers are handled by their agent or manager.

- Record label executives and producers can influence who gets signed to a label, what songs are recorded, what recording studios are used, and what studio musicians are hired.
- Agents and managers can influence who gets signed to record deals, who gets signed to representation agreements, who gets booked on what shows, and what special opportunities for exposure (television, radio, film, etc.) a performer or songwriter can get.
- Promoters can influence other promoters, record labels, agents, and managers on which performers to work with or hire again.

The point is that you need to establish and maintain relationships with anyone who potentially has a positive influence on your target customers. This may be as simple as sending a periodic newsletter or as complicated as staging a private "thank you" reception for key people. A consistent program of "staying in touch" can go a long way toward optimizing your other promotional activities.

Tool 8: Identity Items

"Identity item" is the generic term for tangible promotional gifts that include your identity (name, logo, message) and have some intrinsic value beyond pure promotion. The item is actually *useful* to the recipient. Other common names for identity items include "advertising specialties," "tschotschkes" (find *that* in the dictionary), and "swag." Examples include:

- Wearables, ranging from the legendary T-shirts to jackets, jewelry, backpacks, briefcases, caps, or other clothing.
- Non-wearables, such as CD/DVD openers, guitar picks, pocket knives, clocks, sculpture, flower arrangements, wall plaques, calendars, calculators, PDAs, MP3 players (loaded with your songs), refrigerator magnets, and luggage.
- Edibles, including candy, fruit baskets, gourmet assortments, wine, steak, bottled hot sauce ("We're the hottest act in the industry"), or virtually any food or beverage that can accompany your promotional message or be imprinted with your identity in some way.

Music people are human beings, and they remember thoughtful gifts. The challenge is to choose appropriate items that are both affordable and have the right impact. A performer's key ring with a logo on it may not land a recording deal, but it may remind promoters that the act is serious about its business and cares for its fans.

Some identity items are also products that can be sold to fans. Virtually all wearables and non-wearables (see lists above) can be merchandised at shows and through your direct marketing efforts.

Tool 9: Showcase Performances

In bygone days, there were "auditions," live performances in front of someone who might hire a musician or act. These ranged from individual singers and instrumentalists vying for a spot in a band or orchestra to whole ensembles looking for club or concert bookings. These days, recordings, especially video, have streamlined the audition process. Instead of booking a hall for a day and staging a series of live auditions, a producer often pre-screens applicants via audio or video, and then interviews only the final candidates.

The audition process is different from that of a showcase performance. A showcase is an unpaid live performance with a commercial motive, such as:

- Performer: Secure future bookings, close a recording deal, attract an agent or manager, build a fan base, develop an image.
- Songwriter: Place songs with recording artists, close a publishing or recording deal, attract an agent or manager.

Any live performance, paid or unpaid, is potentially a showcase if the right people show up. The point is that live showcases are one of the promotional tools available to you. In building your marketing plan, choose wisely the quantity and quality of unpaid gigs.

Tool 10: E-Commerce

It's been interesting to follow the development of the Internet as a music industry promotional tool. Since the mid-1990s, performers, agents, and record labels began using Websites and e-mail lists as low-cost alternatives to sales literature and direct mail. Since 2001, a Website and e-mail campaign is considered essential to any music business, even that of an individual performer or songwriter. Before 2001 Websites like MySpace, YouTube, Facebook, and Broadjam simply did not exist.

As we approach the second decade of the twenty-first century, there are more online promotional vehicles than ever before. Hundreds of thousands of acts post songs, bios, and itineraries or host blogs and forums online. A performer or songwriter without an online presence is missing a key opportunity.

There are three basic types of Websites:

1. Informational. This is the most rudimentary site, sometimes called "read only" because it does not allow interaction. Informational sites are online alternatives to sales literature. You can post bios, photos, itineraries, sample contracts and riders, and sample audio or video clips. These can be viewed or downloaded by prospective customers, fans, press, and your competitors.
2. Interactive. This type of site generally includes the features of an informational site, but adds the ability for customers or fans to interact. The most common example is e-mail feedback. A visitor to an interactive site can send

a message to you directly from within the site. Further interaction includes online forums, chat rooms, and surveys.

3. Transactional. This type of site includes the ability to conduct sales transactions online. This is especially valuable to performers and songwriters who sell records, identity items, or tickets, or other merchandise to the general public.

Like publicity, e-commerce can be relatively inexpensive, but it is not free. Take into account the initial production costs, online service fees, and the time it takes to maintain the site adding new content. While not "free," these costs are definable and represent a good value, especially when planned in conjunction with other promotional tools.

THREE KEY QUESTIONS ABOUT YOUR PROMOTIONAL STRATEGY

As you review the many promotional options available, you may wonder what combination of tools is best for you.

> *While the sheer number of promotional opportunities can be daunting, take comfort in knowing that you have control over your own situation.*

As you plan the promotional link in the marketing chain, ask yourself three key questions:

1. Do I have to use all ten categories of promotional tools? The answer is "probably not." There is some overlap. Think of your promotional toolbox as a checklist of options, not a prescription.
2. What can I afford? The range of promotional expense budgets for most music businesses is one percent to ten percent of total revenue. Some businesses spend more, some less. If you are spending less than one percent of your total revenue on promotion, you are probably not promoting enough. If you are spending more than ten percent you are either spending too much or your promotion is not effective.
3. What if I'm no good at writing marketing copy, graphic design, or promotional strategy? This is a big question, and points to the value of building a team of people with promotional expertise. Your team can be made up of employees, freelancers, marketing service companies like ad agencies or publicists, or a combination of all three. Someone needs to do this work, and if you cannot, then find someone you can pay to do it.

Note that I did not specify a dollar amount for your promotion budget, but rather a percentage of total revenue. It is much better to back into the promotion budget after planning total revenue than it is to commit to promotional efforts and then figure out how to pay for them. If you are just starting up and have little or no revenue, plan your promotional expenses judiciously in the context of what you want to accomplish.

Many performers or songwriters get burned by spending too much on the wrong things in the early stages of their business. Retreating with a sour taste of the promotion world, they go too far the other way and don't use the ten tools effectively. You can prevent this problem. The checklists and templates in the Reference Section and on the CD-ROM provide a starting point for planning your promotional strategy, costs, and milestones over time.

KEY POINTS IN THIS CHAPTER

1. Promotion is the process of delivering controlled messages about you and your products to your target customers, audience, and other stakeholders. "Controlled" is the key concept here. *You* make decisions about what information to send and when.

2. Branding is the creation of indelible images of you and your products in the minds of your target customers, audience, and other stakeholders. Promotion helps you build your brand.

3. Advertising is often the first thing that comes to mind when people think of promotion. While advertising is a key element, it may or may not be appropriate for your marketing plan. You have many other options.

4. There are ten categories of tools in your "promotional toolbox." They are: (1) advertising, (2) publicity, (3) sales literature, (4) demo recordings and other collateral materials, (5) direct marketing, (6) trade events, (7) key influencer relations, (8) identity items, (9) showcase performances, and (10) e-commerce.

5. Many music businesses rely heavily on publicity, demo recordings, identity items, showcase performances, and e-commerce.

6. There are more online promotional vehicles today than ever before. Performers and songwriters use e-mail, networking sites, and their own Websites and e-mail lists to great advantage.

7. Your promotional mix will depend on your unique set of marketing and sales objectives, budget, and capacity to implement your promotional strategy. You do not need to use tools in all ten categories.

8. Budget from one to ten percent of your total revenue for promotional expenses. While some music businesses may spend more or less, start here for planning purposes

9. Someone needs to do the promotional work. Options include yourself, your employees, freelancers, ad agencies, publicists, or a combination.

10. Use the Internet as a cost-effective international promotional tool. Music businesses are expected to have Websites and e-mail capability. If you don't, you won't be taken seriously and lose a valuable tool to build your brand on a global basis.

CHAPTER TWELVE

YOUR PLACE OF BUSINESS

The fourth link in the marketing chain involves the physical environment in which business is conducted. The marketing textbooks call this "place" or the fourth "P," after product, pricing, and promotion. In this chapter we will discuss three aspects of place and how they relate to your marketing strategy.

WHY PLACE IS A MARKETING STRATEGY

Where you conduct business has an impact on all the other links in the marketing chain. These are the three dimensions of place to consider: (1) geographic territory, (2) performance venue and distribution channel types, and (3) your workspace—office, studio, or other day-to-day business headquarters.

Now that we are into the fourth link in the marketing chain, we'll start to see how all of the links work together. Sometimes this gets a little murky. Is a venue type also a target customer? As a songwriter, does my publisher's office location have an effect on my ability to sell songs? Will customers actually visit my home studio? Should I sell my records only direct to my fans, or through record retailers?

We'll address the answers to these questions in this chapter and in Chapters Thirteen and Fourteen. For now, the key points are:

- You decide where you want to work.
- Your decision has three dimensions: geographic location, venue, and workspace.
- The strategy changes over time.
- Place is a marketing strategy because it has an impact on all the other links in the marketing chain.

Let's look at each of the three dimensions.

Place Dimension 1: Geographic Territory

Where do your customers live and do business? Is it just in your community, or the whole world? The geography that you cover is called your "trade area." The options are:

- Local—your community and surrounding area
- Regional—several states or provinces
- National—the whole country
- International—more than one country (Note: "International" implies more than one continent, like North America plus Europe.)
- Global—everywhere worldwide
- Interplanetary—coming soon

For some music people, the prestige of performing or trading nationally or internationally is compelling. For others it's scary or unnecessary. For example, if you are a part-time performer with a day job, it is not practical to be a national act. Or, if you are a full-time performer with long-term career plans, you may start regionally and branch out over time as you develop an audience.

If you are a songwriter, the practical aspects are simpler to handle. You do not need to physically visit or perform in every venue in order to get paid. Still, the element of *focus* factors into the strategy. Can you develop and maintain customer relationships (read: artists, producers, publishers) over a wide area? Understanding time zones, foreign languages, and different business cultures are critical to your success when making geographic territory decisions.

Place Dimension 2: Performance Venue Type

"Channel of distribution" is the business term for the type of venue where you work or sell products. Consider a manufacturer selling consumer electronics equipment, from boom boxes to high-end home theaters. The manufacturer has several choices of "dealer channels, including, superstores, independent specialty retailers, boutiques, or systems contractors. Which channel is appropriate depends on the product, the pricing, and the rest of the strategic marketing links presented in this book.

In music, it's easy to plug record sales into the example above. Records are sold everywhere from supermarkets and convenience stores to iTunes and other Web-based specialty retailers. The record label (which may be you) chooses the channel or combination of channels that optimizes sales, manages expenses, and sends the right positioning message to the market.

Consider the following:

- Performers target venues by size and format. These range from small coffeehouses and private residences to clubs, colleges, large arenas, stadiums, and outdoor festivals. Which one you choose depends on the style of music, the target audience, your act's drawing power, and the positioning statement that you want to make.
- Songwriters pitch songs to publishing companies, record labels, producers, managers, and directly to artists. Each of these represents a "channel" toward the ultimate goal: to get songs recorded and performed publicly.

Songwriters and composers may choose to specialize in a specific performance format like records, film, games, or television. This decision also has an impact on channel.

- Agents sell acts directly to venues, to show producers, or through other agents. The choice may depend on the act represented and the other strategies described. While on one hand, a venue or event producer is a target customer, the channel decision has other dimensions. For example, an agent who books on the local or regional level may affiliate with other regional or national agencies to optimize touring opportunities for an emerging national act.

- Managers sell acts to agents, producers, record labels, and promoters. The manager decides whether to use a single agent or multiple agencies depending on the performer's specific situation and needs. Also, managers influence their clients (performers and songwriters) on what types of venues to play and when. This points to the need for a clear channel/venue strategy agreed to by each party (manager, agent, performer/songwriter).

As a performer or songwriter, should I use an outside agent, or play the role of agent myself? The answer relates partly to the channel strategy and partly to the profile of the salesforce as discussed in Chapter Thirteen.

Concert and event promoters make venue and channel decisions as well. The range of venue choices parallels that of performers: clubs, concert halls, and the full spectrum of alternative performance spaces. Promoters sell tickets through venue box offices, ticket bureaus and brokers, mail order, and online.

Are you a club act or a concert act? Do you work exclusively with a specific agent, or nonexclusively with multiple agents? Do you co-market with other artists? These are all examples of channel or venue strategies. The answer is often "all of the above" and depends on the specific situation.

Place Dimension 3: Your Workspace

The term "workspace" refers to the physical place where you do what you do on a regular basis. Here I am referring to offices, recording studios, and rehearsal halls, as opposed to performance venues. Many performers and songwriters work at home. Others work "on the road," in cars and vans, hotel rooms, restaurants, and airport boarding lounges. While this decision is often driven by practical concerns, it is your choice nonetheless.

Workspaces need to have certain basic elements in order to be viable. For all music people those elements include:

- Access to communication tools: telephone, fax, high-speed Internet connection
- Access to files and business records
- Access to reference materials
- Privacy

- Comfort
- Storage space for everything from instruments and stage gear to promotional materials and merchandise

These are operational issues as opposed to marketing strategies. From a marketing standpoint, your workspace needs the following:

- Enough space to conduct necessary meetings
- Décor and amenities that are pleasant for you and anyone who meets with you at your workspace
- A location that is secure yet easy to find; with convenient parking
- A location in a part of town which is consistent with the image you want to project

Here are some examples:

- Performers need a place at home for computer, instruments, equipment, and business records. Depending on your family situation, this may be a separate room or part of the garage or basement. Rehearsals can be held at home or a designated rehearsal space, depending on the nature of the act.
- Songwriters and composers generally need to record what they are writing. Their physical workspace may be a home studio, an office away from home, or a commercial recording studio.
- Agents, managers, and promoters may need less space for storing gear, but often need more space for customer meetings and storage of business records and materials. Business offices range from small rooms at home to shared space in office suites to customized office buildings.

THE PROS AND CONS OF HOME OFFICES

Do I need plush offices in the high rent district? Can I work from a desk in my spare room? Does it matter?

The answers to these questions do matter to both you and your customers. Like the other two dimensions of place, the characteristics of your workspace will change over time. Think of your workspace as part of your marketing strategy in addition to the purely practical or operational space considerations.

Your workspace and the surroundings say a lot about you and your business. Thankfully, the home office revolution started in the late 1980s is still going on today. There is little or no stigma attached to working from a home office, as long as it has the space and resources required to do the job.

Advantages of home offices include:

- Relatively low cost. Assuming you have space, you do not need to incur extra rent, utilities, or building expense to operate from home.

- Convenience. The "20-foot commute" is enviable, especially if the alternative is sitting in traffic for long periods every day.
- Amenities. It's nice to have "all the comforts of home" at your fingertips.

Disadvantages of home offices include:

- Distractions. Your household situation (family, roommates, etc.) may not allow you the privacy required to focus on your business.
- Logistics. Your residence may be too hard for others to find, or too small for you to conduct business.
- Possible zoning problems. It may be illegal to conduct business from your home. Check local laws governing commercial versus residential zones. Note: This generally applies only to businesses that have employees or customers coming and going on a regular basis.

Regardless of where your workspace is, remember that it is a part of your marketing strategy, and will change as your business needs change.

YOUR EVOLVING PLACE STRATEGY

A quick review: A strategy is a decision that affects future activity. How does your future business strategy have an impact on place: geography, channel/venue, and workspace? Do you always want to perform in small listening rooms, or do you see yourself moving up to larger venues? Do you want your songs used for traditional records, or do you want to move into film and television?

Remember that there are no right or wrong answers to these questions. What you do evolves as your business strategy changes over time. And it will change over time.

KEY POINTS IN THIS CHAPTER

1. Where you conduct business has an impact on your overall marketing strategy.

2. "Place" has three dimensions: (1) geographical territory, (2) channel or venue, and (3) personal workspace.

3. Geographic territories can be local, regional, national, international, or global.

4. "Channel of distribution" is a term that comes from manufacturing but is relevant to any place strategy. You choose the channel and/or type of venue where you plan to work.

5. Performance venue types range from private residences to clubs, colleges, arenas, stadiums, and festivals.

6. Examples of channels for your services may include agents, producers, publishers, record labels, or promoters.

7. Examples of channels for goods include record stores, bookstores, supermarkets, coffee shops, performance venue concession stands, mail order, or Internet retailers.

8. Workspaces have practical elements, such as access to tools and privacy, as well as positioning elements, such as size and location. Home offices have both advantages and disadvantages for music people.

9. Like other links in the marketing chain, your place strategy changes over time. Your business plan helps you anticipate those changes and moves.

CHAPTER THIRTEEN

PORTRAIT OF A SALESFORCE

N ow let's look at your salesforce strategy, the fifth link in the marketing chain. Your salesforce is the person or persons who handle your business's sales functions as described in Chapter Eight. As with the other marketing links, your salesforce strategy evolves over time. We'll demonstrate how to optimize the fit of the salesforce to the product by creating a profile of the ideal salesperson.

EVERYONE PLAYS A SALES ROLE

Regardless of your product or your role in the music industry, you are involved in sales, whether you like it or not. Agents and promoters tend to be natural salespeople. They chose those roles because they enjoy them. Performers and songwriters may be less likely to enjoy the role of salesperson, and often delegate sales responsibility to an agent or manager. Managers, while often responsible for sales, are in between agent and performer in terms of their proclivity for sales.

Everyone sells something at some point.

- Performers need to sell themselves to agents, managers, and producers in order to work. Many performers represent themselves for live performance bookings, and actively play an ongoing sales role in addition to the performer role. Whether they are conscious of it or not, performers sell themselves to their audiences every time they perform.
- Songwriters sell their songs to artists, publishers, record producers, film and TV music supervisors, and record label people. Music publishers play a sales role on behalf of songwriters, analogous to the agent/performer relationship. Still, songwriters need basic sales skill to get "in the door" with a publishing firm or record producer.
- Agents sell acts to event promoters. This is the most direct connection between an industry role and the concept of a salesforce. In addition, agents sell their services to the performers they represent.
- Managers sell performers and songwriters to agents and producers. Like agents, they also sell their services to performers. Some managers also play the agent/salesperson role and sell directly to promoters and venues.

- Promoters sell tickets and shows to the general public. Like agents, promoters are full-time sales and marketing people. They also sell their company capabilities to venues, agents, managers, and performers.

WHAT IF I DON'T LIKE THE IDEA OF SALES?

Many performers and songwriters have a negative association with sales. Even the word "salesman" conjures an image of an overweight, middle-aged huckster with ill-fitting clothes, bad breath, and worse jokes. Sensationalized stories of music people getting burned by "business types" or "suits" also come to mind. Everyone has heard a horror story. Unfortunately, many of them are true.

Sales is not a "necessary evil." It is a positive process and the lifeblood of any business, music or otherwise. If you are going to succeed in music, it is vitally important to understand this concept. Consider the expression:

"Nothing happens until somebody sells something."

That "something" can be your idea, your act, your song, or your product. If you don't like the idea of sales, you have to make a choice. Here are the options:

1. Hang in there and handle sales even though it's not your favorite thing to do.
2. Have someone who enjoys it handle sales for you.
3. Go out of business, or don't go into business in the first place.

Clearly, #2 above is the best choice. Thankfully, there are many people who are good at selling and enjoy the process. The challenge is to find someone who loves to sell and also loves your product.

A WORD ABOUT INTEGRITY

It is assumed that any qualified salesperson operates legally and ethically. There is no such thing as being "mostly legal" or "sort of ethical." A salesperson's integrity is essential for business success. Infractions are grounds for the salesperson's disqualification or termination.

Regrettably, the music industry is replete with examples of unwitting performers and songwriters being taken advantage of by unscrupulous opportunists. Once again, the popular media consistently present attorneys, agents, pitchmen, and "corporate" types as unscrupulous money-mongers, who will stop at nothing to get rich at the expense of innocent musicians.

Fraud and extortion happens in all industries. Music people, like other creative and technical types, may be more susceptible to deception or more likely to become the victims of unfair dealing than people in other business categories.

It doesn't need to be that way. The clear majority of people in both the corporate and independent music industry are honest, sincere, "normal" folks. Too often, however, they lack fundamental business skills and have a poor understanding of the sales process. (This is not the same as malicious or criminal intent.) A corporate title and a few years of experience do not guarantee that the person is qualified. You are helping to prevent problems and misunderstandings by reading this book.

CHARACTERISTICS OF A GREAT SALESPERSON— THE "THREE C'S"

Great sales people have a set of basic qualities that are essential to sales success. Your sales representatives need strength in the three "C's" of sales: competence, capacity, and chemistry.

1. Competence: the business skills and experience to do the job. These include product knowledge, market knowledge, time management, presentation and negotiation skills, accuracy of communications, prompt follow-through on all matters, and general business acumen.
2. Capacity: time, people, tools, and resources to achieve your sales objectives. This refers to number of sales and support persons, information systems and telecommunications tools, manageable number of acts or products represented, and ability to cover the assigned geographic territory.
3. Chemistry: the human interface. This refers to the subjective, yet vitally important aspects of business relationships including courtesy, attitude, patience, adaptability, sense of humor, and shared vision.

These elements are the basis for evaluating how any individual or firm will fit with your company. Competence and capacity issues can be rated relatively objectively. Chemistry is more subjective and will vary depending on who is doing the evaluation.

THE IDEAL SALES REP

Your sales force, the individual who represents you and handles sales functions, needs to be strong in each key area of competence, capacity, and chemistry. Here is a detailed profile of the ideal sales representative for performers and songwriters.

Competence

1. Product and music industry knowledge. Understands your product categories, and how they fit into the overall music industry. For example, your agent has seen your act perform, knows your repertoire, and can characterize it properly, now and into the future.

2. Knowledge of your target market. Has experience dealing with the kind of customers that you want to reach. Knows who the major industry influencers and buyers are, and how to do business with them. Understands the relevance and workings of music trade associations, from the Recording Academy, PRO's, and the AFM to local music societies that stage concerts and festivals.

3. Time management ability. Makes the best use of both personal and staff time in developing new business and expediting solutions to problems and opportunities.

4. Solid organizational and presentation skills. Able to present you and your product faithfully to customers. Respects diversity among individual customer's schedules and buying patterns.

5. Marketing skills. Able to assist customers with publicity and general promotion. Interfaces comfortably with key market influencers (press, reviewers, bloggers, etc.) on behalf of you and your company.

Capacity

1. Proper ratio of sales staff to clients. The individual or firm must be able to dedicate adequate sales staff time to all clients or projects represented. While it may seem like stating the obvious, too many agents "collect acts" to represent to make their rosters appear impressive.

2. Access to a real live office person for both clients and customers. There is generally so much for an agency or promotion company to do that a full-time office person is a necessity. Agents, managers, and other salespersons are most effective face-to-face with customers, knowing they have support at the office.

3. Business equipment. Computer, fax machine, and telephones (wired and wireless) are minimum tools. As the company grows over time, the equipment needs also grow and change. Make sure that your salesforce has the right gear.

4. Growth plans and adaptability. The person or firm needs to embrace growth and be able to adapt to the changing music market. The best firms have a business plan and are willing to discuss their long-term strategy with their clients.

5. Training and ongoing professional development. Willing and able to take the time needed to learn about new products, programs, and business procedures. As a performer, for example, you may want to branch out into a new market (like state fairs or corporate meetings). Your salesforce, then, must have the time, ability, and capacity to learn about the new market before leaping ahead.

Chemistry

1. **Positive attitude.** This is expressed consistently toward clients, customers, and the music industry in general. No one wants to buy from a jerk or a sourpuss.
2. **Telephone manners and efficiency.** So much sales work is done over the phone that it is essential that the salesperson come across as friendly, sincere, businesslike, and respectful.
3. **Tactfulness.** We'll allow for variations in personal style, but the salesperson should be able to deliver both good and bad news in a professional manner.
4. **Congruent quality image.** Your products are top quality and marketed to special customers. The salesforce's image needs to be consistent with you and your product's image.
5. **Shared vision of the future.** Your salesforce needs to know and believe in your goals and objectives. This is perhaps the most important chemistry-oriented characteristic of the ideal salesperson. The best reps see the full potential for your products and will invest time and energy to help you realize that potential. If your agent does not take you seriously, move on!

WHAT GREAT SALESPEOPLE LOOK FOR IN A MUSIC "PRODUCT"

Great salespeople keep the interests of both their clients and their customers in mind. A good agent wants to keep performers and promoters or venue owners happy, willing to come back for more. It is essential that the salesperson is consistently motivated and positive toward your product. In other words, everybody needs to win in the course of a business relationship.

It is important to understand what salespeople look for in the products they represent. Here are five characteristics of an excellent product, from the salesperson's point of view:

1. **Excellent quality.** Whether selling live show dates, songs, tickets, merchandise, or services, the "product" needs to be of the highest quality. That way the salesperson can stake his or her reputation on it, with confidence.
2. **Longevity.** The more established the product, the easier it is to sell. This also has a future dimension. Salespeople will invest more time developing the market for a product that has a long life ahead of it.
3. **Professional commitment.** While this should go without saying, it needs to be said. Too many music people are unclear or noncommittal about their professional music career. Good agents and managers ask about commitment in initial interviews. They can sense when an artist is or is not ready or fully committed to be a professional.
4. **Marketability.** A good salesperson needs to know your target market or customer. They also need to understand and believe in the fit between your product and your customer base.

5. Financial viability. The salesforce needs to get paid, so they need to understand and believe in your product's "commercial potential." Remember, everyone has their own idea of how much money is enough. There needs to be congruity between your financial objectives and those of your salesforce.

What, if any, of these five elements are lacking? Experienced agents, managers, publishers, and record people simply will not take on performers or songwriters who don't have market potential or are not ready, willing, and able to make a professional commitment. Your marketing plan goes a long way toward attracting the best people to your salesforce. Sharing your business plan with prospective agents or managers also sets you apart from the vast majority of your competitors.

On the other hand, inexperienced salespeople (like the proverbial friend of the band) may mistake talent and sincerity for your act's business potential. It's tough for a spouse, family member, or well-meaning fan to be objective about your business acumen and potential. They may become discouraged quickly when they discover that key elements of your business are lacking or undefined.

It's better to avoid asking friends and family to sell for you unless they have the basic characteristics of competence, capacity, and chemistry. "But it's a labor of love," they might say. What happens when something more important comes along, like their full-time job, or it's time to take the kids to soccer practice? You may be better off representing yourself until your "product" is ready for professional representation.

KEY POINTS IN THIS CHAPTER

1. Performers, songwriters, agents, managers, and promoters alike, are involved in the sales process in some way.

2. If you don't like the idea of sales, that's okay. You can choose to (1) tough it out on your own, (2) delegate sales to someone else like an agent, or (3) go out of business.

3. You can't run a business without sales! It is the lifeblood of any music business. No one gets paid without it. Remember the axiom: "Nothing happens until somebody sells something."

4. Great salespeople have complete integrity. Beware of media stereotypes portraying slick or unscrupulous opportunists feeding on the weaknesses of unsophisticated music people.

5. Great salespeople have balanced strength in the three "C's" of sales: Competence (business skills), Capacity (resources), and Chemistry (positive personality traits).

6. Great salespeople represent great products. They look for five primary characteristics: (1) excellent quality, (2) longevity, (3) professional commitment, (4) marketability, and (5) financial viability.

7. If any of these are weak or lacking, the fit between your product and your salesforce may be compromised.

8. Beware of inexperienced sales people, like friends and family members, who are willing to work for you, despite a lack of skills on their part or marketability and long-term financial viability on your part.

9. Your marketing plan will go a long way toward attracting the best sales people. Your business plan is a good way to set yourself apart from most of your competitors.

CHAPTER FOURTEEN

THE WHO, WHAT, WHEN, WHERE, WHY, AND HOW OF YOUR CUSTOMERS

Here we come to the sixth link in the marketing chain: customers. We'll outline how to create customer profiles, and how to apply them to your marketing plan.

First, a quick review. In Chapter Two, we identified the need to understand who your customers are, even before you go into business. Here are those three key strategic questions again:

- What's the business or product?
- What's the market or target customer?
- How does everyone get paid?

We also offered a simple definition of a customer: the one who pays for your product. In other words, your primary customer relationship is determined by "where the money changes hands."

UNDERSTANDING BUYER CHARACTERISTICS

Whoever pays you for your product has a set of identifiable characteristics that makes up a "customer profile." The elements of the profile include:

- **Demographic information.** Demographics include age, gender, marital status, and education level. For example, a "boy band" may target 11- to 15-year-old female students. An opera company or symphony may target college-educated men and women age thirty-five and older. A performing songwriter may target a wider age range but focus on gender or education level, depending on song content or themes.
- **Economic information.** This includes household income levels and discretionary spending ability or "buying power." For example, some people will pay up to $20 for a concert ticket or record while others can afford $200 or more. On a "business to business" level—like agents selling acts to promoters—the economic portion of the profile is where you identify the budget range of your target customer. For example, a 300-seat club with a $2,000 budget for a main act is unlikely to book a $50,000 auditorium act.

Nor would it book a $250 coffeehouse act that might not draw enough to fill the room.

- **Geographic information**. Where do your customers physically live? This element is most important to performers. The smaller the geographic "trade area," the easier it is to focus and control costs like travel and promotion. You can choose to be a local, regional, national, international, or global act. Songwriters have greater flexibility in the geographic location of your customers. Most business can be conducted via telephone, e-mail, and at occasional trade events. Still, you may decide that your target customers live and work in a specific area that is music-friendly or where there is a larger population of music people, such as Los Angeles, New York, Nashville, Chicago, Miami, Austin, Vancouver, Toronto, and other focal points of the music performing, recording, and publishing world.

- **Psychographic information.** Psychographics deal with what your customers think about and believe. This includes social traits, religious or spiritual beliefs, political views, and hobbies or personal interests. For example, a topical songwriter may target recording artists, labels, and publishers who accept and specialize in socio-political material. Gospel musicians may target specific church denominations that are more receptive to their musical message.

Note: Agents, managers, publishers, and record labels may choose to represent artists whose lifestyle and political views are compatible with their own. Promoters may choose to present acts they believe in to audiences who are receptive to a specific style of music.

A WORD ABOUT STYLE: THE BLUES BROTHERS EXAMPLE

Understanding your audience's taste in music is fundamental to your long-term success. The psychographic element is the one that music people often think of first. Why? Because it relates to *style* or *genre* of music. What separates country from bluegrass? Rock from rockabilly? Jazz from blues? Rap from hip hop? Folk from world? Classical from avant-garde? The answer is that there are stylistic differences that are relevant not only to the audience, but to performers and songwriters, plus their agents, managers, and promoters. Those differences include not only the sound of the music and the look of the performers and audience, but the interests and values of everyone involved.

Remember the movie *The Blues Brothers*? Whether you've seen it or not, you can imagine this scene:

A blues band shows up for a booking at Bob's Country Bunker, a roadhouse tavern that normally features country acts. During the band's first number, the crowd, expecting their favorite style of country music, throws beer bottles at the band members. Thank goodness there was floor-to-ceiling chicken wire in front of the stage.

In the movie, it's pretty funny. In real life, it's pathetic. The business lesson: Understand your target customer's interests and values before you make the sales pitch. The problems inherent in the Blues Brothers story can be prevented by creating a customer profile in advance and using it as a guiding element in the marketing mix. It is relatively common, and often wise, to organize everything about a music business around a style, or narrow range of styles, of music.

BUYING HABITS AND PREFERENCES

How do your target customers like to buy? Do they have special needs, habits, or preferences? The answers to these questions are additional elements in your target customer profile. The examples that follow, while not an exhaustive list, will give you ideas of what to look for.

- If you perform at weddings, corporate meetings, or other private events, be prepared to commit to future dates far in advance. The ability to guarantee that the act will show up on time, look good, and perform the right material a year from now is a set of purchase criteria that transcends demographics, economics, geography, and style.
- Promoters may choose to only book acts that they have seen in person. Be prepared to audition live, play a showcase gig for little or no money, or invite and transport the promoter to see you at another venue—or don't work for that promoter. Remember that you always have a choice.
- Music publishers, film and TV music supervisors, and record producers have established criteria for how to submit material: number of songs, recording format, or even time of year that they are open to submissions.
- Agents and managers may or may not be seeking new acts to represent. If they are, find out what the criteria might be for submitting your act for consideration.
- Promoters may have a geographical limit on dates booked in competitive venues. For example, if you (as a performer) or your agent are looking for a show date within a specific time frame, you may have to guarantee that the promoter has an exclusive within a 50-mile radius plus or minus thirty days.
- If you sell recorded music, be prepared to offer it in a variety of formats or packages. While digital downloads have become mainstream in the early twenty-first century, there are still fans who prefer to buy CDs or vinyl.

These are examples of special buying criteria or characteristics. There are two business points here. First, understand your customer's buying habits. Second, incorporate positive criteria—the ones you can live with—in the profile of your target customer.

INDIVIDUAL VS. INSTITUTIONAL CUSTOMERS

Another important aspect of customer profiling is to understand who actually makes the buying decision. Is it a single person or a group? Does the person you are selling to have the authority to make the commitment, or does it require a vote or "blessing" by someone else? In this context, there are two types of customers: individual and institutional.

Individual customers make the decision to buy on their own and are usually spending their own money. Examples include:

- Clubs, private parties, or other venues where the owner books the acts
- Independent record labels or publishing companies run by the owner
- The general public when they buy show tickets or records

Institutional customers make buying decisions in groups and are often spending an organization's money. Examples include:

- College and university "activities committees"
- Major corporate record labels and publishing companies
- Large global music companies like Live Nation or AEG

Is one type of customer better or worse than the other? That depends on your ability do deal with the special circumstances—buying preferences and characteristics—inherent in each situation. The point is to be aware that each of the two types of customers behave differently, have different buying criteria, and need to be marketed and sold to differently as a result.

WHAT ABOUT NON-VIABLE CUSTOMERS?

As you develop your target customer profile, you are likely to think of the bad examples along with the good—the "customers from Hell." When you identify the buying criteria that you can't live with, the "deal-breakers," you are creating a profile of a non-viable customer. This is a valuable exercise. Here are a few examples of deal-breaker attributes:

- Doesn't like or understand your style of music
- Can't pay any price, let along what you are asking
- Won't sign a contract ("Don't worry, you can trust me.")
- Non-communicative; doesn't return phone calls or e-mails in a timely fashion
- Doesn't understand or acknowledge your production needs (sound, lights, dressing rooms, etc.)

You get the picture. Many music people think that they have to live with bad customer relationships as part of "paying your dues" in the music industry. While there is some value in living through challenging experiences, most music people "learn the hard way" (trial and error) and either move on to viable clientele or get out of the business. Understanding your own tolerances and comparing them to your customer profiles helps prevent problems and optimizes results.

HOW TO SLICE THE PIE

Your customers can be organized into natural segments. Think of a segment as a "slice of the orange" or a "piece of the pie." Market segmentation, as it's called in the business world, is the process of efficiently organizing and focusing your approach to target your customers. This is especially important in today's fragmented music industry. There are so many performers, songwriters, genres of music, and buyer profiles that it is impossible to target them all.

If you were to define your target audience as "all music lovers" or "all buyers of talent," where would you start? How would you know if your publicity and collateral material is on target? How would you know who to call first? The idea is to narrow the focus to a group of prospective customers who (1) you understand, (2) have demonstrated interest in your type of product, and (3) are "target-able" from a marketing communications and promotional standpoint.

Let's talk about "target-able" a little more. Targeting involves reaching out to current and prospective customers via telephone, e-mail, Websites, trade shows, and the media as described in Chapter Eleven. Remember that your customers are not likely to come after you. You need to go after them. To that end, do you start with the local phone book and start calling everyone, or use an industry directory or networking tool to narrow the focus? Obvious answer: Using a pre-qualified list of prospective customers is much more efficient and potentially rewarding.

As we discussed earlier in this chapter, the music industry is oriented toward styles or genres of music. That often becomes the first market segmentation principle. The other principles flow naturally from the remaining categories of customer information: demographic, economic, geographic, and psychographic. What happens when you segment your market is that you not only focus on customers who are attractive to your business, but you also intentionally *avoid* unqualified or unattractive customers. That's where the efficiency kicks in.

For most music people this is intuitive and simple to understand. You might be thinking, "I'm already focusing on my genre of music in a geographical area that makes sense to me right now." Any performer who has traveled to a distant gig where the venue and audience was expecting something else (like Bob's Country Bunker) knows what I mean.

Yet, it is tempting to take that festival or college booking four states over, even though you will lose money due to the time and travel expenses involved with making the gig. Your options are to work the date and pay the price or respectfully decline the offer, citing the current geographical focus of your act. Most promoters understand the rationale and will keep the door open to discuss future work as your business grows and your trade area expands. Just remember that you have a choice.

Here's another marketing rule of thumb. You can only focus on one or two segments at a time with any degree of efficiency. If you are trying to "walk the walk and talk the talk" of too many types of customers at one time, things can get out of hand. The exception is an organization with multiple products and the capacity to focus each product on a limited number of customer segments simultaneously, such as:

- Booking agencies or management companies representing acts in multiple musical genres
- Songwriters and publishing companies who cross over numerous musical styles
- Promoters who present multiple musical styles to multiple audience profiles

DEVELOPING YOUR TARGET CUSTOMER PROFILE

Take a few minutes now for this exercise: write the "five-bullet" profile of your target customer. In the boxes below, there is space to add a few words to describe your customer in each of the main parameters we have presented in this chapter. Notice that there is also a column for non-viable customer characteristics. You'll find that the process of profiling viable and non-viable customers at the same time is both illuminating and liberating. Note: This exercise is also included on the CD-ROM, so you can write it as many times as you need to. For now, start with one product and one target customer type and see how it goes.

Customer Profiling Exercise

Profile Element	Viable Customer	Nonviable Customer
Musical genre or style	_____	_____
Demographic information	_____	_____
Economic information	_____	_____
Geographic information	_____	_____
Psychographic information	_____	_____
Special buying criteria	_____	_____

How did it go? Any new insights? Hopefully you are now able to say with confi dence, "There are enough viable customers out there that I can avoid the non-viable ones."

DON'T LET YOUR "DEAL-BREAKERS" PUT YOU OUT OF BUSINESS

We mentioned the concept of deal-breakers earlier. Those are the criteria that make a customer non-viable for you. You've just listed a few in the exercise above. The point of mentioning it again is: Beware of having such a narrow focus that there are not enough customers to support your business. Let's say that you are a performer and your target customer profile is "left-handed heart surgeons who love zydeco music and are willing to pay $50,000 for a private performance." If you find one, let me know. If you find enough to make a sustainable living, it's a miracle.

While that may be an extreme example, I encourage you to apply the thought process to your own situation. By going through the profiling exercise several times, you'll find the balance between the ideal and the practical and be able to proceed from there. You'll also be better equipped to leave the non-viable customers for your competition . . .

KEY POINTS IN THIS CHAPTER

1. The sixth link in the marketing chain is the understanding of customers. A customer is the "one who pays for your product," or "where the money changes hands."

2. Customers have identifiable characteristics that can be organized into a "customer profile." The four main categories of customer characteristics are demographic, economic, geographic, and psychographic.

3. Demographic information includes age, gender, marital status, and education level. You need customers who are consistent with your preferences or needs in these areas.

4. Economic information includes income, buying power, and budget guidelines. You need customers who can afford the price of your product.

5. Geographic information means where the customer physically lives or conducts business. You need customers who are in your trade area.

6. Psychographic information refers to what customers think about and believe: their social traits, religious beliefs, political views, and hobbies or personal interests. You need customers who find your product consistent with their own interests and values.

7. Each customer also has a definable set of buying criteria, habits, and preferences, such as preferred modes of communication, timing, or capacity guidelines.

8. There are two basic types of customers: individual and institutional. Individual customers make the decision to buy on their own and are often spending their own money. Institutional customers make buying decisions in groups and are often spending an organization's money.

9. As you develop profiles of target customers, you will identify "deal-breakers" or characteristics that make some customers non-viable for you. This valuable exercise helps you prevent problems.

10. Market segmentation, or slicing the pie, is the process of efficiently organizing and focusing your approach to target your customers. It is vital to segment your market in today's fragmented and dynamic music industry.

11. Customer profiles in the music industry generally include musical style or genre preference as a vital organizing principle. By starting there and adding demographic, economic, geographic, and psychographic information, you can quickly develop profiles of target customers that enhance your marketing plan.

12. Savvy marketers focus on only one or two market segments or customer profiles at a time. It is difficult and inefficient to be all things to "all music lovers" or "all buyers of talent."

13. Conversely, beware of establishing customer profiles that are so narrow you don't have enough qualified buyers to support your business.

14. You can't make a sale without a customer. Understanding in advance the purchase criteria of various customer types or segments saves you time, money, and headaches.

CHAPTER FIFTEEN

UNDERSTANDING YOUR COMPETITION

The seventh and final link in the marketing chain is the competitive analysis. In this chapter we'll target the competition and learn how to understand the competitive environment. We'll identify who your competitors are and provide tools for understanding their strengths and weaknesses.

THE COMPETITIVE ENVIRONMENT

You and your competitors have one key characteristic in common: you are both going after the same target customer. As we discussed in Chapter Three, there are two basic kinds of competition: direct and indirect. Here's a quick review of the definitions:

- Direct competition: similar businesses in your product category
- Indirect competition: any product from outside your product category that goes after the same target customer's attention and money

The total competitive environment includes both the direct and indirect competitors. While this may seem obvious, I've found that most music people focus primarily on one or the other. Consider these two scenarios:

Scenario 1: "Oh, music people are one big happy family. It's sports and other leisure activities we need to worry about." This is both idealistic and unrealistic. Other performers and songwriters are going after your target customers all the time, and may not view you as "family."

Scenario 2: "If people aren't interested in music, I don't care about them. My problem is that there are so many performers (songwriters or whatever) going after my customers." This narrow view is also unrealistic. Who do you know that is not interested in music in some way? While sports fans may spend more on game tickets than concert tickets, that does not mean they are completely out of the market. Why do you think the half time show at the Super Bowl features music?

Sure, these are generalized examples, but how real are they for you? Too many music people focus only on one type of competition to the exclusion of the other. We need to focus on both in order to fully understand the competitive environment.

IDENTIFYING YOUR DIRECT COMPETITORS

It's tempting to oversimplify when identifying your direct competitors. If you are a performing songwriter, you might conclude that *all* other performing songwriters are competing for the same gigs. In a general or abstract way, that's true. However, remember the "customer profile" in Chapter Fourteen? We saw that there are many different customer profiles, which allows you to target your direct competitors much more accurately and precisely. Consider these examples:

- You are the leader of a jazz-fusion band that performs in clubs and theaters in a five-county area surrounding your home metropolitan area. Other acts that focus on different styles of music (like classical, folk, or gospel), different target audiences, or different geographical areas are only marginally competing with you.
- You are a songwriter seeking alternative country and Americana acts that record and perform all original material and tour internationally. You focus your efforts on producers and record labels that are known for their work with similar acts. While other songwriters are indeed direct competitors, an R&B lyricist (for example) is likely to focus on a different set of producers while looking for a recording or publishing deal.
- You are a pop cover band looking for "general business" or "casual" gigs: weddings, proms, private parties, and retail promotions within a 100-mile radius of where you live. Your direct competitors include similar local bands and mobile disc jockeys, but not touring acts looking for showcase club or concert work in your trade area.

Here's the point once again. While it is idealistic to think that all music people are "like a family" and not in competition, it is illuminating, even essential, to understand potential competitors' target customers. That is the first step in developing a competitive strategy.

UNDERSTANDING INDIRECT COMPETITION

Let's go back to the sports versus music example. Local sports teams are competing with music promoters for both ticket sales and audience attention. In addition to distracting fans, they tie up the press and may even make venues unavailable.

This has an impact on the performers, agents, and managers involved, too. In other words, the impact of indirect competition crosses over music industry roles. If a fan spends three hours and $90 attending a basketball or football game, he or she did not spend that time and money on a concert, club date, or record purchases. The same can be said of other entertainment forms, including movies, theater, museums, dance, reading, games, and comedy.

There are additional non-entertainment sources of indirect competition. Indirect competitors who target the general public as the customer include:

- Hobbies and leisure activities—from coin collecting to balloon rides
- Educational pursuits—from sending kids to private schools (often using discretionary funds) to enrolling in seminars or continuing education programs
- Home improvements—from buying furniture and appliances to adding rooms or remodeling
- Vacation travel— from camping to cruises
- Health and fitness activities—from exercise to extreme sports

These activities take time and money. Similarly, there are indirect competitors who target businesses or institutional customers. They may distract your target customer:

- A company who had traditionally hired a dance band for its holiday party may cancel the event altogether and give employees a cash bonus instead. The competition is not another performer, but another kind of bonus or reward for their employees.
- Upgrading computer hardware, software, and systems may distract or prevent a corporate client from using music at its annual sales meeting. The competition is not another act or agent, but time and money spent on company infrastructure.
- A publishing company may be in the process of being sold to one of the majors, forcing a freeze on signing new acts until the deal is done. The competition is not other songwriters trying to place their songs, but time and legal fees spent on the acquisition.

EXERCISE: IDENTIFY YOUR TOP FIVE DIRECT AND INDIRECT COMPETITORS

By now you have a feel for how to identify competitors. Let's put that knowledge to work. In the spaces on the following page, write down the names of your top five direct and indirect competitors. Note: A similar template is included in the Reference Section and on the CD-ROM.

Top Five Direct Competitors

1. _____

2. _____

3. _____

4. _____

5. _____

Top Five Indirect Competitors

1. _____

2. _____

3. _____

4. _____

5. _____

WHY INDIRECT COMPETITION IS SCARIER THAN DIRECT COMPETITION

Now look at the two lists above. How do you feel about each? Most people find the indirect competitors to be more mysterious and intimidating—*scarier*—than the direct competitors. This is true in any category of business, not just the music industry.

Many business people view their direct competitors as predictable and vulnerable—nuisances as opposed to threats. Yet the indirect competitors, like the National Football League (sports), the City of Paris, France (tourism), or Microsoft (computer software) can cause real competitive anxiety. A typical response is, "Yikes! My direct competitors are tough enough to deal with, but these others are just overwhelming."

Why is this the case? No mystery here. It's because indirect competitors are often large, capable, and able to distract our target customers with power and consistency. In most cases, there is nothing that you can do by yourself to impact indirect competitors. That's the job of trade groups like the PRO's, RIAA, Recording Academy and Musician's Union. The point is to recognize and learn to deal with *both* direct and indirect competition as part of your overall marketing plan.

COMPETITIVE STRENGTHS, WEAKNESSES, OPPORTUNITIES, AND THREATS

So what do we do about competition? How can we determine where we stand relative to key competitors? An important tool in understanding your market position relative to that of competitors is to conduct a "SWOT" analysis. SWOT is an acronym for Strengths, Weaknesses, Opportunities, and Threats. Strengths and weaknesses are about your company or the "internal environment." Opportunities and threats are about both your company and the market or "external environment."

Here are working definitions of each of the four concepts:

- **Strengths:** superior resources and skills that can be drawn on to exploit opportunities and deal with threats. Every business has strength beyond "product." Examples include production capability, marketing capability, financial resources, management capability, information systems, and people.
- **Weaknesses:** deficiencies that inhibit the ability to perform or achieve results, and must be overcome to avoid failure. Every business also has weaknesses. Any of the items mentioned as possible strengths can be weaknesses if the item is holding the company back in some way.
- **Opportunities:** environmental trends with positive consequences. Opportunities may suggest a new basis for competitive advantage or present a possibility of improved performance (increased efficiency, sales, profits, or market share) if pursued. Examples include overall market growth, emerging customer segments, vulnerable competitors, political and cultural trends, technology trends, and economic trends.
- **Threats:** environmental trends with potentially negative impacts. Threats may impede implementation of strategy, increase risk, increase the people or cash resources required, or cause us to reduce expectations for business results. Threats are also called risks. The examples of opportunities mentioned above can also be threats if they have potentially negative consequences.

Note: The music market is full of opportunities and threats that can have an impact on *all* competitors. The key point: While each music business has a unique set of strengths and weaknesses, there are market opportunities and threats facing us all. How you manage the balance is what makes you more competitive or less competitive.

YOUR COMPETITIVE INTELLIGENCE SYSTEM

How do you secure information on competitors? Isn't it difficult to get accurate and useful data? Two key points here:

1. Virtually all information about the market and competitors is readily available.
2. The information is often free or inexpensive to gather.

So where does competitive intelligence come from? A detailed prescription is beyond the scope of this book, but here are some pointers to get you started.

Public Sources of Competitive and Market Information

The public sources listed below are generally free or inexpensive.

- Websites, blogs, and collateral material of competitors and their fans
- Industry directories
- Trade publications
- Trade shows, events, and associations
- The general media
- Published research studies

Private Sources of Competitive and Market Information

Private sources of information allow you to screen out "junk" data by asking specific and detailed questions that are relevant to your competitive analysis. Be prepared to pay for information and service.

- Your network of personal contacts in the industry
- Third party informants
- Insider newsletters, forums, and conferences
- Market research firms and information brokers

YOUR COMPETITIVE DATABASE

Your competitive intelligence system may consist of a simple file folder with scribbled notes or a computerized database with detailed records on every direct and indirect competitor. Regardless of how you store the information, here are the basics to have at your disposal.

1. Basic profiles of leading direct competitors. In addition to name and contact information, the profile includes each competitor's product description, estimated sales volume, growth trend (up, down, or flat), and key strengths and weaknesses.
2. Estimated total market segment size and growth. It is important to see where you and your competitors fit in the overall market. When you know the size of the total market segment and each competitor's estimated sales revenue, you can calculate market share. "Segment" is a key word here, since the global music industry is so multi-faceted.

3. Market trend information. Secure and organize information on economic, cultural, political, and technology trends that can impact you and your competitors.
4. Source information. Create a list of places to go for further information when you need it. Examples include publications, Websites, or people in the know.
5. Sample materials. In the music industry it is relatively simple and inexpensive to secure recordings, promotional material, agency rosters, concert schedules, and publicity clippings on each of your key direct competitors. Keeping this on file not only keeps you in touch with their activities, but can also provide ideas for what to do or what to avoid in your own product and promotional strategies.

Success tip: Use a system to keep track of competition. Make sure that your files are up to date and that you dedicate time on a regular basis to update your information on new competitors or changes in strategy among your core competitors.

USING THE SEVEN LINKS

Now that you understand the seven links in the marketing chain, let's use them to develop even more detailed competitive profiles. Here's a shortcut to understanding your competitors: Write down the essence of their marketing plan.

Try this exercise. Fill in a few words about yourself and each of two more direct competitors in the table shown on the following page. This exercise can be sobering, motivating, and inspiring all at the same time. Note: This template is included in the Reference Section and on the CD-ROM.

Profile Element	You	Competitor One	Competitor Two
Product description	_____	_____	_____
	_____	_____	_____
	_____	_____	_____
Price range and strategy	_____	_____	_____
	_____	_____	_____
	_____	_____	_____
Promotional strategy	_____	_____	_____
	_____	_____	_____
	_____	_____	_____
Place/geographic territory	_____	_____	_____
	_____	_____	_____
	_____	_____	_____
Salesforce strategy	_____	_____	_____
	_____	_____	_____
	_____	_____	_____
Target customer	_____	_____	_____
	_____	_____	_____
	_____	_____	_____
Key strength	_____	_____	_____
	_____	_____	_____
	_____	_____	_____
Key weakness	_____	_____	_____
	_____	_____	_____
	_____	_____	_____

What did you learn from the above exercise? Are your competitors really what they seem on the surface? More or less formidable? The answers will inform your marketing strategy in a big way.

In Section Four, we'll begin putting the pieces of your business plan together.

KEY POINTS IN THIS CHAPTER

1. Competitors are other businesses or individuals who are vying with you for the same target customer or buyer. It is essential to understand your competitors to succeed in music.

2. Direct competitors are businesses that are in your product category (such as other performers or songwriters).

3. Indirect competitors are any products (goods or services) in any field that pursue the same target customer's attention and money.

4. Direct competitors are generally easier to identify and understand than indirect competitors. As a result, indirect competitors are often perceived as mysterious or intimidating.

5. To identify leading direct competitors, it is helpful to refer to your target customer profile. For example, one performer or songwriter may target a substantially different set of customers from another, thus reducing the immediate competitive threat.

6. Every competitor (including you) has a unique set of Strengths, Weaknesses, Opportunities, and Threats. Constructing a competitive SWOT analysis is a helpful tool in preparing competitive strategy.

7. Strengths and weaknesses refer to an individual company. Opportunities and threats refer to overall market conditions that can have a positive or negative on all competitors.

8. Details about the market and about specific competitors are readily available. Most market information is relatively inexpensive. Your "competitive intelligence system" allows you to understand market conditions and see how you and your competitors are dealing with them.

9. Public sources of information include Websites, collateral material, the general media, published research studies, and trade publications, events, and associations. Private sources of information include your network of personal contacts, insider newsletters, and market research firms.

10. Your competitive database should include (a) basic profiles of leading direct competitors, (b) estimated total market size and growth, (c) market trend information, (d) source contact information, and (e) sample materials.

11. The dossier for each leading competitor includes information on product mix, price range and strategy, promotional strategy, place or geographic territory, salesforce strategy, target customer profile, key strengths, and key weaknesses.

APPLYING THE FUNDAMENTALS IN YOUR MUSIC BUSINESS

CHAPTER SIXTEEN

DOING THE NUMBERS–SETTING REALISTIC GOALS AND OBJECTIVES

Performers and songwriters are often driven by creative or artistic goals and dreams, and frequently downplay their financial and personal aspirations. Having realistic written goals and objectives is the best tool for managing the inherent challenges in balancing music, business, family, and other interests.

How much do I want to earn? How hard do I want to work? What am I willing to risk to get what I want? Many music people have never really addressed these questions. This chapter will provide a framework for setting realistic goals and objectives that are consistent with your mission, vision, and values.

THE IMPORTANCE OF GOALS AND OBJECTIVES

There's an old expression that goes, "What gets measured, gets done." This is an important business truism. Having *written* business goals and objectives is essential for:

- Strategic planning
- Marketing and sales planning
- Creative development
- Personal development
- Congruity with personal values
- Financial success

You may be thinking, "I have my goals in my head. I don't need to write them down." It's good that you have goals. It's better yet to write them down and turn them into a set of actionable objectives with milestones. That's what this chapter will show you how to do.

QUICK REVIEW: HOW ARE GOALS DIFFERENT FROM OBJECTIVES?

Here are those definitions again:
- Goal: a desired result; often long-term; something good that you aspire to over a long period of time.

- Objective: an aspect or subset of a goal that is specific, measurable, and achievable.

For example, many people have a goal to "get rich and retire young." That's a desirable result and likely to be a long-term proposition. As we began in Chapter One, let's continue turning this goal into a set of objectives.

Objective: "Own a $2 million investment portfolio by age sixty and be able to live on the interest or dividends."

This is a clear statement of objectives. It is *specific* ($2 million in investments by age sixty), *measurable* (can be tracked over time), and *achievable*.

Remember the definitions of strategy and tactics, from Chapter One? Let's review them.

- Strategy: a decision made now that affects future activities. In other words, a strategy is a thought process leading to a decision and commitment, not necessarily the behavior or work itself.
- Tactic: an activity designed to achieve a desired result. Tactics are what you do to implement a strategy. Where strategy describes "what," tactics describe "how to."

In this context, goals relate to strategy; objectives relate to tactics. You need both. Since things change over time, it's important to keep a short-term *and* long-term perspective.

SETTING GOALS IN THREE CATEGORIES

Goals and objectives relate to all aspects of your music career and your personal life, not just finances. For most music people, goals fall neatly into three categories: creative, financial, and personal. Let's look at examples.

In each of the three categories below there is a list of possible goals. The part in quotes ("be a _____") is aimed at helping you articulate your goals for that subcategory. You do not necessarily need goals in all of these sample categories. In addition, you are likely to think of goal categories that are important to you but are not listed here. Remember this is just a starting point.

Creative Goals

Creative or artistic goals are the long-term results that you desire, whether you make money from them or not. Goals in the creative category define the business playing field before adding the financial elements. Note to performers and songwriters: Creativity is not limited to composition and performance. Agents, managers, and promoters are creative and have creative goals, too. Examples of creative goals may include:

- Songs written, published, and recorded—"be a successful songwriter"
- Records produced and released—"be a successful recording artist"
- Airplay on radio, television, or online—"expose my music to the public via broadcast media"
- Show dates performed—"expose my music to the public via live events"
- Award nominations and wins—"win a Grammy or other music industry award"
- Interviews, articles, and reviews published in the media—"be recognized in the media for excellence in the music industry"
- Endorsements and sponsorships—"earn a part of my income from promotional fees"
- Website visitors and fan club members—"have a network of loyal fans connected via the Internet" or "Have a million friends on MySpace"
- Participation in benefit shows or other pro bono work—"give a part of my time and talent back to charitable causes"

These are examples to get you thinking about your own creative goals. Let's move on to financial goals.

Financial Goals

Even if you are working in music part-time or on a not-for-profit basis, you need financial goals. Your financial goals need to tie to your creative goals. Once you "do the numbers," you will get better grounded in reality. Your financial goals may include:

- Revenue from song royalties—"earn all or part of your living as a published songwriter"
- Revenue from record royalties—"earn a living as a recording artist"
- Revenue from live performances—"earn a living as a stage performer or promoter"
- Revenue from endorsements and sponsorships—"earn money from promotions"
- Revenue from merchandising or other sources—"have a catalog of merchandise that sustains the operation between tours or projects"
- Largest, smallest, and average target revenue by source—"build my reputation to command increasing prices, allowing me to be selective on projects"
- Profit (revenue minus expenses)—"be profitable; have something left over to save or invest"
- Return on Investment (ROI)—"make a return on my cash and time investment that is as good or better than putting money in a savings account"

These examples should get you thinking about your financial goals. Let's continue with personal goals.

Personal Goals

Your creative and financial goals need to be consistent and in harmony with your personal goals. By identifying these goals up front, you can optimize all results and prevent problems down the road. Personal goals may include:

- How much you work in the course of a year—"work enough to make a living and get ahead while preventing burnout"
- How much vacation time, and what you do on vacation—"take a vacation that does not involve work"
- Family time, projects, and relationships—"have plenty of time for family and personal life"
- Community involvement and activities—"contribute to or be involved with my community"
- Spiritual growth and activities—"have time to develop my spiritual beliefs" or "be active in my church"
- Educational development—"have time to learn new business and non-business skills"
- Health maintenance—"stay youthful and live long"
- Exercise and fitness activities— "have time to stay fit"
- Hobbies and recreational activities—"have time to pursue my favorite leisure activities"

EXERCISE 1: YOUR THREE-YEAR GOALS

Where do you want to be in three years? Or looking at it another way, what do you need to do over the next three years to be satisfied with your progress? Write down the top three to five goals that come to mind in each of the three major categories. The idea is to articulate your primary goals so that you can turn them into objectives and milestones.

How long should you spend to articulate your goals? When I present live seminars, I give the audience six minutes, knowing they need more time. By starting the process with limited time, your mind will prompt you to list the most important things first. I suggest taking a few minutes now to write down whatever comes to mind, then go back and refine this later, using the template in the Reference Section and CD-ROM.

Creative Goals

1. _____
2. _____
3. _____
4. _____
5. _____

Financial Goals

1. _____
2. _____
3. _____
4. _____
5. _____

Personal Goals

1. _____
2. _____
3. _____
4. _____
5. _____

Now look at what you just wrote. What did you learn? Even a six-minute goal setting exercise is a clarifying experience. Among performers and songwriters that I've encountered, the three most common reactions are:

- "I need to focus more on achieving my financial goals."
- "My business goals are not compatible with my personal goals."
- "Now I know exactly where I need to change!"

TURNING GOALS INTO OBJECTIVES: WHEN IN DOUBT, QUANTIFY

When those uneasy feelings bother you (like wondering if your goals are realistic), it's time to do the numbers. Quantifying your goals is the first step in designing a set of objectives that are specific, measurable, and achievable.

Everything, including non-financial goals, can be quantified in terms of number of units, pricing or revenue, expense budget, and timing or date the results are achieved. As they become quantified, your creative, financial, and personal goals turn into objectives. Here are a few examples of solid trackable objectives in each of the three categories:

Creative Objectives

- Write ___ new song (s) each month
- Release ___ new record (s) each year
- Perform ___ shows each year

Financial Objectives

- Earn $ _____ from publishing, recording, or performing each year
- Increase average performance fee from $ _____ to $ _____ by _____ (date)
- Earn $ _____ from non-traditional sources (endorsements, merchandising) by _____ (date)

Personal Objectives

- Work ___ days per year (the rest is free time)
- Contribute $ _____ or _____ (time) to my local charity, church, school, or community
- Get my weight to _____ pounds and cholesterol level to _____

THREE KEY QUESTIONS ABOUT SETTING OBJECTIVES

Your personal goals and objectives are unique. While circumstances may dictate what is feasible to some degree, you have control over your objectives. To that end, here are three key questions to ask yourself as you turn your goals into objectives.

1. How much do I want to earn?
2. How hard do I want to work?
3. How much am I willing to sacrifice?

The answers will help keep you focused. They also serve as "checks and balances." For example, if you want to make a lot of money but not work very hard, you'll need to determine if that is feasible. Likewise, the "risk versus reward" concept discussed in Chapter Two comes into play. If you are too risk-averse, it may limit your earning capability. There are no right or wrong answers here. Use the three questions to guide your thinking.

WHAT'S ACTUALLY ACHIEVABLE?

How much can I possibly earn in music? Do I need to aspire to stardom to make it all worthwhile? Most music people want to at least be able to "pay for their habits." Others want to make a modest living creating or performing music full-time. Others want to "get rich and retire young." Theoretically, all of the above are possible, assuming that you have the talent. Your business plan, including goals and objectives, is your single most important tool for achieving what you want and staying in control throughout the process.

THE SCHOOLTEACHER PARADIGM

Let's set the media-induced, "get-rich-quick schemes" aside for the moment. Consider the example of a typical public school teacher in North America. Good teachers have creative skills and goals. They are respected in the community and often viewed as underpaid and under-appreciated. Sound familiar? Let's compare the characteristics of a schoolteacher to those of a music person and see where it takes us. This comparison can be made easily for performers, song-writers, agents, managers, and promoters alike.

Item	Schoolteacher	Music Person
College education	Required	Not required
Certification or license	Required	Occasionally required
Preparation for the job	Lesson plans, materials	Songs, rehearsal, planning
Communication skill	Required	Required
Deal with tough crowds	Occasionally	Occasionally
Term of contract	Minimum one year	Minimum one performance
Health plan, other benefits	Full coverage	Infrequently
Retirement plan	Teacher's pension	Social Security maybe
Pay scale	$30K–$50K per year	Varies widely
Vacation	Two months with pay	As long as you want, unpaid

Here's the point: It is entirely fair and realistic to work toward schoolteachers' wages and benefits as a basic model for "modest" business success in the music industry. While many music people aspire to, or are earning more, too many music people settle for less!

As you set your financial objectives, keep the following in mind:

- In terms of prevailing wage standards and cost of living, there are geographic variations across North America and around the world. Adjust your objectives to your location.
- After accounting for all the time put in on the job, many music people make less than the federal minimum wage. This relates to the question "how hard do I want to work?"
- Regardless of what you are earning *now* through music, plan to increase or at least control how much you earn relative to your time and cash investment. Pay attention to inflation and changing family needs, as well as your long-term goals in the three categories above.

HOW TO FORECAST SALES REVENUE

Sales don't just happen by accident. You need a revenue plan—a set of financial objectives—that is specific, measurable, and achievable. Here is a simple formula for forecasting revenue:

Total revenue $ equals units sold times average $ revenue per unit

Units and revenue per unit are calculated differently, depending on your role in the music industry. Detailed forecast methodology for all types of music business endeavors is beyond the scope of this book. However, the basic principles illustrated here apply to your planning process, whether you are already budgeting and forecasting or not. Here's a quick reference table to define what we mean by "units."

Industry Role	Unit of Measure	Basis for Average $ Revenue per Unit
Performer	Live show dates performed	Average performance fee per date
Songwriter	Airplay or record sales for each song in catalog	Royalty rate per performance or record sold
Agent	Show dates booked for each artist	Average commission $ per date booked
Manager	Represented artists	Average commission $ based on artist's total earnings.
Promoter	Show dates or events presented	Average ticket sales per show (ticket price x paid attendance)

While this book is geared to performers and songwriters, it is essential for you to understand how agents, managers, and promoters get paid so that you can relate to them in a business sense as well as personally.

USING THE FIVE-YEAR WINDOW™ TO FORECAST REVENUE

How far can you look into the future? How can you base your revenue plan on a semblance of reality? In our consulting practice, we recommend looking three years into the future, supported by last year's actual history and this year's likely results. We call this the "Five-Year Window." Using a four-piece band as an example, here's a sample forecast template based on this approach:

Item	Last Year	This Year	Next Year	Year 2	Year 3
Number of show dates	24	36	60	90	120
Average price per date	$500	$ 750	$1,000	$1,500	$2,500
Total performance revenue	$12,000	$ 27,000	$60,000	$135,000	$300,000
Expenses @ 50% of revenue	$6,000	$ 13,500	$30,000	$67,500	$150,000
Gross profit margin	$6,000	$ 13,500	$30,000	$67,500	$150,000
Number of band members	4	4	4	4	4
Average $ per member	$1,500	$3,375	$7,500	$16,875	$37,500
Target $ per member	$1,500	$3,000	$6,000	$15,000	$35,000
Variance $ per member	$ –	$375	$1,500	$1,875	$2,500

This quick forecast is *not* a full-blown budget; that would be beyond the scope of this book. Still, you can estimate business expenses (50 percent of gross revenue is a good rule of thumb) and calculate how much revenue is left over per person. This is the money that you have to live on, or contribute to your personal budget.

If you were the act in the above scenario, you might ask, "Where are we going to get 120 gigs that pay an average of $2,500 each?" If your average performance fee this year is $750, it might be unrealistic to increase that much overnight without a hit record or other windfall. But by looking three years into the future, you have time to 1) develop your brand so that it is worth more to promoters and audiences and 2) develop customer profiles leading to relationships with viable buyers as described in Chapter Fourteen.

EXERCISE 2: YOUR THREE-YEAR OBJECTIVES

Using the above format, let's plan one key financial objective for you or your company over a three-year period. Choose an objective category that has real revenue potential for you—your "bread and butter." For performers, I suggest using show dates as in the example above. For songwriters, I suggest using mechanical royalties based on record sales for cuts that you have placed (as of 2006, the rate is $.091 per cut). If you are splitting royalties with your publisher, scale the per-unit royalty accordingly.

As described above, it's a good idea to use the Five-Year Window: the previous year, the current year, plus three years into the future. Last year and this year are reference points that help you to get started. If you are just now entering the business world, leave the "last year" column blank.

Success Tip: The sequence is important. Fill in last year's history first, then your estimate for the current year. Rather than going on to next year, look ahead to year three, then go back to fill in next year and year two. When you "suspend disbelief" (using the dramatic and cinematic term) about what you can accomplish in three years, you are more likely to stretch a bit. This helps you set your sights higher, while being informed and guided by your current situation. The numbers above the following columns indicate the recommended sequence.

Sequence	1	2	4	5	3
Item	Last Year	This Year	Next Year	Year 2	Year 3
What (your product)					
Number of units					
Average dollar ($) per unit					
Total dollar ($) revenue					

This exercise is designed to get you thinking three years in advance. It helps you understand the variables (like units and pricing) and the extent to which you can or cannot control them. You can also use the exercise in reverse. Try setting a target for revenue and then create the number of units and pricing that are necessary to reach your objectives.

THE LURE OF THE ENTERTAINMENT INDUSTRY— ARE MY GOALS REALISTIC?

If your music business information comes primarily from the general media— television, radio, newspapers, and magazines—you would conclude that all music people are either rich or dead. That's a bit of an exaggeration. Still, think about it. People working in the music industry are rarely mentioned in the media. This is especially true of songwriters, agents, managers, promoters, and other "behind-the-scenes" music people.

Some people are lured to the music field by the promise of "sex, drugs, and rock 'n' roll," along with the "American dream" scenario of getting rich doing something glamorous. The popularity of the *American Idol* television show (and others like it) adds fuel to the flame. If you have read this far, I trust you understand that the chances of getting rich quick in music are about the same as in any other business category: pretty low.

Is there a middle ground between celebrity and oblivion? You bet. In fact, that's where most of the approximately three million people in the music industry in North America are: somewhere in between. The point is, you don't need to be a superstar to make a good living in music. Be careful as you observe or attempt to emulate the portrayals of music-business celebrities in the media. They can be illustrative and entertaining, but seldom serve as a real business model.

SHARING YOUR GOALS WITH OTHERS

Who do I share my goals and objectives with? Who needs to know and at what level of detail? There are three basic types of relationships to consider in addressing these questions.

1. Family and friends. You are likely to be most comfortable sharing goal information with those who know you best and are close to you. While they may not be interested in the short-term objectives and the fine details, they are generally interested in understanding where you are headed long-term from a creative, financial, and personal standpoint.
2. Business associates. Your business partners, investors, and key creditors are especially interested in your financial goals and objectives. While less concerned with creative and personal issues, they are likely to care about understanding how the financial pieces of your business fit together. Your business plan becomes the medium for sharing the information.

3. Your support team. Staff, service vendors (like publicists, arrangers, and recording engineers), and coworkers need to know where you are headed. For example, if you are a performer or songwriter working with an agent or manager, it is important for you to share detailed goals and objectives and monitor progress together actively.

A WORD OF CAUTION

Your competitors would love to know all about your plans for success, just as much as you would like to know theirs. Be careful how much information you share and with whom. Long-term goals like "be a successful performer and song-writer" are benign enough, but details on how you plan to achieve those goals are proprietary or confidential. In other words, tell family, friends, business associates, and support team just enough to satisfy their needs. That's where the expression "need-to-know basis" comes from.

KEY POINTS IN THIS CHAPTER

1. Goals and objectives are essential for business planning, marketing and sales planning, creative development, and personal development.

2. Writing down goals and objectives is a powerful exercise that provides clarity and the ability to communicate the information with others. "What gets measured gets done."

3. A goal is a desired result that is often long-term. An objective is an aspect or subset of a goal that is specific, measurable, and achievable.

4. Goals drive the strategy—what you are going to achieve. Objectives drive the tactical operating plan—how you are going to achieve results.

5. Goals can be organized into three categories: creative, financial, and personal. Congruity among all three types of goals is important in business.

6. Once you have written goals in the three categories, they can be turned into a set of objectives. Both financial and non-financial goals can be quantified in terms of number of units, pricing or revenue, expense budgets, and date the results are achieved.

7. You have control over your objectives as long as you keep them realistic. Ask yourself three important questions: (1) How much do I want to earn? (2) How hard do I want to work? and (3) How much am I willing to sacrifice or risk to achieve my objectives?

8. The range of objectives in the music industry, like any other business, is wide. Some music people want to make a living in music, others want to work part-time. Still others aspire to "get rich and retire young." All need well-defined goals and objectives to remain grounded in reality.

9. Your sales forecast flows from financial and creative objectives. The formula for forecasting sales is: Total revenue $ equals units sold times average $ revenue per unit.

10. When creating a sales forecast, start by recognizing actual sales results for last year and this year, then plan three years into the future. This is called the "Five-Year Window."

11. The media portrays music business celebrities as rich and famous. In reality, a relatively high percentage of performers and songwriters work part-time and/or make a modest living from their music business pursuits. Beware of the influence of media stereotypes as you set your goals and objectives.

12. Beware of revealing private goals and strategy to your competitors. Share your goals and objectives with your friends and family, business associates, and support team on a selective or "need-to-know basis."

CHAPTER SEVENTEEN

COMMON SENSE BUSINESS LESSONS FOR THE UNCOMMON WORLD OF MUSIC

In my consulting work, I often get questions like, "That planning stuff all sounds good, but where are the shortcuts? How can I get rich and retire young without having to do all that stuff?" My answer is that there are no gimmicks or secrets in the world of business. Planning is the best "shortcut," and it is a lot less costly than the trial and error alternatives.

In this chapter, we'll look at six common sense business lessons that will help you optimize your planning along with the other fundamentals of business. See if you can relate to any of the "common pitfall" examples cited throughout the lessons.

LESSON 1: "WHEN IN DOUBT, QUANTIFY."

I present this lesson first because it is probably the one you will use the most frequently. Ever wonder if your goals or objectives are realistic? Have a knotty problem to solve? Wonder where the money is going to come from? We've all felt uneasy about things like this. The first thing to do when you feel anxious is to pinch yourself, remember this lesson, and take a look at the numbers.

Common Pitfalls

Here are examples of danger signals that lead to business problems:

- Having no budget or financial tracking. You'll never know how you are doing if you don't keep track. For some music people this is obvious, for others it's a revelation.
- Not understanding how long things take or how much things cost. How many hours do you spend in rehearsal or traveling to gigs? What's your hourly rate when you factor everything in?
- Making decisions based on a gut feeling, intuition, or how others have done things. Intuition is very important, but it is essential to apply reason to decisions involving money and time commitments.
- Not knowing the revenue potential of what you are doing. For example, let's say that your share of a songwriting cut on a hit record is 50 percent of the mechanical royalty rate, with the other 50 percent going to the publisher.

A million-selling record will eventually pay $91,000 ($.091×1,000,000) at current rates. Your share is $45,500—pretty good if it comes all at once and quickly. However, it's likely to take some time, and you may need to pay your agent or manager a percentage of your share. Also recognize that it will take *1,000* thousand-selling cuts to pay the same amount over time.

Recommended Action

Most music is logical, systematic, and mathematical, making it less of a stretch for musicians to "do the numbers" than for many other creative types. Use this to your advantage. Start with a basic revenue and expense forecast for any project before going to work. Think of your budget as an "original composition," something that you create and have control over. When thinking through your three-year goals and objectives, see what expenses are feasible in the first year, regardless of where you want to be in year three. Do the math and let the numbers guide you.

> *Some performers or songwriters may say, "I'm the creative force in my business. I need someone else to deal with the money."*

While that may be true, there will be times when you are called upon to make decisions that involve time and money. In anticipation of that, remember the lesson: "When in doubt, quantify."

LESSON 2: "THE CHAIN IS ONLY AS STRONG AS THE WEAKEST LINK."

Remember this age-old expression? We hear it all the time. We've already begun to apply it to your music business. Chapters Nine through Fifteen discussed the Seven Links in the Marketing Chain. We've already made the point that each of the seven links is important, and if one link is weak or missing, it compromises all results. Here are some more examples:

Common Pitfalls

- Thinking that the music is all that matters or that a strong song, stage show, or record can make up for weakness in other areas. For example, as a performer, you could have the best act in the world, but if you don't get enough bookings at the right price, it doesn't matter from a business perspective. Each link needs to be strong.
- Focusing on one area of the business to the exclusion of the others. This challenge extends well beyond the marketing plan. Your business, even a one-person company, has five functional areas: (1) marketing and sales, (2) finance and accounting, (3) product development, (4) production and

operations including information systems, and (5) general management. Weakness in any of these areas jeopardizes overall results.

- Promoting to the wrong audience. You may have a great act and solid promotional materials, but if they are geared to an audience that is too small or doesn't exist, you won't achieve your goals. This relates to understanding your customers and how they buy (more below).

Recommended Action

Go for balanced strength in each of the key areas of the business. You have already taken the first step: to be aware of what it takes to run a business. You now know that a business has five functional areas and the marketing chain has seven links. If you pay attention to each of those elements, you can be confident that you are covering the bases.

LESSON 3: "THE BUSINESS STUFF—ESPECIALLY SALES—IS A FULL-TIME JOB."

If you already operate a music business, you know how true the above statement is. When was the last time you worked a 40-hour week? Even if you work for someone else, you know that operating a music business is demanding and time-consuming.

Many aspiring musicians work "day jobs" and pursue their musical business interests on a part-time basis. This is fine if your goals and objectives are consistent with the practical realities. There's a point at which you will *need* to quit your day job in order to focus full-time on the music business. Additionally, you will need to hire or contract with additional people as the business grows.

Focus, expertise, and image with customers all come into play here. While it is tempting to "let someone else handle the business," you need to understand the risks.

Common Pitfalls

- Hiring friends or relatives, even on a part-time basis. There's nothing inherently wrong with this, but the risk is one that is common to the music business. Remember the band story in our Overview? It's common for performers to have a spouse, relative, or friend do booking, bookkeeping, or other support functions, only to find out that the person lacks the skill or time to make a positive long-term difference.
- Assuming that all business people are selfish crooks. Some music people think that agents, managers, accountants, and promoters are "only in it for the money" or are "rip-off artists." Every business has its share of opportunists and criminals. The media reminds us of those in the music and entertainment industry because of the glamour associated with performers. However, there are plenty of reputable and qualified music business agents, managers, accountants and promoters with integrity.

Recommended Action

Recognize immediately that no one person has all the skills and time needed to build a music business. If you try to do everything yourself, you may succeed to a point and then find that you can't grow beyond a certain point—creatively, financially, or personally. Build your team with people who are well qualified in their respective areas.

LESSON 4: "BUILD ON STRENGTHS AND DELEGATE THE WEAKNESSES."

Remember the SWOT analysis in Chapter Fifteen? It is important and helpful to identify your company's strengths and weaknesses. Once you understand them, what do you do next? For many people, the natural inclination is to go to work on the weaknesses.

For example, let's say you are a songwriter with strength in composition, lyric writing, and recording, but weakness in the areas of accounting and finance. One approach is to drop what you are doing and learn accounting and finance. Go to night school, buy computer software, practice in your spare time, and hope you get it right. After six months, you are likely to have marginally improved in finance. In the meantime, your other work may have suffered. It's also possible that your self-esteem may be dampened as you struggle with the new material.

It is generally a better alternative to delegate any tasks that require experience and knowledge that you don't have. Focus on what you do best and hire other people to do the same. If you are weak in finance or other aspects of your business, find an expert (accountant, business manager, attorney) to pick up the slack rather than trying to become an expert in a new area yourself.

Common Pitfalls

- Failing to identify strengths and weaknesses objectively. This works both ways. Some people exaggerate their strengths, others exaggerate their weaknesses. You may need outside feedback from customers, staff, friends, or family for a clearer perspective.
- Setting unrealistic expectations on how long it takes to learn special skills. Whatever you are good at now probably comes easily to you. Can you learn sales negotiation as easily as you learned songwriting? Will it take as long to create a marketing plan as it does to secure a record deal? Understand that new things take longer to learn than you might imagine.

Recommended Action

First, beware of isolated self-assessment. Use input from your team, friends, or family as a "reality check" when preparing your SWOT analysis. Work at what you are good at and enjoy doing and delegate the rest. Remember that virtually any task, from vehicle maintenance to promotion, can be performed by someone outside of your organization. While you'll have to pay for professional services, you are likely to save both time and money now and in the long run. You don't have time to learn or master brand-new skills quickly enough to make a difference in the fast-paced business world.

Consider the example of the self-represented performer or songwriter. Should you do all your own bookings and negotiate recording and publishing deals on your own, or engage an agent, manager, or lawyer to represent you? The answer becomes clear when you write down your specific goals and objectives as discussed in Chapter Sixteen. It's a matter of planning and timing, more than cost.

Here's a true story to illustrate this idea. A friend of mine is a performing songwriter and has been a full-time professional for over thirty years. He complained to me that he was spending too much time packing CDs and promotional material and taking them to the post office. It bogged down his spirit and took up valuable creative time.

I suggested that he hire a part-time clerk to support his one-person business. In addition to handling mail and courier packages, this person could keep the contact database up to date, relay phone and e-mail messages, and serve as a sounding board for creative and business ideas. I advised him to find someone locally who 1) likes your music, 2) has clerical skills, and 3) will work hourly on a per-project basis (a contractor, rather than a salaried employee).

By being freed up from these tasks, my friend was able to consistently book more gigs, write more songs, make and sell more records, and enjoy life more. Focus on your strengths and delegate the rest.

LESSON 5: "UNDERSTAND YOUR CUSTOMERS AND GIVE THEM WHAT THEY WANT, PLUS A LITTLE MORE."

Your customers have needs and expectations. They will evaluate your performance (musical or business) based on a set of criteria. As you complete the customer profiling exercise discussed in Chapter Fourteen, you develop an increased understanding of their buying criteria.

There is both a risk and an opportunity here. If you fail to deliver what your customers want, they may not come back for more. Adding to the risk, they may not tell *you* what went wrong, but they are likely to tell others (like prospective customers, competitors, blog readers, or the press). If you deliver slightly above their expectations, they are more likely to want more, and also more likely to tell others about you.

Common Pitfalls

- Undefined target customer profiles. If you don't understand your customers, you will never know if you are meeting their needs. You run the risk of promoting to the wrong audience.
- Assuming that "if we create it, they will buy it." For example, experienced promoters know that simply booking name acts is not enough. The venue,

date, promotion, pricing, and logistics (like audience parking or transportation access) all need to be consistently good in order to please the crowd and keep them coming back for more. Likewise with performers and songwriters. You need to exceed your customers' expectations in terms of communication, quality of materials, timeliness, and follow through. You need to do more than simply have a good act or write a good song.

- Cutting corners on promotion materials to save money. Being "penny wise and pound foolish" generally does more harm than good. Consistently providing quality materials makes a good impression and is appreciated as a "pleasant surprise" by your customers.

Recommended Action

First, establish a clear definition of your market and focus your efforts on those customers. Don't worry about the "mass market," because there isn't one. Your target customers have needs and buying criteria that are unique to them, but they can be identified up front.

Once you've done that, it is relatively simple to exceed your customers' expectations for quality and consistency in whatever you do. Don't your target customers deserve something better than the photocopied bios and demo CDs with hand-written titles that your competitors use?

LESSON 6: "UNDERSTAND YOUR COMPETITORS AND DIFFERENTIATE YOURSELF FROM THEM."

If you are *exactly* like your competitors, the ultimate purchase criterion becomes either lowest price or closest personal relationship. Is your act just like all the rest? Do your songs sound just like those of _____ (fill in famous songwriter's name here)? As a performer, are you offering shows that provide an excellent entertainment value when compared to sports, movies, or theater (in addition to competitors' shows)?

In Chapter Fifteen, we discussed how to identify and understand your competition. The point here is that to be better, you need to be different. Being different *for its own sake* does not necessarily mean that you are better, but you can't be better by being the same.

Common Pitfalls

- Assuming that you need to be just like your competitors in order to succeed. This is an error in logic. It's fine to learn from competitors and develop comparable strengths, but copying can lead to problems.
- Ignoring competition, especially the indirect kind. "We have no competition." Think again. Remember all those examples of direct and indirect competition? Whether you are looking for show dates to play, artists to record your songs, or fans to buy your records, someone else is going after your customers' time and money.

Recommended Action

The first step is to conduct your competitive analysis. Identify the top five competitors in each relevant category, including their strengths and weaknesses. List the similarities and differences between you, and focus on promoting the positive differences in your marketing plan. Remember that you need to be as good as the competition before you can be better, but that does not mean direct copying or promoting the similarities.

Do the six lessons above sound like common sense? Hopefully the answer is "yes." The idea here is to reinforce what you already know so you can apply it to your music business with confidence.

KEY POINTS IN THIS CHAPTER

1. The only secret to success in business is that there are no secrets. Business principles apply to the music industry just as they do to other fields.

2. There are no gimmicks or "get rich quick" schemes in modern business. Apply common sense to what you know rather than look for shortcuts.

3. Lesson 1: "When in doubt, quantify." Understand how much things cost and how long things take to accomplish. "Do the numbers."

4. Lesson 2: "The chain is only as strong as the weakest link." Strengthen your business with balance in each of the five functional areas: marketing and sales, finance and accounting, product development, production and operations including information systems, and general management.

5. Lesson 3: "The business stuff—especially sales—is a full-time job." No one person has all the skills and time needed to build a music business. Build your team with people who are well-qualified in their respective areas.

6. Lesson 4: "Build on strengths and delegate the weaknesses." Do your SWOT analysis with input from your team, friends, or family as a "reality check." Then, work at what you are good at and like doing, and hire out the rest.

7. Lesson 5: "Understand your customers and give them what they want, plus a little more." Establish a clear definition of your market, focus your efforts on those customers, and exceed their expectations.

8. Lesson 6: "Understand your competitors and differentiate yourself from them." Identify your leading competitors, including their strengths and weaknesses. List the similarities and differences between you, and focus on promoting the positive differences in your marketing plan.

CHAPTER EIGHTEEN

PUTTING IT ALL TOGETHER

If you've gotten this far, you have been exposed to each piece of a business plan. Before moving on to budgets and financial schedules, let's review what we've covered so far:

SECTION ONE: THE ART OF MAKING GOOD DECISIONS

Mission and motivation: understanding why you are in the music business

- Preliminary planning: understanding what's involved in starting a new business
- Market overview: understanding the scope and structure of the music industry
- Risk analysis: deciding when to quit your day job

SECTION TWO: CREATING YOUR ESSENTIAL BUSINESS PLAN

- Rationale: eight reasons to have a business plan
- Contents: five "chapters" of your business plan and their relative importance
- Planning flow: from mission statement to daily action list

SECTION THREE: BUILDING YOUR BRAND

- Marketing versus sales: understanding key functions of the two related disciplines
- The seven links in the marketing chain: (1) product strategy, (2) pricing strategy, (3) promotional strategy, (4) sales channel strategy, (5) salesforce strategy, (6) customer profiles, and (7) competitive environment

SECTION FOUR: APPLYING THE BUSINESS FUNDAMENTALS IN YOUR MUSIC BUSINESS

- Goals and objectives: realistic milestones on the road to success
- Common sense: six lessons from the business world applied to music

Where are you now in terms of your planning process? If you have not done so already, this is a good time to start putting the ideas and material for your business plan together. This applies to you whether you are:

- In business already but don't have a written plan
- In business and have a partial plan
- In business, have a plan, and are contemplating growth or the launch of new products
- Not in business yet, but thinking about it

YOUR BUSINESS PLANNING CHECKLIST

In Chapter Seven, we identified the five primary elements or stages of the planning process:

- Plan Element 1: The Mission Statement
- Plan Element 2: The Brand Positioning Statement
- Plan Element 3: The Three-Year Product Plan
- Plan Element 4: The Operating Plan
- Plan Element 5: The Daily Action List

What else do you need? Here are the additional elements:

- Operational strategy. Creating the product is important, but delivering it consistently and profitably points to your business's operations: ability to execute the plan. This ties to Plan Element 4 and the financial schedules.

  Operational elements include:

  » Location and infrastructure: workspace, computer systems, vehicles, equipment, telecommunications

  » Licenses and business registrations: any required state, local, or federal authorization to conduct business; partnership, LLC, or corporation documents if applicable

  » Staff organization and benefits: payroll, insurance, employee policies and evaluation procedures, reporting structure

» Marketing plan: tactical implementation plan (specific methods and costs) for the strategies discussed in Section Three of this book

» Accounting and success measurement: management, financial, and tax reporting policies and procedures

- Financial schedules. The forecasting exercise in Chapter Sixteen got you thinking about revenue three years into the future. In addition to your revenue plan, your business plan includes expense budgets and income statements (also called profit and loss or "P&L" statements). Note: While detailed discussion of how to do budgeting is beyond the scope of this book, we have included simplified financials in the Reference Section and on the CD-ROM.
- Sources of working capital. When you start or develop a business, there is seldom enough revenue from basic sales operations to cover initial expenses and the costs involved in growth. Many businesses fail because they cannot cover expenses in the early days. Identify in advance where your working capital will come from.

Note: The items above are presented in checklist form in the Reference Section and on the CD-ROM.

WHERE CAN I GET THE CASH I NEED TO BUILD MY BUSINESS?

Your cash needs also change over time. Understanding your future cash flow is another benefit of planning three years ahead rather than one year or not at all. "Where will I get the money?" The answer depends largely on how much you need. Your business plan will point you in the right direction. For review, see the section in Chapter Four about viable and nonviable sources of working capital. To refresh your memory:

- Most music businesses have a difficult time qualifying for traditional bank financing. Many performers and songwriters use money from savings, credit card advances, or day jobs to support their music.
- Backers or angel investors will eventually want a return on their investment. Even your "rich uncle" deserves a decent return on investment, or ROI.
- You won't know who to approach for funding until you know how much you need. That's why it is essential to do the planning first.

FREQUENTLY ASKED QUESTIONS ABOUT BUSINESS PLANS

Here are the answers to common questions about the process of constructing a business plan.

1. *Who's going to read the plan?* First and foremost, it's for you and your team. Both the strategy and the operating details are foundations of your business. If you are a one-person business, it is essential to write things down and keep the details organized. If you have investors or are seeking financing, remember that those people will need to review and understand your plan. In most cases, stakeholders like investors or financiers require a business plan as a condition for funding.

2. *How long and detailed should the document be?* There is no standard business plan length. It depends on the complexity of the business, how much preparation or "homework" you have done, and your personal style. That said, most people won't read a long document, even if they have a financial stake in the business. They want the essence, the highlights, the bullets, the executive version. To that end, the best plans have four primary sections.

Section 1: Strategic overview. This section includes the five "chapters" as described here in Chapter Six. This should be no longer than ten to fifteen pages.

Section 2: Tactical marketing plan. This section covers the seven links in the marketing chain, spelled out for the next twenty-four months. This should be no longer than six to ten pages.

Section 3: Financial schedules. The essence of the financials and key metrics are presented in the strategic overview. The financial section includes detailed summaries in spreadsheet form, by account (income and expenses) by month, for the next twelve months of the fiscal year, plus annual summaries for the following two years. The pages of the financial section include (a) revenue plan, (b) expense budget, (c) cash flow analysis (including sources of cash in addition to normal business operations), (d) income statement or profit-and-loss (P&L), (e) capital expense budget, and (f) balance sheet. See the Reference Section and CD-ROM for samples of this format.

Section 4: Appendix or reference section. This is the place to put sample promotion materials, market statistics, publicity reprints, detailed competitive analysis, job descriptions, employee policies, or any other items that you want to have organized and in the same place as the rest of the plan. Keep your audience in mind: financial people like to see market statistics and trend information; employees like to see vacation policies and insurance benefit program details.

Table: Estimated Business Plan Page Count

	Low	High
Strategic marketing	10	15
Tactical marketing	6	10
Financials	6	6
Reference	5	50
Total Pages	27	81

Final result: The main document is twenty to thirty pages of text, six pages of financials, and the appendix items, which could range from five to fifty pages of additional material.

3. *What about an "executive summary"? Do I need one? How long should it be?* A true executive summary is a two-to-five-page document that includes the essence of the whole business plan. In addition to the text, the executive summary needs to include a one-page "key metrics" spreadsheet with the numbers in Five-Year Window format. It is helpful when seeking financing, especially when many people are reviewing the plan. Executive summaries are generally not necessary for internal staff or your own use.

4. *What format is best?* Ring binders are fine, but I suggest the coil or spiral binding that you can get at a copy shop. Why? Two reasons. First, a ring binder is clunky and hard to use unless you spread it out on a big desk or table (makes it hard for your rich uncle to read on an airplane). Also, contents of ring binders mysteriously disappear or get rearranged, which is not good. A more subjective reason involves the initial impression of the document. A bound book simply looks better and sends the message that you are committed and have done your homework. By the way, the production cost for the two formats is about the same.

5. *How often should I update the plan?* Annually, with semi-annual adjustments to the revenue plan and expense budgets. While mission statements and multi-year product plans change very little, the operating plan needs to be updated regularly. The idea is to do a revised three-year plan every year. Remember the "five-year window," how we looked at one year back, the current year, plus three years? If you do that every year, you are revising an existing plan rather than starting from scratch each time. Each year, one year of history drops off and a new year is added on. As you revise, you'll notice your original thought process. This allows you to monitor your own progress and accuracy in forecasting as time goes on.

6. *How long does it take to write a business plan like this one?* The range is big here, depending on how much preparation you've already done and how comfortable or experienced you are with writing. Once you have thought through the strategic issues, writing the plan down and running numbers can take anywhere from 20-60 hours, spread out over a two- to four-week period. Your first plan will take longer than the next annual revision. I also suggest working on the plan steadily for a few weeks rather than sporadically for several months.

Does twenty to sixty hours seem like a long or short time to you? Consider how long it takes to develop your musical chops, create and rehearse a performing act, or write great songs. Doesn't your business idea deserve the same attention in order to prevent problems and optimize your chances of success? Remember, business chops are learned skills, just like your musical, creative, or technical chops.

KEY POINTS IN THIS CHAPTER

1. The planning process applies to new or existing music businesses alike. You can apply the principles in this book whether you are already in business or just thinking about it.

2. Your business planning checklist includes elements from each section in this book and from the five "chapters" of a business plan described in Chapter Six. Before writing the plan, pull all the elements—your notes, figures, and other materials—together in one place.

3. Operational strategy includes details covering (1) location and infrastructure, (2) licenses and business registrations, (3) staff organization and benefits, (4) marketing plan, and (5) accounting and success measurement.

4. Most music businesses need cash to pay the bills, or operating capital that does not come from day-to-day sales revenue. There are viable and nonviable sources of cash.

5. The audience for your business plan starts with yourself, and includes your team and other stakeholders like investors or financiers. Write the plan with the assumption that it will be shared, even if you are currently a one-person business.

6. Concise business plans include four sections: strategic overview, tactical marketing plan, financial schedules, and appendix or reference section. The grand total ranges from about twenty-five to eighty pages, depending on the complexity of the business and your style. Brevity is a virtue, especially in the executive summary (two- to five-page version of the plan plus one page of key metrics).

7. A coil or spiral binding is better for presentation than a ring binder. The production cost of the two formats is about the same.

8. Revise the operating plan including the financials once every year, so you are always looking at a "five-year window" —one year back, the current year, and three years into the future.

9. Once you have thought through the strategic issues and completed the basic preparation, the actual writing of a business plan takes twenty to sixty hours, which can be spread over a two- to four-week period.

10. You and your business deserve the effort that it takes to put the plan together.

11. "If it's not written down, it's not a plan." As we've said throughout, the details need to be documented in writing so they can be shared with others. Like writing a song, the plan-writing process is a clarifying and creative experience.

CHAPTER NINETEEN

WORDS OF ENCOURAGEMENT— MORE COMMON SENSE LESSONS

For some of you, this chapter may reinforce things you already know. For others, it may be the most important part of the book. It contains five more common sense lessons from the world of business, all of which are relevant and applicable to any performer, songwriter, or participant in the music business.

LESSON 1: "PLANNING IS YOUR FIRST AND BEST BUSINESS INVESTMENT."

The expression, "Ready, fire, aim" describes people who jump into a project without knowing what they are doing. Throughout this book, we've discussed how to plan and the benefits of writing down your plans. What happens if you don't? The biggest risk is that you may waste time and money—yours and others'—pursuing the wrong business path.

Common Pitfalls

- Leaping ahead without the benefit of market knowledge. You simply cannot make strategic marketing decisions without understanding the market. "But I don't know how much to charge, let alone how to promote myself, so I'll just take whatever they are offering." This is how music people get exploited by the unscrupulous criminals that unfortunately do get into the business.
- Asking for investment capital without knowing how much you need, where it will be spent, or how it will be paid back. "I know a rich guy who likes my music. I'll ask him to be my backer." Any investor who is worth a long-term relationship will ask what you are going to do with the money, and how you are going to provide a return on the investment. Sure, parents and friends may kick in some gas or rent money once in a while, but that is not enough to build and sustain a music business. Further, most investors will not advance money to pay for expenses you have already incurred, like the utility bill that you charged on your credit card.
- Making decisions on gut feelings or by copying others' mistakes. "I just know this will work. It's the same thing that _____ (your friend or an admired

colleague) did." Go back to Lesson 1 in Chapter Seventeen: "When in doubt, quantify." You may not think you are in doubt, but did you run your numbers? The person or business you admire *may not be as successful as you think they are,* not to mention the fact that their situation is different from yours.

Recommended Action

This book is all about planning and taking conscious steps to move your music business in a positive direction. Follow the template provided here: define the business, understand the market, and analyze the risk, as outlined in Section One. Then go on to construct your business plan and marketing strategy, as discussed in Sections Two and Three.

LESSON 2: "NO PRODUCT SELLS ITSELF."

Can you relate to any of the following?

- "We'll play a lot of shows and build our fan base, then make a record and get rich."
- "I'll get my songs recorded by big acts. All I need is one hit in order to make a fortune."
- "Our show is so strong, we'll have to turn down gigs."
- "Everything lines up for this deal. The backer loves me and is ready to write the check."

I've heard versions of these scenarios many times. They are all making the faulty assumption that the product sells itself.

Common Pitfalls

- Assuming that "if we provide it, they will buy it." You can't bank on sales based solely on your reputation or the strength of a product that you and a few others believe in. This leaves you vulnerable to both direct and indirect competitors.
- Assuming that buyers will pick up the phone and call you. Anyone who's "worked the phones" knows that customers are hard to reach and even harder to get to respond. Relying only on incoming inquiries is a fatal mistake.
- Failing to follow-through on sales contacts and operational details (contracting, paperwork, promotion). The follow-up is *your* responsibility. Sure, there are a few truly professional and personable customers who pick up the slack if you don't. But there aren't enough out there to build and sustain your business. The good ones get tired of doing your work for you, and will ultimately move on.

Recommended Action

Be sure that the sales function of your business is covered by someone who likes to sell, knows how to sell, has all the sales tools, and is properly compensated. This relates to the profile of your salesforce as described in Chapter Thirteen.

LESSON 3: "ARTISTIC INTEGRITY AND COMMERCIAL VIABILITY ARE INTRINSICALLY COMPATIBLE."

This is element #2 in the Business Chops Philosophy. I coined this phrase several years ago while sitting through a tedious panel discussion at a music trade show. At issue was the future growth and development of an entire genre of music. People in the discussion were concerned that "if we get too successful the music will suffer." For many music people, the idea of "suffering for the music" is so ingrained, that achieving commercial or financial success is almost incomprehensible. To do so would require "selling out," or compromising artistic integrity for the sake of money.

Run that by me again? Where does it say that music people have to work three part-time, non-music jobs to pay the expenses for the "privilege" to play low-paying gigs *so the music will sound better*? This entire book is about getting over those feelings and moving on. You can have *both* musical and financial success. They are not mutually exclusive.

Common Pitfalls

- Believing that the rules of business do not apply to the music industry. "Music business? That's an oxymoron. You can't apply common sense to music. I'll never be successful, but I love doing it."
- Assuming that business is evil and that music overcomes evil through its art. "All agents, managers, record labels, accountants, and lawyers are crooks. I got burned once, so they must all be out to get us."
- Believing that for the music to sound good, the musicians must be "starving artists." This applies to the "suffer for the music" scenario described above.

Recommended Action

Many successful people in the music business lead rich, positive lives and create great art without compromising their values. You can certainly recognize the work of music industry people who have become role models for their peers and children, as well as major contributors to social, political, and religious causes.

LESSON 4: "THE BIGGEST MARKETING CHALLENGE IS STANDING OUT FROM THE COMPETITION."

Whether you are a performer, songwriter, or involved in any other aspect of the music business, you have competitors. We discussed the competitive environment in detail in Chapter Fifteen. Why bring it up again now? Because many music people seem to forget that their customers have too many positive choices. If all of those choices blur together, the customer is likely to succumb to the lure of the indirect competitors with more resources.

Common Pitfalls

- Assuming that fans and colleagues hear about your act, song, record, or show by mental telepathy. "We made a record but it didn't go anywhere. I still have 950 of them in boxes in my garage." How was it promoted and distributed? Did you tell anyone other than your family and friends that it was available?
- Forgetting about indirect competition. Remember, the sports, film, and game industries also want music fans to spend leisure time and entertainment money with them. What are you doing to rise above their din?
- Assuming that people have an infinite supply of time and/or money. "It's been three weeks and they haven't returned my call. It must be because they don't care." Not necessarily. How much discretionary time do *you* have? Put yourself in the position of a promoter, record label, or manager who is bombarded with information from acts and songwriters that want gigs. They can't possibly check out every act. That's why some companies return unsolicited materials unopened. It's not about you, it's about priorities. Time and attention are a finite resource for every one of us.

Recommended Action

Focus on customers who are targetable, not the "mass market." Review the customer profiling techniques discussed in Chapter Fourteen. Once you've identified your target customers, promote positive differentiation of your product to set yourself apart from the pack. While there are no guarantees, you will improve your chances of rising above the "noise level" and getting closer to your objectives.

Also, understanding and mastering time management is essential for success in the music business. By respecting your own and others' time, you will develop ways to make it easy for people to decide to buy what you are selling.

LESSON 5: "IT'S OKAY TO BE RISK-AVERSE."

Throughout this book, we've talked about both the risks and the opportunities inherent in the music industry. Let's be clear: the concept of risk applies to any business, music or otherwise. Some people thrive on risk; others tolerate and manage it. Some individuals can't handle any level of risk. As we discussed in Chapter Four, you can enjoy a successful career in music regardless of your tolerance for risk. Simply put, it's okay to be risk-averse.

Common Pitfalls

- Leaping into business without assessing your feelings about risk. "I just had to do it. I couldn't wait any longer. After I spent my life savings on producing the CD, I freaked out. Now I'm applying for jobs in other fields. At least I'll get benefits and a steady paycheck."
- Assuming that the only way to be involved in the music business is to start or own your own business. "I can't imagine anyone wanting to book me, so I'll handle it myself." Or, "My style of music isn't mainstream enough, so I'll go it alone." Or, "I don't know anyone who I could handle working for. I have to be my own boss."

Recommended Action

First, acknowledge that taking risks is tough. It's not for everyone. Determine your level of risk tolerance in each of the areas described in Chapter Four: time, money, reputation, and self-esteem. If you can handle "putting everything on the line," then going into business for yourself is viable from a risk standpoint. If you prefer lower stress but still want to be involved in music, look for a job with an existing company or wait for your personal situation or market conditions to change.

APPLYING WHAT YOU'VE LEARNED

We're approaching the end of this book. How do you feel now compared to when you started reading Chapter One? My aim has been to inform and inspire by providing a set of tools for you to use. If you invest the time completing each exercise, you will be better prepared to make good business decisions, construct a business plan, develop a comprehensive marketing strategy, and set realistic goals and objectives.

You are now ready to apply what you've learned. I suggest that you begin by reviewing the "Key Points in This Chapter" list at the end of each chapter. You will likely say to yourself, "Now I get it . . ." Then go to work.

KEY POINTS IN THIS CHAPTER

1. Lesson 1: "Planning is your first and best investment." As demonstrated throughout this book, planning up front saves time and money. You can't afford *not* to plan.

2. Lesson 2: "No product sells itself." Beware of the tendency to minimize the role of sales and marketing in your music business. Make sure your sales are handled by someone who likes to sell, knows how to sell, and is properly compensated.

3. Lesson 3: "Artistic integrity and commercial viability are intrinsically compatible." (Business Chops Philosophy #2.) Beware of music industry myths that exaggerate the need to "suffer for the music." You don't have to compromise quality or limit yourself to musical or business stereotypes.

4. Lesson 4: "The biggest marketing challenge is standing out from the competition." Focus on targetable customers as discussed in Chapter Fourteen. Promote positive differentiation between you and your competitors.

5. Mastering time management is essential for success in the music business. Start by understanding that you and your customers have a finite amount of time, attention, and money.

6. Lesson 5: "It's okay to be risk-averse." Your decision to either develop your own music business or work for someone else relates directly to your feelings about risk. Determine your tolerance level for risk in each of the four areas in Chapter Four: time, money, reputation, and self-esteem.

7. Make decisions for yourself, don't just "go with the flow." Your situation, like every business situation, is unique. While you can *learn* from the successes and failures of others, it is virtually impossible—and not advisable—to simply copy them verbatim.

8. Once again, there are no secrets or gimmicks to business success. Hopefully, applying what you have learned in this book, along with your common sense, can get you further down the road to succeeding in music.

CHAPTER TWENTY

A LOOK TO THE FUTURE: PERSPECTIVES ON OUR EVOLVING INDUSTRY

You may have read the news in the music trade publications on October 16, 2007: Madonna signed with Live Nation for a comprehensive "360 deal" worth $120 million over ten years. This is one of many recent music industry developments that underscore how dynamic things are right now. Will The Beatles sell their songs on iTunes? Will record companies eventually stop marketing CDs and album-length work in favor of single tracks and ringtones? Will concert promoters sign artists just like Hollywood studios sign actors? What will happen to the independent side of the music industry?

In this final chapter, I'll share perspectives and make a few suggestions on what you can do to deal with changing times in the music industry.

RECORDS VS. MUSIC

Is the record industry dying? With physical CD sales declining (and digital media on the rise), it's easy to jump to conclusions. But let's take a deep breath and remember what "record" means. It's an abbreviation of the word "recording" that has been in use for over 70 years. Even in the 1950s, there were multiple record formats: 78 rpm, 45 rpm, and 33⅓ rpm discs, and reel-to-reel tapes. In the 1980s, record companies offered 33 rpm vinyl LPs, CDs, and cassette tapes. Today, the choices include digital downloads and portable digital media (like music, video, and liner notes on pre-recorded USB drives) in addition to standard CD, SACD, DVD-A, and yes, vinyl LPs!

Then there is the issue of albums versus singles. In the early days of recorded music, there were *only* singles, recorded on shellac-covered canisters. Later, "albums" became big notebooks with multiple 78 rpm discs, allowing the listener to enjoy more songs by a favorite artist in one purchase transaction.

Today we have, in addition to all of the above, box sets that range from a few CDs in a jewel box to elaborate multi-media extravaganzas with audio, video, print, and online components (check out Ray Charles "Pure Genius—The Complete Atlantic Recordings 1952-1959" for a fun example). The content is still *music*, regardless of the packaging or format. And the "record" is still an art object, not a commodity.

DIGITAL VS. ANALOG

Will CDs and other physical media be entirely replaced by downloads and other digital media? In 2008, Forrester Research projected that the adoption of digital media will grow substantially over the next few years, and that half of all recorded music sales in the U.S. will be digital by the year 2011.

According to SoundScan, 10.2 billion albums were sold between 1991 and 2006. While CD sales through traditional retail outlets have declined, "non-traditional" album sales (defined by SoundScan as Internet, venue/mail order, non-specialty retail, and digital downloads) have increased significantly. What this means for artists and record labels is that offering digital delivery of music is no longer optional, but an essential alternative. It also means that there is life left in CDs and other non-digital formats for the foreseeable future.

THE VALUE OF A SONG

Do you remember 45 rpm "singles"? Each disc had two songs on it. When I started buying records in the 1960s, the street price of a single was $1.00 and an album with ten to twelve songs and 35 minutes of music sold for about three dollars. Accounting for inflation, a 1967 dollar is worth $6.00 in 2008—a 600 percent increase over a forty-year period. But a "single" goes for less than $6.00 these days.

Has the value of music decreased in the past forty years? That is a difficult question to answer. Music is unquestionably a great entertainment value; the purchase price of a song is less today than years ago. For reference, a digital download single sells in 2008 for $.99 and an album for $9.99 on iTunes. While there are no liner notes or packaging, and sound quality is compromised, this is all offset by a high level of convenience.

Compact discs are a bit closer to the six times multiple at $18.98 list/$12.98 street price. Albums contain far more music on average (a CD holds up to seventy-eight minutes worth) than vinyl LPs did in their heyday. There are also more choices for music fans today than ever before. Today's music industry is a classic "buyer's market"—virtually infinite supply versus limited, albeit large, demand.

MULTIPLE REVENUE STREAMS

Back to the Madonna deal. This isn't just about records. It's about multiple revenue streams. Here's a quote from the press release:

> ***The deal with Live Nation encompasses future music and music-related businesses, including the Madonna brand, albums, touring, merchandising, fan club, Web site, DVDs, music-related television and film projects, and associated sponsorship agreements, the statement said.***

From the public's standpoint, there are two ways to consume music: live and recorded. It's not one or the other, but both. As a result, just about all performers and songwriters have multiple revenue streams. That's a good thing, and is unlikely to change in these dynamic times. It's also not a new idea.

RECORD COMPANY VS. MUSIC COMPANY

Here are three business trends that are worth watching:

- Record companies are becoming music companies (again). Much like Motown Records in the 1960s, record companies today are looking for (you guessed it) multiple revenue streams. To accomplish this, they are redefining themselves as music companies, and stand to earn a share of song royalties, merchandising revenue, and live performance revenue from signed artists.
- Concert production companies are becoming music companies. Live Nation's core business is live entertainment. The Madonna deal takes them into records, merchandise, and publishing, thus making them a "music company."
- Artist management companies are becoming music companies. While artists' managers have been paid on multiple revenue streams in the past, many are now developing their own record labels and concert production divisions— still another version of a "music company."

Independent performers and songwriters might be thinking, "I've always handled my own booking, recording, merchandising, and management." Which proves that "being a music company" is not a new idea, but a proven business model with new validity in the twenty-first century.

DIVERSITY IS GOOD

As I was working on this chapter of *Succeeding in Music*, I attended the fiftieth annual Grammy Awards show and watched the eightieth annual Oscars; both took place within a two-week period during February 2008. What a change from previous years! The diversity of the nominees, award winners, and live performances was startling in a good way.

- The 2008 Grammy Album of the Year was awarded to jazz artist Herbie Hancock for *River: The Joni Letters*. It was the only the second time in fifty years that a jazz album won the prestigious award; Stan Getz and Joao Gilberto won the Grammy in 1964. Hancock, age sixty-eight, was stunned by the award, especially considering the younger and more mainstream nominees in that category—Foo Fighters, Vince Gill, Kanye West, and Amy Winehouse.
- The 2008 Oscar for best song in a motion picture was awarded to Glen Hansard and Marketa Irglova for the song "Falling Slowly" from the movie

Once. The entire film was produced for $100,000 and tells a story about a performing songwriter. In his acceptance speech, Hansard proclaimed "Make Art!" and got a standing ovation from the Hollywood crowd.

- Also while watching the 2008 Oscar show on television, a commercial for JC Penney's "American Living" brand featured music by Alison Krauss and Robert Plant, from their platinum-selling *Raising Sand* album on Rounder Records.

IS IT JUST ME?

Is it just me, or are the times changing? Hmmm, let's see. A jazz album that pays tribute to a performing songwriter wins a major music industry award. A self-produced song by two relatively unknown performing songwriters wins a major film industry award. A TV commercial for a fashion clothing line includes roots-based music from two radically disparate artists, recorded by an independent label. This could not have happened ten years ago. As Stephen Stills' classic song lyric goes, "Something's happening here, and what it is ain't exactly clear."

WHERE IS IT ALL HEADED?

Whether you are a performer, songwriter, agent, manager, record label, promoter, or producer, you need to pay attention to changing business models in our industry. The public loves music and will pay for it. If there were no music created or sold, there would be no music industry. Here's what you should focus on:

1. Take stock of your situation. Are you achieving your creative, financial, and personal goals and objectives? Will you be able to sustain your own music business over time as the industry changes? Are you willing and able to take the risk?
2. Update your business plan. As I've said so many times in this book, your plan is your best competitive weapon and keeps you in control of your business. Make sure that it is always up to date and written down.
3. Be flexible. The rules are changing. There is no single best business model; there are many options for success. For some people this is scary, for others it is exciting.

How much is music (live or recorded) worth in the grand scheme of things? Business wisdom says that the *price* of anything is whatever the buyer and seller agree upon. The price of a particular song may be $0.99 as a download, or more than five dollars if included as part of a live concert ticket. That said, the *value* of music ranges from worthless to priceless, depending on the buyer's point of view.

What will happen to the value of music between now and tonight's eleven o'clock news? Anything can happen. Keeping your options open is essential for success. Stay in control of your business through planning, objectivity, and flexibility.

KEY POINTS IN THIS CHAPTER

1. The music industry continues to grow and change. How business is conducted today is different from how it will be in 2020.

2. Recorded music, from CDs and DVDs to digital media, will continue to be offered in multiple formats.

3. Adjusting for inflation, the selling price of a recorded song (about one dollar) has decreased from what it was forty years ago. Album selling prices have kept pace more closely.

4. Artists, record labels, concert production companies, and artist management companies are all examples of music companies. They often have multiple revenue streams and are looking for ways to grow through increased diversification.

5. Independent and non-mainstream music is more readily available and prominent than ever before. The diverse tastes of the global music audience combine with modern promotional tools (like e-mail, social networking sites, and alternative record distribution outlets) to create new and evolving business opportunities.

6. Three suggestions for dealing with changing times: 1) Take stock of your situation; 2) Update your business plan; and 3) Be flexible. The rules of the music industry are evolving.

TWO KEY QUESTIONS REVISITED

In Chapter Two, I posed two strategic questions that you should now be able to answer and address fully.

Question 1. What do I want to accomplish?

Assuming that you have articulated your mission, vision, goals, and objectives, you have the answers. It is likely that those answers are now somewhat different from when we first addressed the issue. That's part of life in the music business—or any business. Things change.

Question 2. How much am I willing to risk?

We talked about the need to understand the risks and rewards inherent in the music business and how they affect your time, money, reputation, and self-esteem. While there is risk in every business situation, you are now equipped to understand and manage risk better than you might have been before reading this book. And as the saying goes, when in doubt, quantify.

Answering these two questions comes more easily for some people than others. Some either never address the questions, or keep searching for the perfect answers. Trust the process, and remember that there is no perfect path or outcome—just ongoing examination, reassessment, and improvement.

I've tried to make it easier for you to create a music business plan that allows you to fully understand what you want to accomplish, what the challenges are in achieving your goals and objectives, and what tools are available to help you control both risks and opportunities. I hope it's been helpful and rewarding for you.

THREE FINAL POINTS

How would I summarize *Succeeding in Music*? Here is the essence:

1. *Double the planning time and cut the implementation time in half.* This is an old time-management rule of thumb. It's easier, faster, and less costly to do the planning up front than to learn everything by trial and error. Construct your business plan early in the game.

2. *The biggest challenge is competing for attention.* We are continually bombarded with information today, and this is unlikely to change. Remember the absolute necessity of your marketing plan in the overall scheme of things.
3. *Someone has to manage the business.* If not you, find someone who will. Identify your strengths and weaknesses, and then build your team.

Let me know how things are going. Visit the *Succeeding in Music* Website at www.succeedinginmusic.net, and stay in touch. Good luck!

FIVE

REFERENCE, WORKSHEETS, AND RESOURCES

REFERENCE SECTION

Here's additional information to help you in your quest for success in the business of music. The material in this "workbook" section is organized in three primary areas: sample business plan, worksheets, and resources. Note: All of this material is on the CD-ROM that accompanies this book. You'll be able (with the help of Microsoft Word and Excel) to edit the sample forms and worksheets to suit your needs.

SAMPLE BUSINESS PLAN

We'll re-visit our friends from "The Band Story," give them a name and a fresh start. The business plan includes the following:

- Vision, mission, and values statements
- Brand positioning statement
- Market overview
- Product plan
- Staff and team organization overview
- Operations and infrastructure overview
- Marketing plan including trackable business objectives
- Key milestones for the coming year
- List of basic financials and appendix items

WORKSHEETS

This section includes blank forms and planning templates from the book:

- Risk analysis checklist
- Business plan contents checklist including appendix items
- The five-year window key objectives matrix

RESOURCES

This section includes information and tools for further study:

- Glossary of key terms, concepts, and buzzwords
- Bibliography: books, magazines, trade associations, and Websites
- Contents of the accompanying CD-ROM

SAMPLE BUSINESS PLAN

This section includes a sample business plan written for a band. You can easily adapt it to your situation whether you are a solo performer, songwriter, or leader/manager of a large musical organization. As you review the sample, please keep the following in mind:

- While the story of "Our Band" is fictitious, it includes concepts and situations that are universal and may be applicable to you.
- The entire contents of this plan are included on the CD-ROM. You can start your business plan by renaming the file and editing to suit yourself.
- The wording is chosen to demonstrate the principles from *Succeeding in Music.* Feel free to adapt to your own style. Go for it!

Disclaimer: The people and events described below are fictional and included here for educational purposes only. Any resemblance to real people living or dead is coincidental.

"OUR BAND" BUSINESS PLAN

This is the business plan for Our Band in fiscal years (FY) 2009-2011. The band was founded in 2002 by Ricky and Ronnie Williams to provide an outlet for musical creativity and a source of extra income beyond our day jobs. In the years since, the company has grown, expanded in scope, and performed hundreds of show dates.

This document is the basis for further growth of Our Band's business. It is intended to serve as the foundation for decision-making on all levels: finance, sales, marketing, product development, operations, staff organization, and management. The audience for this plan includes Our Band members, staff, and select advisors, and is otherwise confidential.

I. Vision

Changes in musical trends, technology, and culture have had a significant impact on both business and private life. As we look to the future, we envision the following:

- Music will continue to be a significant element of world culture and the entertainment industry. People simply love to listen, dance, and be entertained.
- Individuals (fans) will enjoy a gradually increasing amount of discretionary time, both on and off the job. While many people work long hours, they still have some scheduling flexibility. This creates an opportunity to enjoy both live and recorded music for entertainment.
- The music industry will continue to diversify. There is no single "most popular" musical style, as there has not been a "mass market" for many years. This opens the door to unique musical entertainment and music businesses that did not exist or could not flourish before.
- The relationship between the business world and the creative world will stabilize over time. As we learn and develop business skills, business people will come to understand the value of our music and its role as entertainment in daily life.
- Business and music will peacefully co-exist. In other words, a music person or group like Our Band does not need to "sell out" (compromise quality) in order to be financially successful.

II. Mission

The mission of Our Band is to enhance the quality of life through music and entertainment. To do this, we strive for the following:

- We write, perform, and record music with positive messages that are meaningful to our target audiences.
- We build our business by charging fair market value for our products.
- We continually invest in the growth of Our Band, our company, and our community.

III. Values

Our values drive our business. Our Band believes the following:

- Music is a universal language that helps performers and their audiences enjoy life fully.
- The music business is a people business. It is important to understand and deal with the human factors on all levels, from staff to customers to suppliers.
- Change is a prerequisite for growth. To be better implies being different; being different points to the need for change.
- Being the best in music includes having a unique combination of musical ability, entertainment ability, and common sense business chops. We strive for strength in all three areas.
- Truth and objectivity go hand in hand. Accurate analysis of current and future situations requires steadfast, often brutal honesty. As a result, "the truth shall set you free."

- Personal relationships form the foundation for all business. Computers, factories, offices, and mobile phones are examples of tools for doing business—all operated by real people. Strong relationships make for strong business.
- We learn continually: new material, new licks, new skills. Both knowledge and experience are essential to success. All three—knowledge, experience, and success—increase over time.
- Communication skills form the basis for all success in business and in life. Poor communication ability spells danger. Compromised communication impedes all life functions. Superior communications skills represent a competitive advantage.
- There is an abundance of opportunity and prosperity available to all who choose to embrace that view of the music business environment, as opposed to taking the scarcity view. We choose to create win-win prosperity scenarios for all our stakeholders rather than view situations as "win-lose" or "zero-sum."

IV. Brand Positioning Statement

Our Band is in the business of providing music and entertainment services on a contract basis. Our clients include promoters, record labels, and fans worldwide. We focus on those customers (promoters and fans) who share our love of dance and pop music of the 1980s and 1990s.

Our fans are motivated by a combination of needs, including:

1. The need for entertainment with positive messages
2. The need to dance as well as listen
3. The need to identify with artists who present a positive image on a consistent basis

We provide our fans with a special blend of cover and original material in both live and recorded performances. We can entertain virtually any audience—young or old, hip or square. We consistently exceed fan and promoter expectations and are uniquely competitive in the following areas:

- Quality of the music. We are expert songwriters, arrangers, and performers. We are well-rehearsed and cohesive entertainers.
- Adaptability and flexibility. We integrate easily within each promoter's unique environment. We are versatile and work comfortably in most performance situations.
- Marketing and promotion. We provide high-quality promotional materials and participate willingly in interviews and showcases. Our representatives maintain the highest standards of creativity and cooperation in making events successful for promoters and fans alike.
- Attention to detail. We know that the little things count. We take pride in our thoroughness and accuracy in communication, professional image, and follow-up.

- Timeliness and accountability. We show up on time and work within schedules. We understand the time value of money and the monetary value of time, and work closely with our clients to optimize resources.

Promoters and fans regard Our Band as a friend and musical resource. We write, record, and perform. Depending on the situation, we provide one, two, or all three of these core products. While project lengths vary, relationships are long-term.

We are acknowledged by the music industry, by clients and competitors alike, as a leading band. Our success is measured in terms of our promoters' ability to make money and our fans' ability to be entertained.

V. The Market Overview

Target Client Profiles

While our fans buy tickets, records, and merchandise, our clients include live music venues, promoters, and record labels. Key segments include:

1. Showcase and dance clubs ranging from 300 to 1,000 seats
2. Promoters of special events in the corporate world: trade shows, special meetings, store openings, etc.
3. College and university activities programs
4. Record labels with a focus on danceable pop music and target acts that sell 10,000 or more records per year

While we have performed for private events (weddings, parties, reunions, etc.) we do not target them in our current marketing efforts.

Our target clients have the following characteristics:

- In business at least two years
- Present and promote our kind of music regularly
- Potential for exceeding the guarantee and increasing fees on repeat engagements
- Properly financed and solid business skills—no hobbyists or sharks
- Demonstrate that they value their customers, employees, and vendors

Market Size and Growth

The live music industry brings in over $2 billion each year. While there are no specific statistics that break out our target segments, we estimate that there are over 2,000 clubs, 3,000 campuses, and 500 special events promoters who use live dance and pop music each year in North America alone. The total number of show dates promoted is unknown.

The record industry sells an estimated 400 million albums and one billion digital tracks per year, according to SoundScan. While the industry is in flux, there are more records released and songs recorded now than at any point in history.

This market allows for ample growth of Our Band's business for the next three years.

Competitive Environment

The music business has become increasingly competitive since Our Band was founded in 2002. There are more performers and recording artists than ever before, each going after increased sales volume and market share. Direct competitors fall into three categories:

1. Professional acts. These include other full-time performers and recording artists who do what we do.
2. "Performing Engineers." These include deejays and mixers who take the place of a live act with "two turntables and microphone."
3. Amateur performers. These are "nuisance factor" competitors who call themselves bands but are really part-time hobbyists.

Indirect competitors include a wide range of entertainment service providers who target the same client profiles as we do. Examples include:

- Sports events and promotions
- Hypnotists, jugglers, magicians, and novelty acts
- Karaoke machines
- Movies, theater, and film festivals
- Travel and leisure activities
- Games

VI. Product Plan

Over the past five years, Our Band has focused on two primary sources of revenue: live performance fees and record sales. In that time, we have also developed original songs that can potentially be recorded by others or sold as ringtones.

As we begin to look to the future, we will continue to rely on performing and recording as primary product areas. In addition, we plan to develop the following products:

- Line of merchandise including shirts and novelty items (2009)
- Catalog of original songs to pitch to other artists (2010)
- Fan club with membership revenue through our Website (2011)

We also will continue to integrate new cover material into our live shows in addition to original songs.

VII. Our Band Team Organization

Band Members
- Ronnie Williams: cofounder, guitar, vocals, songwriter
- Ricky Williams: cofounder, keyboards, vocals, songwriter
- Jennifer Jackson: bass guitar, vocals, songwriter
- Desmond "Sticks" Cremona: drums, vocals, songwriter
- James Lee: sound engineer, driver, all-around technical guru

Management
General management of Our Band is handled by the two founders, with duties as follows:

- Sales: Ronnie Williams
- Marketing: Ricky Williams
- New product development: Ronnie and Ricky Williams with help from Our Band
- Finance: Ronnie Williams
- Operations (information systems, human resources, facilities): Ricky Williams

See the appendix for brief biographical information on Ronnie and Ricky.

Staff and Vendors
We currently have no staff on the payroll other than the band members mentioned above. Over time, we plan to add part-time staff in bookkeeping, merchandising, and coordination of communication between the band and the rest of the business team.

The Our Band team is supported by key vendors and subcontractors:

- Booking agent: Richard Adams at Dancemeisters Agency
- Publicist: open
- General legal counsel: Jerry Smith of Smith, Smith, and Smith Attorneys LLC
- Music business and intellectual property attorney: open
- Recording engineer/producer: Mike Fishman
- Home base club: "Gyrations"
- Computer system and mobile communications expert: United Technologies
- Market research and promotional writing: Currently seeking additional vendors
- Accounting and tax advisor: Acme Accounting Services
- Human resources and employee benefits advisor: The HR Company
- Insurance programs: Independent Underwriters Agency
- Financial advisor: open
- Graphic designer: open

- Webmaster: open
- Spiritual advisor and famous chocolate chip cookies: Linda "Mom" Williams

While none of the above is a full-time position, we consider them to be key members of the Our Band team.

VIII. Operations and Infrastructure

Office and Rehearsal Facilities

Our Band sublets two rooms from Ronnie Williams. One room is set up for band business: communications, meetings, files, and storage of promotion materials. The other room is set up for group songwriting, demo recording, and rehearsals.

When we need a full stage and sound system for rehearsals, we use our home club, Gyrations. As our business grows, we plan to move more of the business functions out of the Williams household and into the offices of our team members.

Information Systems

Our Band members are equipped with computers and wireless music phones (mobile phones with music storage and playback capability). This allows each member to create song files as well as business documents and share them easily.

- Each band member is equipped with a tested, reliable, full-featured computer, printer, and software.
- Workstations are wired to the Internet via "always on" DSL service.
- Wireless phones also provide broadband Internet access while traveling.
- Software allows us to read and write in both Macintosh and Windows platforms.
- Our Band fan database, Website, MySpace page, and financial records can be accessed from anywhere.

Special Equipment and Technology

Since we are active in the music industry, we are conscious of and have access to a wide range of instruments and equipment. In addition to basic computers and telephones, Our Band's offices include:

- Audio/video playback systems with capability to reproduce most media formats, including DVD, MP3, Blu-Ray, audio cassette, audio CD, phonograph, and standard radio and television
- Media server for storage and playback of record masters, live shows, and recorded work in process (audio and video)
- Communications tools including multi-line telephones with conference and speaker phone features, fax machine, mobile telephones, and caller ID

- CD and DVD burners capable of duplicating data, music, and multimedia disks
- Scanner

Band members own and maintain their personal instruments and stage rigs. The company owns a basic sound reinforcement system and uses house systems for most shows. The rehearsal room is equipped with a basic demo recording system. We use other recording equipment owned by Mike Fishman and other studios that we use from time to time.

IX. Marketing Plan

As we look to the years ahead, some aspects of the marketing mix will stay the same, some will change, and some will be added. This section describes how we will market over the next three years.

Product Concepts and Rationale

Emphasis in 2009 will be in two primary areas:

- Personal appearances ranging from $1,500 to $2,500 per day—our "bread and butter"
- Record sales including one new release added to our current catalog of two prior records

Future revenue streams include:

- Royalties and advances. To date we have produced and merchandised our own records. We plan to look for a record label in 2009 and hope to sign a deal by the end of the year.
- Merchandise sales. We plan to offer a line of T-shirts and Our Band logo novelty items for sale at shows. We'll introduce this late in 2009. We are looking into ringtones and sample songs stored on a logo USB drive as a possible item for sale.
- Fan club. We've developed a mailing list of over 6,500 fans who have either attended shows or bought records over the past two years. We plan to develop this into a membership organization with its own marketing plan in 2010 for launch in 2011.

Key Product Benefits

Our fans and promoter clients look to us for the following benefits:

For Fans
- Exciting shows. Instrumentally, vocally, and visually, we put on a great show. Fans are energized and entertained.

- Positive messages. Our lyrics and image are upbeat without being sentimental. People have a good time and forget their troubles when they listen to our songs.
- Consistency. We're there for our fans and keep coming back to entertain. They can count on us to deliver. We want you to be a fan for life.

For Promoters
- Spending crowds. We draw people who buy tickets and like to party. They buy food, beverages, and merchandise in addition to paying for show tickets and cover charges.
- Promotional support. We provide photos, press materials, Web links, and records as part of our standard package. This puts our promoter clients in a position to market our shows more competitively.
- Empathy. We understand enough about the music business to understand what our customers are going through. Offstage, we talk their language and can relate to their situation enough to form lasting business and personal relationships.

Our Unique Competitive Advantage

Our Band offers both musical and business integrity. Our musical ability is complemented by our team's business chops. This unique combination of musicianship and professionalism helps us stand out from our competitors in a positive way.

Essence of Our Band's Marketing Strategy

In 2009 and beyond, we will focus on three primary marketing and sales initiatives:

1. Upgrade our presentation package. We are investing in updates and enhancements to our Website, MySpace page, brochure, and other collateral material. We will create a new photo and press kit; our press kit was last updated in 2004.
2. Find a digital record label as a marketing partner. We will continue to sell our self-produced records, and use them to establish a label relationship by the end of 2009. The label needs to be progressive not "old school." This goes along with the development of new collateral materials.
3. Use merchandise for revenue in addition to promotion. We have given away limited runs of Our Band T-shirts in the past. As our fan base, Web presence, and record sales grow, we will add the sale of logo identity items to our revenue base.

Note: Preliminary "how-tos" for each of the above are included in the tactical marketing plan below.

Pricing and Financial Assumptions

1. Personal appearances are based on daily performance rates.

- **Average** club rate: $1,500
- **Average** campus or corporate rate: $2,500

2. Expenses are not reimbursed by clients. Our fees need to cover travel and overhead in addition to personal compensation.
3. Selling price for records is $15 each, including postage and handling. We only sell direct to fans. Digital tracks sell for $.95 (lossless and no DRM!) to be competitive with iTunes.
4. Bookkeeping is done on a cash basis.
5. We meet monthly to review results and adjust forecasts and tactical plans to reflect current reality.
6. The fiscal calendar is January 1 through December 31.

Key Metrics: Trackable Business Objectives

	FY 09	FY 10	FY11
Performance revenue	$425K	$500K	$650K
Fixed marketing expense budget	$35K	$40K	$50K
Number of personal appearances	200	210	220
Records sold	7,000	12,000	25,000
Records in our catalog	2	3	4
Mailing list	7,500	10,000	15,000
Fan club members	N/A	N/A	2,000
Number of publicity hits/reviews	20	30	50
MySpace Friends, etc.	3,000	5,000	10,000

Tactical Marketing Methods

1. Essence of the selling strategy

- Continue to work with Dancemeisters to sell increasingly high-quality dates. Support them with the new press kit, live show DVD, and mailing list.
- Focus on corporate parties as better paying gigs than private parties.
- Find a progressive record label in 2009 so we can record a new album in 2010.

2. Product mix

- Live performance fees are the foundation of our revenue.

- Increase record sales as a percentage of total band business.
- Plan for merchandise line in 2010 and fan club in 2011.

See the sales budget in the appendix for details on sales by product and client category.

3. Pricing model and strategy
Our rates are in the middle of the high end in our part of the country. We are able to get a little more per date than competitors because of our draw and exciting shows. We plan to increase prices as we record more and develop our mailing list and online network into a fan club.

4. Promotion plan.
Forecasted promotional expenses are included in the fixed marketing expenses budget in the appendix. Key elements of the promotion plan are listed below.

- *Advertising media.* We do not advertise directly, but we supply photos, bios, audio and video clips, and support materials to promoters, who can use those materials in their advertising and promotion.
- *Publicity.* Work with Dancemeisters' publicist to develop a new press kit based on updated collateral package. Send press releases on key showcase dates and growth of the band to the music trades as part of the effort to locate a record label.
- *Sales literature.* Update the current brochure, press kit, photos, demo DVD, and collateral package in the first quarter of 2009.
- *Demo recordings and other collateral material.* Use our latest record ("Live at McDill's") in lieu of auditions and for in-club promotion. Make compilation video from our live show footage. This may also turn into a "for fans only" product that can be sold.
- *Direct marketing.* Continue "Our Band Notes" print newsletter series twice in 2009. Include order forms for records with each mailing. Start to make the newsletter interactive with a link to an online survey. Make decision on phasing out print newsletter in lieu of all online by the end of 2009.
- *Trade shows and special events.* Attend the *Billboard* Magazine Dance Summit and *Keyboard* Magazine "Keyboard Day" events in 2009.
- *Key influencer relations.* Leverage our relationship with the Rockin' 80s Band to get an introduction to Pop King Records and their producer Laurence "DJ Prog" Michelson.
- *Wearables and identity items.* Produce a high-class gift for key clients and record label prospects in the third quarter of 2009. May accompany holiday greetings sent in the fourth quarter. We are thinking of a high capacity USB drive that includes our logo, recent album, live show video clip, and press kit. Use T-shirts and other merchandise for promotion as well as for sale.

- *Showcase performances.* Showcase at the National Association for Campus Activities convention to help secure premium college dates. Do two local benefit concerts in our home club and invite the press and prospective corporate event planners as our guests.
- *Website and e-commerce.* Upgrade our Website to allow online record orders, including digital tracks, digital albums, and traditional CDs. Send special newsletter to fan base with e-mail addresses in addition to traditional "snail mail" newsletter. Enhance our MySpace page and look for additional opportunities on music-related networking sites.

5. Geographic territory

Most performing work is done in a 200-mile radius of our home base. That way we can drive to all gigs, and focus promotional efforts regionally until we record for a label with national distribution.

6. Salesforce strategy

Sales of show dates are handled by Richard Adams at Dancemeisters Agency for clubs, colleges, and corporate events. Ronnie Williams is the band contact for sales; he is also responsible for heading up our quest for a record label. We are looking for part-time clerical help to support our merchandising efforts as our catalog grows.

7. Attractive end-user segments

- College campuses with 1,000 to 5,000 students. We can position ourselves as "stars" on the medium sized campuses.
- Dance and show clubs with 500 to 1,000 capacity. The size means that we can command a larger fee while not competing with national touring acts. In some of the larger clubs, we can share the bill or open for name acts.
- Corporate event planners in low-tech industries. We go over great at parties and store openings in the fashion retail, automotive, and fast food world.

While we have done work with small clubs and private parties in the past, we do not target them for future growth.

8. Direct competitors

- Dance bands, including the Rave Mongers, Dancing Beasts, and Banyan Tree
- Performing engineers and deejays including Steve Wilson, DJ Twister, and Tofu Berger
- Weekend warriors including The Garage Band, The Amy Phillips Trio, and Bar and the Dogs

Schedule of Key Milestones for 2009-2011
(Note: Q1, Q2, Q3, and Q4 refer to the first, second, third, and fourth quarters of the year.)

Q1 2009
- Upgrade photos, press kits, and sales materials
- Q1 revenue = $95 K

Q2 2009
- Our Band Notes (newsletter) Issue #5
- Q2 revenue = $100K

Q3 2009
- Develop new T-shirt and merchandise line
- Play first $5,000 gig at sales meeting for corporate client
- Q3 revenue = $120 K

Q4 2009
- Our Band Notes Issue #6 and decision re: 2010 publication format
- Holiday package to promoters and vendors including logo gift item
- Secure record deal
- Q4 revenue = $110 K
- Total year performance revenue = $425 K
- Total record revenue = $85 K
- Total merchandise revenue = $10 K
- Grand total revenue = $520 K
- Band members quit day jobs (finally!)

2010
- Record and release new record with nationally distributed digital label
- Average gig greater than $2 K
- Total performance revenue = $500 K
- Total record revenue = $130 K
- Total merchandise revenue = $50 K
- Grand total revenue = $680 K

2011
- Launch Our Band Fan Club online
- Average gig price greater than $3 K
- Total performance revenue = $650 K
- Total record revenue = $250 K (includes advance, royalties, downloads, and direct sales)
- Total merchandise revenue = $100 K
- Grand total revenue = $1,000 K (Wow, that's a million bucks!)

X. Financials

Detailed financial schedules are included in the appendix section as follows:

- Revenue plan and key objectives FY (fiscal year) 2009-11
- P&L / expense budgets FY 2009-11
- Detailed fixed marketing expense budget FY 2009-11
- New equipment priorities FY 2009

XI. Contents of Appendix

A. Organization chart and team contact list

B. Job descriptions and band bios

C. Master client history spreadsheet ranked by total sales

D. Product plan spreadsheet and tracking matrix FY 2007-11

E. Historical data: FY 2008 final reports

F. Sample promotion materials including newsletter and press clipping

WORKSHEETS AND CHECKLISTS

H ere are blank worksheets that will help you develop your business plan. Electronic versions are included on the CD-ROM, ready for you to go to work.

RISK ANALYSIS CHECKLIST

Answer the following questions, knowing that you are the only judge. The more *yes* answers you have, the more prepared you are to take the risk of going into the music business for yourself.

The market is big enough to support my music business; people are ready to buy what I'm selling.

       Yes   No

I understand my competitors (direct and indirect) and can differentiate myself from them.

       Yes   No

I know who will handle each of the key elements of my business: sales, marketing, accounting and finance, operations, product development, and general management.

       Yes   No

I have a written business plan that looks three years into the future.

       Yes   No

I have sources of funding to cover my business and personal expenses for one year or more.

       Yes   No

My risk tolerance is moderate to high.

       Yes   No

Best case scenario is that you answered "yes" to all six questions. If not, go back and see what it would take to do so. You are probably closer than you think.

Success Tip: The question "What's it going to take?" is more important than "Can I do it or not?" It forces you to think through the issues and find solutions.

Business Plan Contents Checklist

Use this section as a guide and checklist to be sure that you have thought through and written down all the elements of your business plan.

Vision, Mission, and Values Statement

We believe that the future of our business is bright because:

_____

_____

_____

_____

We are in business to:

_____

_____

_____

_____

We believe in the following business values and operating principles:

_____

_____

_____

_____

Brand Positioning Statement

The brand positioning statement is the foundation of your marketing plan and clearly establishes how you are different from your competitors. It is a one-page document that answers the following four questions accurately and succinctly: Use this page as a worksheet, then refine from there.

What business are we in?

_____

_____

_____

_____

Who are our customers?

_____

_____

_____

_____

What makes us special?

_____

_____

_____

_____

What's in it for everybody (customers, vendors, community, owner/investors, us)?

_____

_____

_____

_____

The Three-Year Product Plan

Your products (goods and services) are what your customers pay you for. Whether you are a performer or songwriter, you are likely to sell more than one category of product. In addition, your product mix is likely to change over time. Use this worksheet to think through the products you plan to offer over the next three years. Start by filling in what you are already offering in the "Last Year" and "This Year" columns. Then "suspend disbelief" and go out to Year Three. Fill in Next Year and Year Two after that. This is the Five-Year Window process in action.

Sequence	1	2	4	5	3
Product	**Last Year**	**This Year**	**Next Year**	**Year Two**	**Year Three**
Show Dates Performed					
Songs Written					
Songs Recorded					
Records Released					
Merchandise Sold					
Other (Specify)					

Operational Elements

Creating the product is important, but delivering it consistently and profitably is critical to your business's operations, or ability to execute the plan. Think through each of the following, and estimate costs and time needed. Use this worksheet as a quick start and checklist. Create financial spreadsheets and other documentation as your business plan comes together.

	Estimated Cost $	**Who's Responsible**	**Deadline Date**
Location (workspace and infrastructure)			
Licenses and business registration/incorporation			
Staff organization and benefits			
Marketing plan			
Accounting and success measurement			

The Detailed Operating Plan Document Package

Once you've got the first three elements—mission/vision/values, brand positioning statement, and product strategy—you are in a position to create an operating plan. This is the part of the plan that most people think of when they think of a business plan. Let's make a distinction here. Remember the definition of strategy vs. tactics? A strategy is a decision. A tactic is a method. In a strategic business plan, *both* strategies and tactics are articulated.

Organize all of the above, plus financial information and other documentation, into a concise written plan. Note: Taking this step assumes that you have decided to start or continue the business. Elements of the plan include:

1. Detailed revenue forecast. Revenue equals units sold times average selling price, by product, by month.

2. Marketing plan. Use the marketing plan outline from the sample business plan for "Our Band" to guide you.

3. Budgets and pro forma financials. These are the hardcore financial schedules, related to both income (revenue forecast) and expenses in all areas. The words "pro forma" come from Latin and imply that portions of the material are hypothetical (future) as opposed to actual (real history). Examples of financial material include departmental or project expense budgets, income or profit and loss (P&L) statements, and balance sheets.

4. Organization plan. This includes a listing of each staff position, the reporting structure (best illustrated in a graphical organization chart), job descriptions for each position, and a description of employee benefits provided by the company. Benefits include: (1) insurance (health, life, disability, liability), (2) paid holiday schedule, vacation and personal day policies, (3) retirement, profit sharing, or stock options, and (4) any extras not covered elsewhere, like day care, fitness counseling, on-the-job training, or tuition reimbursement. Sound a little corporate? That's okay. These are the kind of things that help you differentiate your company from your competitors. If you can't afford everything right away (likely), create a placeholder in your plan for future benefits.

5. Capital purchase schedule. Capital purchases are those items which the company buys that have a useful life of longer than one year. In most cases, the Internal Revenue Service requires that capital purchases be depreciated, that is deducted from taxable revenue over the useful life of the item rather than all at once. Examples include vehicles (cars, vans, trucks, buses), equipment (like stage gear, instruments, and recording equipment), and real estate.

6. Appendix items or supplemental material. The plan document should include material that illuminates the text and numbers without cluttering things up. You decide what items are most important for your purpose.

Examples include:

- Organization chart
- Job descriptions and team member bios
- Information policy (how long to keep data, who gets access, etc.)
- Master client history spreadsheet ranked by total sales
- Product plan spreadsheet
- Historical data: prior years' financial reports
- Customer profiles and target customer criteria
- Sample promotion materials, press clippings, awards, Website content
- Employee handbook including company policies and benefits
- Market research reports and statistics
- Detailed profiles of competitors

GOALS AND OBJECTIVES: USING THE FIVE-YEAR WINDOW TOOL

What gets measured gets done. The worksheets below are a place for you to log in your key goals and objectives in the three categories discussed in Chapter Fifteen.

Success Tips:

- Remember that goals are long-term desired results. Objectives are aspects of goals that are specific, measurable, and achievable.
- List your goals first, without time constraints. Then break them down into trackable objectives, looking three years into the future.
- The Five-Year Window tool allows you to fill in last year and this year for reference and focus. Then look ahead to Year Three, allowing yourself to stretch a bit.
- The category descriptions below are offered as prompts. Feel free to adapt them to your specific situation.
- These worksheets are also included on the CD-ROM. You can streamline the worksheets by taking out anything that does not apply and adding in the details that are meaningful to you.

Top Five Creative Goals

1 _____

2 _____

3 _____

4 _____

5 _____

Creative Objectives	Last Year	This Year	Next Year	Year 2	Year 3
Songs written by me					
Songs written and recorded by me					
My songs recorded by others (cuts)					
Records released					
New material in stage show					
Music association award					
Grammy award					
Other award					
News/press clippings in trade media					
News/press clippings in general media					
Radio airplay					
Radio interviews/appearances					
Television airplay					
Television interviews/appearances					
Record reviews					
Song reviews					
Largest venue I performed in					
Smallest venue I performed in					
Largest audience					
Smallest audience					
Fan testimonials					
Promoter testimonials					
Competitive testimonials					
Number of fan club members					
Website unique visitors					
Benefits or pro bono shows					

Top Five Financial Goals

1 _____

2 _____

3 _____

4 _____

5 _____

Financial Objectives	Last Year	This Year	Next Year	Year 2	Year 3
Songs recorded by me or others					
Average royalty income per song					
Total royalty revenue					
Smallest revenue for one song					
Largest revenue for one song					
Records sold—all titles in release					
Average royalty or margin per record					
Total revenue from record sales					
Smallest revenue from one record					
Largest revenue from one record					
Number of show dates performed					
Average revenue per show date					
Total live performance revenue					
Smallest revenue from one show date					
Largest revenue from one show date					
Product endorsement revenue					
Corporate sponsorship revenue					
Merchandising and other revenue					
Grand Total Revenue $					
Allowance for Expenses $ (50%)					
Left Over to Pay People $					
Number of People					
Average Share $					
Target Average Share $					
Variance $					

Top Five Personal Goals

1. _____

2. _____

3. _____

4. _____

5. _____

Personal Objectives	Last Year	This Year	Next Year	Year 2	Year 3
Number of days worked	_____	_____	_____	_____	_____
Average revenue per day	_____	_____	_____	_____	_____
Number of hours worked	_____	_____	_____	_____	_____
Average revenue per hour	_____	_____	_____	_____	_____

Vacation objective: **Last year:** _____

This year: _____

Next year: _____

Year 2: _____

Year 3: _____

Family objective: **Last year:** _____

This year: _____

Next year: _____

Year 2: _____

Year 3: _____

Community Objective: **Last year:** _____

This year: _____

Next year: _____

Year 2: _____

Year 3: _____

Spiritual objective: **Last year:** _____

This year: _____

Personal Goals and Objectives

Next year: _____

Year 2: _____

Year 3: _____

Educational objective: **Last year:** _____

This year: _____

Next year: _____

Year 2: _____

Year 3: _____

Health objective: **Last year:** _____

This year: _____

Next year: _____

Year 2: _____

Year 3: _____

Exercise and fitness objective: **Last year:** _____

This year: _____

Next year: _____

Year 2: _____

Year 3: _____

Hobby and recreational objective: **Last year:** _____

This year: _____

Next year: _____

Year 2: _____

Year 3: _____

Other personal objective: **Last year:** _____

This year: _____

Next year: _____

Year 2: _____

Year 3: _____

Sources of Working Capital (cash to fund the business)

When you start a business, there is seldom enough revenue from sales operations to cover initial expenses and the costs involved in growth. Many businesses fail because they cannot cover expenses in the early days. Identify in advance where your working capital will come from.

Funding Source	Year One	Year Two	Year Three
Savings			
401k/IRA			
Sale of assets: real estate, securities			
Second mortgage or home equity loan			
Credit card cash advance			
"Rich uncle" (friends and relatives)			
Bank loan			
Private investor or "angel"			
Reinvested profits (your business)			
Other			

Success Tips:

- Be prepared to answer the top three questions that funding sources will ask:

1. How much do you need?
2. What are you going to spend it on?
3. How do we get paid back?

Your business plan answers all of these questions and presents the details in a professional way. That's why I suggest that you do the planning before you ask anyone for money.

- Banks view musicians as bad credit risks; they are unlikely sources of working capital, unless the loan is secured by real estate, cash on deposit, or guaranteed in some way. This is not a personal reflection on you, so don't take it personally.

- Angel investors or "backers" need to have three key characteristics in order to be viable for you: 1) they have the amount of money that you need, 2) they understand the music industry, and 3) they share your sense of urgency and will give you a prompt disposition. If any of these are missing, look elsewhere.
- Investors and other funding sources have dollar ranges that they are comfortable with and willing to invest. For any amount under $20,000, I suggest using your savings, sale of assets, or a home equity loan. Save the investor pitches for the larger amounts that you might need in future years.
- Fund-raising can be a full time job. Build the time that it will take into your business plan.
- Beware of people who say they can raise the money for you and charge you a commission for doing so. While there are reputable fund-raisers out there, most of the good ones are focused on other industries.

Branding and Promotion

A brand is a symbol that causes your audience or customers to connect with you in a positive way. The stronger your brand, the stronger your competitive position, and consequently your sales and profits. The name and identity of your act is a brand.

- Your brand brings to mind unique characteristics.
- Your brand highlights differences rather than similarities.
- Your brand message should be short and easy to remember.
- Branding relates to visual, as well as verbal identity.

Stiernberg's Top Ten Branding Tips

1. Make your brand message simple and memorable. Refer to your brand positioning statement for the concepts and copy points.
2. Make it accessible to your target audience. Use language and visual images that appeal to the people that matter to you.
3. Make it fit on a business card (not too long). Your business card should include your logo, contact information, and a few memorable words—not your entire bio and history.
4. Deliver the message consistently across all media (print, Website, press kit, product packaging, etc.). Make sure that the words and images that you use tell the story accurately, regardless of medium.
5. Make small adjustments over time, instead of radical changes. Things will change, and it is a good idea to refine your brand message as you go along. Just be careful to introduce changes gently.
6. It's okay to state the obvious. This is a key point in telling your story. What's obvious to you (like your style of music, instrumentation, history, etc.) is fresh information for your customers and fans.

7. Get feedback from others before you promote your brand. Do a test with customers who know you. Ask for critical comments and suggestions.

8. Get professional help where necessary, unless you already are a professional. The costs of first class graphic design, copy writing, editing, and production are relatively small. Weigh the risks or consequences against your goals and objectives. A sloppy or amateurish look is likely to turn off far more prospective clients than you might think.

9. Representation (examples: manager, agent, publicist) has two advantages: time management and positioning. Your plan is to be a performer or songwriter and you want to spend your time doing things that only you can do. From an image standpoint, artists with representation position themselves as the real pros. The "I wear many hats" approach can cost more money than it saves.

10. Build a sales community. Your database and network of fans, business contacts, and buyers becomes an extension of you and your brand. Telephone, e-mail, and online networking tools help you to do this in a cost-effective way.

Optimizing Music Trade Shows, Seminars, and Conferences

As a performer or songwriter, you may have attended or plan to participate in one of the many excellent music business seminars, conferences, and trade shows that are offered all year round. Perennial favorites include South by Southwest, Taxi Road Rally, Midem, NACA, and the various genre conferences (e.g. IAJE, IBMA, Americana, Folk Alliance, etc.). New ones continually crop up; there are opportunities all over the world in virtually every music genre.

Whether you are an exhibitor, panelist, or attendee, the seminar, trade show, or conference represents an important business opportunity. How do we prepare to take advantage of that opportunity? How do we optimize our time during exhibit or networking hours? How do we track results and evaluate the success of the conference experience from a business standpoint? This section addresses these topics.

Why Trade Shows?

Why have a trade show in the first place? Isn't a music conference all about the music? Well, yes, but it's the *business* of music that brings people together to most events. Here are some fundamental principles that apply to any music trade show or networking event.

- Trade shows are great marketing opportunities because they allow *face-to-face* interaction among vendors and customers. A lot can be accomplished via phone, fax, and e-mail, but there is no substitute for getting together in person to do business.

- Further, shows and conferences are events. In our consulting work, we have an expression that goes like this: "Events are the catalysts that lead to consciousness shift." A consciousness shift is a change in thinking, awareness, or attitude. It's human nature to remember events. Those events are naturally associated with changes or shifts in our thinking or consciousness.

- Consider the following two voice mail messages from a booking agent to a festival promoter:

Message One: "This is Richard Adams calling from the Dancemeisters Agency. I'd like to introduce myself and discuss the possibility of booking some of our acts on your festival. Please call me back . . ."

Message Two: "This is Richard Adams calling from the Dancemeisters Agency. Hey, it was good to meet you at the NACA regional in Austin. I'm calling to follow up our conversation there regarding the date we talked about. Please call me back . . .

Which of the two is more likely to get the call back? Whether you are buying or selling, the same psychology applies.

The Three Keys to Trade Show Success for Both Buyers and Sellers

There are three keys to business success at conferences and shows: 1) planning, 2) presentation, and 3) follow up. Whether you are "working the room" or "working the booth," the same principles still apply. You need to project a good appearance, have a story to tell, and leave something behind to facilitate follow up. Further, you can evaluate competitors by seeing how well they stack up in the three areas described below. Remember that buyers and sellers need each other and the fundamentals of marketing apply to both.

1. *Planning* your show activities starts with your business objectives. Ask yourself the following questions at least three months in advance of the event:

- Who do I want to see? The answer is both specific (actual names) and general (profiles or categories).
- How many contacts are realistic? Is it five? Fifty? Five hundred? This depends on the attendance at the event and on how much time you spend in each conversation or meeting. Set a realistic objective in advance and plan your time accordingly.
- How do I measure success? Whether you are buying or selling, this has both financial and non-financial (read as "positioning") dimensions. While you need to recoup your investment and balance the budget, it is also important to measure the intangibles like possible long-term alliances or industry "buzz" created by your presence.

2. Your *presentation* is what people remember you by in a business environment. As either an exhibitor or attendee, there are three key presentation elements:

- Exhibit booth or table. The appearance, sound, and feel of your booth combine to create your first impression. It needs to be both orderly and inviting, and convey your message visually. If you are an attendee, this also applies to your personal appearance and demeanor.
- Sales story. Know your company "pitch." Be able to answer the following three questions in a concise and friendly way.

  » What are you selling here? If you are an exhibitor, this is sometimes expressed to you as "What's new this year?" If you are an attendee trying to sell something (like an artist looking for a recording or publishing deal), be prepared likewise.

  » Why is your product good for me? Alternatively, "Why should I buy your product (act, record, song, service, etc.) as opposed to someone else's?"

  » What do I do next? Assuming that your prospective customer shows some interest, prepare them for follow up after the show. Send information? Call on the phone? E-mail? Let them know what to expect and when.

- Take away materials. It's human nature to want a souvenir to remember a positive event, even if that event is as brief as a conversation in an elevator. If you want your contacts to remember your conversation longer than the time it takes for them to get to the next conversation, plan to give them something tangible. Examples include business cards, press kits, bio sheets, CDs, DVDs, or even identity items like caps, shirts, fly swatters, pens, USB drives, etc., with your logo on them.

3. *Follow-up* is the third essential key to trade show success. There are three time frames for follow-up.

- During the show. Some follow-up occurs before you go home. You may have second meetings with hot prospects, both in and out of the exhibit hall, seminar room, or showcase venue. In addition, it is beneficial to make notes on what you will need to do when you get home, so you don't forget key details.
- Upon return. Immediately after you get back home, list and prioritize your follow-up activities. Do you need to make phone calls, send e-mails, ship materials, write contracts, all of the above? Before you do the first task, create a list of all follow-ups so you can put them in the proper priority sequence.
- Three months later. Trade show veterans get in the habit of evaluating their results about three months after the end of the event. That is usually enough time to determine if your show activities have paid off. How do you know? Go back to your planning notes and pre-show objectives. What came true?

What didn't? What will you do differently in the future? This exercise is the true key to continuously improving business results.

Optimizing the Conference Exhibit Hall and Networking Opportunities

Music trade shows and conferences are so much fun that it is tempting to forget that we attend them primarily to do business. The good news is that we can do both: have fun and conduct business throughout the conference. In that spirit, here are five success tips for optimizing your business results as you work any event's exhibit hall or other networking events.

Success Tip 1: Make appointments. Already know that a key contact is going to be at the show? Set up a meeting in the exhibit hall in advance. If you approach someone in a booth who is busy, ask discreetly for a good time to meet. Then be sure to show up on time.

Success Tip 2: Be there the entire time. Many conference schedules are organized with only minimal time conflicts between the exhibits and other activities like seminars, showcases, banquets, and organized jam sessions. In other words, exhibit hall time is precious. Plan to work the hall during its full hours of operation, remembering that things change over the course of the event. While you may be able to walk up and down all the aisles in a few hours, it's the people contact that keeps things lively each day.

Success Tip 3: Talk it up. Did you meet one of the hot new showcase acts in their booth? Make contact with a music supervisor who is working on a movie that will use a lot of original music? See one of the visiting music legends in person? Tell your friends and colleagues. That creates the "buzz" that helps maintain a high energy level in the hall.

Success Tip 4: Carry materials with you. Whether you are exhibiting or not, carry your basic business material (cards, brochures, records, etc.) with you at all times. You never know who you will run into in the aisles, at the bar or at the concession stand.

Special note on business cards: When I meet performers and songwriters, too often I am (unpleasantly) surprised when I ask for a business card and get a blank stare followed by "I don't have one." Running out is bad enough, but not even having a business card to exchange at a music business event sends the message: "I don't really know why I'm here." This is easy to remedy, if you plan ahead.

Success Tip 5: List your contacts and follow-ups *every day*. Still wired after that late night showcase? That's a good time to make a few notes, such as who you met that day and what follow-up is necessary. Two big advantages: 1) you capture the details while they are still fresh in your mind, and 2) you jump-start the follow-up process so you can hit the ground running when you get home.

RESOURCES

GLOSSARY OF KEY TERMS, CONCEPTS, AND BUZZWORDS

Here are the most important words and phrases used in this book, presented here in alphabetical order for quick reference.

360 Deal: an all-encompassing (360 degree) agreement between an artist and a music company. Not limited to a particular revenue stream, 360 deals may include touring, recording, publishing, film, television, merchandising, and licensing.

Advertising: the act of delivering a paid promotional message to a target audience. A key word here is "paid." You pay someone to deliver the message to a predetermined or target audience on your behalf.

Amateur: no compensation—a labor of love.

Angel investor: a type of funding source that 1) can provide the amount of money that you need, 2) understands the music industry, and 3) shares your sense of urgency relative to investing in your business; also called "backer."

Art: human expression in sensuous form, often "for its own sake." The word "expression" is very important, because it implies that the motivation comes from within the artist rather than somewhere else.

Assumption: the answer to the question, "How did you get the numbers?" Assumptions are key elements in business plans, as they illuminate and rationalize sales forecasts and expense budgets.

Audience: whoever enjoys the music, whether they are the paying customers or not. Fans who buy tickets are customers of the promoter, but they are the audience for the performer.

Audition: the process of performing without pay with the intention of getting hired. This can apply to individual musicians or entire acts. Demo recordings, especially video, have streamlined this process recently. Also see "showcase performance."

Backer: see "angel investor."

Balance sheet: a financial schedule listing a company's assets, liabilities, and stockholder equity. Also known as a "net worth statement."

Brand: a symbol that causes your audience or customers to connect with you in a positive way.

Branding: the creation of indelible images (logos, trademarks, messages) of you and your products in the minds of your target customers, audience, and stakeholders. Examples of music business brands include your name or stage name, your company name, names of songs, records, festivals, concert series, clubs, and other venues.

Budget: planned revenue and expenses tracked over time; usually presented in monthly increments over a twelve-month fiscal year.

Business plan: a written system of documents that puts your business and its market environment in context over the next several years. It describes what you are going to do, how you are going to do it, and what the consequences are.

Buyer characteristics: common traits that make up the profile of your target customer. Categories of traits include demographic, economic, geographic, and psychographic attributes. This information is used to match the target customer with your product.

Career: business activity or occupation; something done to make a living.

Collateral materials (also referred to simply as "collateral"): those promotional items that work with, but do not take the place of, basic print sales literature. Examples include demo recordings, itineraries, publicity reprints, photos, biographies, agency rosters, etc.

Commerce: buying and selling of goods and services. This implies financial transactions, which further implies a profit motive.

Commodity: any product that is both relatively abundant and virtually un-differentiated among competitive offerings. Traditional examples include foodstuffs, energy, and building materials.

Competitive intelligence system: a set of information that allows you to understand what is going on in the market, and how you and your competitors are dealing with market conditions. Most market information is readily accessible and relatively inexpensive. A comprehensive intelligence system includes information in eight categories: 1) competitors, 2) customers, 3) markets (audiences in the music industry), 4) suppliers, 5) economic trends, 6) legal and regulatory trends, 7) technology trends, and 8) social, cultural, and political trends.

Corporation: a legal classification of business for a company with any number of owners (as few as one) that is organized according to laws and tax codes designed to regulate larger firms. The various owners take shares of stock in the company, and that stock can be bought and sold periodically by the individuals with little or no disruption to the business.

Creative goals: the desired long-term results, whether you make money from them or not. Also called artistic goals, they define the business playing field before adding the economic elements. Must be congruent with financial and personal goals.

Customer: whoever pays you directly; where the money changes hands. For example, if a club owner pays a band to perform, the club owner is the band's customer. If a band pays an agent to secure the booking, the band is the customer.

Day job: what you do outside of music (whether done during the day or at night) to make money to support your musical interests.

Demographic information: age, gender, marital status, and education level of target buyers. Relevant and essential to the creation of buyer profiles.

Differentiation: a pricing and positioning strategy in which the seller charges as high a price as possible, based on the product's features and competitive advantages. Assumes that there are aspects of each competitor's product that can be distinguished easily and are worth paying more for. This is the most common music industry approach (see "low-cost producer").

Direct competition: competition from similar businesses in the same product category. Examples include other performers or songwriters.

Direct marketing: any promotional activity in which direct contact is made with the target customer. Also called "direct response marketing," it allows you to get immediate trackable feedback from your target customers. Common techniques include direct mail, telemarketing, and cold canvassing (also called missionary selling).

EBITDA: acronym for Earnings Before Interest, Tax, Depreciation, and Amortization. This is a key metric for any business because it shows level of profitability from day-to-day operations.

E-commerce (also called e-business): the process of using the Internet as a platform for conducting business. Examples include posting information on Websites, e-mail promotion, conducting surveys, music downloads, or selling merchandise online.

Economic information: household income levels and discretionary spending ability or "buying power" for individuals. Relevant and essential to create buyer profiles.

Elevator test: the challenge of articulating the essence of your brand positioning statement to a stranger in the time it takes to travel ten floors on an elevator. This is a good barometer of how clearly you can describe what you do professionally.

Entertainment: amusement or diversion including public performances or shows. Entertainment, including music, is usually created with the needs of the audience in mind, first and foremost. Non-music examples include movies, television, games, books, and sports.

Executive summary: a one- or two-page document that includes the essence of the whole business plan. Helpful when seeking financing, especially when many people are reviewing the plan.

Financial goals: the set of desired long-term results that are measured in financial terms. Examples include revenue, profit, and return on investment (ROI). Must be congruent with creative and personal goals.

Full-time: geared to making 100 percent of financial income; implies focus and dedication.

Geographic information: where your customers physically live or conduct business. Relevant and essential to create buyer profiles.

Goal: a desired result; often long-term. Something good that you aspire to over a long period of time.

Hobby: leisure-time activity; something done for fun.

Hybrid: a pricing and positioning strategy in which the supplier offers more than one product and uses both the low cost producer and differentiation strategies selectively. Some products may be viewed as "commodities" and subject to competitive market pressures; others can be "differentiated" and priced accordingly.

Identity item: the generic term for tangible promotional gifts that include your identity (name, logo, message) and have some usefulness or intrinsic value beyond pure promotion. Also called "advertising specialties," "tschotschkes," or "swag." Examples include wearables (T-shirts, jackets), non-wearables (key rings, guitar picks), and edibles (hot sauce, candy).

Income statement: a financial schedule which includes a summary of revenue minus expenses, resulting in net income (profit or loss) for a given time period (typically a fiscal year). Also called "P & L," short for profit and loss statement.

Independent or indie: adjective or noun used to describe a record label or other music company that is not owned or exclusively distributed by one of the major label groups or publicly-traded entertainment corporations.

Indirect competition: competition from any product that goes after the same target customer's attention and money, but from outside of your product category. Examples include not only the obvious entertainment specialists (games, cinema, sports), but alternative purchases like furniture, clothing, home improvements, computers, cars, and/or activities like vacations, hobbies, and education.

Individual customers: those who make the decision to buy on their own and are usually spending their own money. Examples include clubs or other venues where the owner books the acts, Indie labels or publishing companies run by the owner, and the general ticket- and record-buying public.

Influencers: people who do not buy from you, but can influence your target customers. Examples include managers, record label personnel, celebrity endorsers, and any other source of referrals or recommendations.

Institutional customers: those who make buying decisions in groups and are often spending an organization's money. Examples include college and university "activities committees," major corporate record labels and publishing companies, and ticket brokers and resellers.

Links in the marketing chain: the seven elements or links of any marketing plan are: 1) product strategy, 2) pricing strategy, 3) promotional strategy, 4) trade area and workplace strategy, 5) salesforce strategy, 6) target customer profiles, and 7) competitive environment.

Limited Liability Company (LLC) and Limited Liability Partnership (LLP): legal classifications of businesses in which the owners' liability for the financial and legal obligations of the company are protected by the partnership agreement, without some of the administrative detail involved in a full corporation. The partners get the liability protection of a corporation with the tax advantages and simplicity of a partnership. Commonly used in structuring ownership deals with angel investors.

Low cost producer: a pricing and positioning strategy in which the seller prices to the low end of the market and earns acceptable profits by controlling internal costs. This is more relevant to manufacturing and retailing than to the music industry, but still an important concept to understand.

Major label: a record label owned or exclusively distributed by one of the Big Four label groups, including EMI Music, Sony BMG, Universal Music Group, and Warner Music Group.

Management: the professional administration of any business, even a one-person operation. Management has four key functional responsibilities: planning, organizing, motivating, and controlling.

Marketing: the act of developing products and exposing them for sale to a specified customer base. Be sure to differentiate marketing from sales, and to understand that marketing has seven key components or "links" —not just advertising and promotion.

Marketing functions: the four functions of marketing in any business are: product planning and positioning, communications and public relations, customer relationship management, and advertising and promotion.

Market segmentation: the process of organizing your approach to target customers for the sake of focus and efficiency. Think of a segment as a "slice of the pie." Music market segmentation is oriented toward styles or genres, but can also be broken down by demographics, economics, geography, and psychographics.

Mission statement: a few sentences or a paragraph that answers the question, "Why are you in business?" This is a key foundation of strategic planning.

Objective: an aspect or subset of a goal that is specific, measurable, and achievable.

Opportunities: environmental trends (both internal and external) with potentially positive consequences, such as a competitive advantage or improved business performance (increased efficiency, sales, profits, or market share).

Part-time: dividing time and focus among various pursuits or sources of income.

Partnership: a legal classification of business in which more than one person owns the company, but it is not set up as a corporation. The partners share the assets and liabilities and are taxed on their share of net company income.

Personal goals: the set of desired long-term results that relate to your health, family, education, recreation, and spiritual pursuits. Must be congruent with creative and financial goals.

Place strategy: the decision about where you conduct business. There are three dimensions of place to consider: geographical territory, channel of distribution or venue type, and your physical workspace.

Planning flow: the concept of doing business planning in a structured sequence to optimize results. The recommended sequence is: (1) mission, vision, and values statements, (2) brand positioning statement, (3) product plan, (4) detailed operating plan, and (5) daily action list.

Product: what you get paid for—whether goods, services, or a combination. Most businesses offer more than one product, like a performing songwriter who gets paid for both live performances and publishing royalties.

Product development: the process of getting the product ready to offer to your target customer base, like rehearsing before going on stage or into the studio.

Product life cycle: each product has a "life cycle" roughly analogous to that of human life, from conception and birth to death. The business world organizes the product life cycle into six phases: research and development, introduction, early growth, late growth or shake-out, maturity or saturation, and decline.

Professional: declared intent to work for pay. May require special training or certification by a third party.

Profit: revenue minus expenses, or the money left over after a business pays the costs of doing business.

Promotional toolbox: a set of tools for building your brand. Examples include advertising, publicity, sales literature, demo recordings, showcase performances, Websites, newsletters, identity items, and related materials.

Psychographic information: what your customers think about and believe. This includes social traits, religious or spiritual beliefs, political views, and personal interests. Relevant and essential to the creation of buyer profiles.

Public company or publicly traded company: a classification of business corporation in which anyone qualified to buy stock can be an owner. Public companies are heavily regulated by the government and subject to strict reporting and disclosure procedures. Very few music companies (e.g. the Big Four) are public versus privately held.

Publicity: the act of delivering an unpaid educational message to a target audience. The key words here are "unpaid" and "educational." While you pay for advertising space or time, you do not pay for editorial placement of publicity.

Revenue: money coming in to your business, calculated as units sold times average selling price.

Revenue stream: where the money comes from. Performer and songwriter examples include show dates (performance fees), record sales, publishing royalties, merchandise sales, and licensing.

Risk: the danger of loss or other negative consequences. In business, the four things at risk are money, time, reputation, and self-esteem.

Risk analysis: the process of determining what is at risk, and how much risk you are willing and able to take.

Sales: the act of causing and expediting a purchase at a specified price, or within a price range. Be sure to understand the difference between sales and marketing, and how the two work together to achieve business objectives.

Sales functions: the four functions of sales in any business are: achieving sales objectives ("hitting the numbers"), event participation, territory management, and general sales administration.

Sales literature: the brochures and catalogs that describe and depict your product. This is the tangible print material you can deliver to prospective customers by mail, online, or in person.

Self-expression: conveyance of personal feeling, as in art. This implies that the feelings, emotions, and personal needs of the artist (composer, songwriter, performer, producer) take the highest priority.

Showcase performance: a live performance by a solo musician or an entire act in front of someone who might hire them or increase promotional efforts if the act is already hired. May be paid or unpaid. Also see "audition."

Sole proprietorship: a legal classification of business, in which one person owns the company and its assets. There is no "stock" as in corporations, so the stock cannot be traded.

Strategy: a decision made now that affects future activities. A strategy is a thought process leading to a decision and commitment, not necessarily the behavior or work itself.

Strengths: superior resources and skills that can be drawn on to exploit opportunities and deal with threats.

Supply and demand: the business principle that asserts that selling prices go up or down based on the balance between *supply*, or product availability, and *demand*, or number of potential customers. The price of secondary market concert tickets goes up because the supply is finite and limited. The price of songs on iTunes goes down because the supply is virtually infinite and inventory is unlimited.

SWOT analysis: a planning tool used to take a snapshot of your company's overall status and capabilities at a given point in time. SWOT is an acronym for *S*trengths, *W*eaknesses, *O*pportunities, and *T*hreats.

Tactic: an activity designed to achieve a desired result. Tactics are the things you do to implement a strategy. Where strategy describes "what," tactics describe "how to."

Threats: environmental trends with potentially negative impacts. Threats may impede implementation of strategy, increase risk, increase people or cash resources required, or cause us to reduce expectations for business results. Threats are also called risks.

Trade events: gatherings of business people designed to make marketing and selling cost-effective by bringing many buyers and sellers together under one roof. Examples include trade shows and conferences. Seminars and panel discussion, while focused on education, also are considered trade events.

Treatment: a one-page business plan. Shorter than an executive summary, a treatment describes the product, the market, revenue potential, and investors' exit strategy. More broadly used in the film and television industry, a treatment may be used in music to get the attention of prospective investors, agents, or producers.

Values statement: your code of ethics or the operating principles that are fundamental to your business and unlikely to change over a long period of time.

Vision statement: a short document that describes your view of the future of the industry or market. Vision statements are part predictions, part trend analysis, part context information.

Weaknesses: deficiencies that inhibit the ability to perform or achieve results, and must be overcome to avoid failure.

Working capital: the cash needed on hand to pay the expenses of your business, whether you are bringing in revenue from product sales or not.

FOR FURTHER STUDY: TWELVE CLASSIC (OR SOON-TO-BE CLASSIC) BUSINESS BOOKS

Want to learn more? A recent amazon.com search on the words "strategic planning" yielded over 41,000 listings! Where to begin? The books listed below expand upon key business concepts discussed in *Succeeding in Music*. While they do not focus on the music industry, they include valuable lessons that can be helpful as you develop your music business.

Anderson, Chris. *The Long Tail: Why the Future of Business Is Selling Less of More.* New York: Hyperion, 2006.

Beckwith, Harry. *Selling the Invisible: A Field Guide to Modern Marketing.* New York: Warner Books, 2001.

Blackwell, Roger and Stephan, Tina. *Brands That Rock: What Business Leaders Can Learn from the World of Rock and Roll.* Hoboken: John Wiley & Sons, 2004.

Hawken, Paul. *Growing a Business: An Insider's Guide to Starting and Building a Business from the Ground Up.* New York: Fireside Books, 1998.

Kawasaki, Guy. *How to Drive Your Competition Crazy: Creating Disruption for Fun and Profit.* New York: Hyperion, 1996.

Moore, Geoffrey A. *Crossing the Chasm: Marketing and Selling Technology Products to Mainstream Customers.* New York: Harperbusiness, 2002.

Phillips, Michael, and Rasberry, Salli. *Marketing Without Advertising: Creative Strategies for Small Business Success.* Berkeley: Nolo Press, 2005.

Porter, Michael E. *Competitive Strategy: Techniques for Analyzing Industries and Competitors.* New York: Free Press, 1998.

Ries, Al, and Trout, Jack. *Positioning: The Battle for Your Mind.* New York: McGraw-Hill Professional Publishing, 2000.

Silber, Lee. *Time Management for the Creative Person: Right-Brain Strategies for Stopping Procrastination, Getting Control of the Clock & Calendar, and Freeing Up Your Time & Your Life.* New York: Three Rivers Press, 1998.

Tracy, Brian. *Maximum Achievement: Strategies and Skills That Will Unlock Your Hidden Powers to Succeed.* New York: Fireside Books, 1995.

Wolf, Michael J. *The Entertainment Economy: How Mega-Media Forces Are Transforming Our Lives.* New York: Times Books, 2003.

MUSIC INDUSTRY REFERENCE BOOKS

Whether you are a performer, songwriter, parent, friend, or colleague of a music person, you can benefit from deeper knowledge of the music industry through studying music industry reference books. A recent amazon.com search on the words "music business" yielded over 22,000 listings! As with the general business titles, it's easy to get bogged down because there are so many choices. Here are five recommended titles:

Avalon, Moses. *Confessions of a Record Producer: How to Survive the Scams and Shams of the Music Business.* San Francisco: Backbeat Books, 2006.

Brabec, Jeffrey, and Brabec, Todd. *Music, Money, and Success: The Insider's Guide to Making Money in the Music Industry.* New York: Schirmer Books, 2006.

Goldstein, Jeri. *How To Be Your Own Booking Agent: The Musician's & Performing Artist's Guide to Successful Touring.* Charlottesville: The New Music Times, Inc., 2004.

Krasilovsky, M. William, et al. *This Business of Music: The Definitive Guide to the Music Industry.* New York: Watson-Guptill Publications, 2007.

Passman, Donald S. *All You Need to Know About the Music Business: Revised and Updated for the 21st Century.* New York: Simon & Schuster, 2006.

WEB RESOURCES

There are tens of thousands of music-related magazines, Websites, and trade organizations. To try to identify and evaluate all of them is futile at best. Thankfully, with the ease of search engines on the Internet today, publishing a comprehensive directory in book form is unnecessary. For example, a simple Google search on the keywords "bluegrass+music+business" yielded over 482,000 listings!

Still, there are some magazines and trade groups that cross genre boundaries and are useful to anyone in the music business. Here are ten Web resources that are relevant to performers and songwriters:

General Information

List of music journals, newspapers, and periodicals: www.music.indiana.edu/music_resources/journals.html

Pollstar—The Music Hotwire: www.pollstar.com
Billboard magazine: www.billboard.com
Performing Songwriter magazine: www.performingsongwriter.com

Performing Rights Organizations (PRO's) and Trade Associations

American Society of Composers, Authors, and Publishers (ASCAP): www.ascap.com

BMI: www.bmi.com

SESAC: www.sesac.com

Society of Composers, Authors, and Music Publishers of Canada (SOCAN): www.socan.ca

American Federation of Musicians of the United States and Canada (AFM): www.afm.org

National Academy of Recording Arts and Sciences (NARAS): www.grammy.com

National Music Publishers Association (NMPA): www.nmpa.org

Nashville Songwriters Association International: www.nashvillesongwriters.com

Just Plain Folks: www.jpfolks.com

Circle of Songs: www.circleofsongs.com

CD-ROM CONTENTS

The CD-ROM that accompanies this book is a great tool for getting started on your business plan. The disc includes the following:

Section 1: Industry Reference Material

- Glossary of key terms, concepts, and buzzwords
- List of general business and music business books
- Web links for music trade magazines and trade associations

Section 2: Business Plan Templates

- Mission, vision, and values statement
- Risk analysis checklist
- Short-form business plan with financials
- Brand positioning statement
- Three-year product plan and sales forecast matrix
- Sources and uses of working capital
- Goal setting and milestone-tracking sheet
- "Our Band" business plan (for you to re-name and start your own plan document)

INDEX

Academy Awards, 171–72
accounting, 31
    operating plan and, 157
administrative tasks, 68
adrenaline, 3
advances, 85
    credit cards and, 157
    music publishing, 85
    recording, 80
advertising, 211
    marketing and, 66
    promotional tool of, 88–89
    sample, 191
    types of, 89
AFM. *See* American Federation of Musicians
agents
    buying habits, considerations for, 115
    channel of distribution for, 101
    commissions for, 16
    influence of, 93
    role of, xvii, 15
    sales of, 105
    workspace considerations for, 102
    wrong assumptions about, 165
amateur, 211
    professional v., 4–5
amazon.com, 63
American Federation of Musicians (AFM), 19, 63
analog. *See* digital v. analog
angel investor, 211
appendix (business plan), 47–48, 158, 199
    sample, 194
Apple. *See* iTunes
Armstrong, Louis, 76
art, 211
    commerce v., 6, 165
    profit and, 7
ASCAP, 19, 63
assets. *See* sale of assets
assumptions, 211
    agents and wrong, 165
    audience and wrong, 164
    business plan and, 45
    competition and wrong, 166
    indirect competition and wrong, 166
    managers and wrong, 165

record label executives and wrong, 165
    time and wrong, 166
attention management, 64–65
audience, 211. *See also* customers; target audience
    for business plan, 158
    competition for attention of, 176
    mistakes in assumptions of, 164
audience profiles, 68. *See also* customer profiles
auditions, 94, 211

backer, 211
balance sheet, 211
bands
    business knowledge ignored by, xv–xvi
    current number of, 19
banks, 30
    approaching, 205
The Beatles, 169
Bennett, Tony, 76
The Blues Brothers, 114–15
BMI, 19, 63
booking agent
    friends/family as, xvi
    pricing strategy and, 79
    products of, 72
    rates of, 80
books, 218–19
brand, 212
branding, 212
    business plan and, 155
    definition of, 87
    importance of, 87–88, 206
    tips for, 66–67, 206–7
brand positioning statement
    business plan and, 52–55, 183–84
    "elevator test" for, 54–55
    features of, 52
    sample, 52–53, 183–84
    uses of, 53–54
    worksheet for, 197
Brooks, Garth, xvi
budget, 56, 199, 212
    advice for, 148
business. *See also* corporate music business;
        independent music business
    bands' ignoring, xv–xvi

music industry, books on, 218–19
music industry, key elements for, 31–32
music industry models changing in, 22
music industry, trends for, 171
organization of, 20–21
record producer's mistakes in, xvi
understanding, xix
world culture's impact on, 181–82
business cards, 210
"Business Chops Philosophy," xviii–xix
business lessons
    for competition, 152–53
    customer understanding and, 151–52
    quantifying for, 147–48
    sales and, 149–50
    strengths and, 150–51
    weaknesses and, 148–51
business plan, 212
    appendix for, 47–48
    assumptions and, 45
    audience of, 158
    benefits of, 38–41
    branding and, 155
    brand positioning statement for, 52–55, 183–84
    cash and, 157
    as catalyst, 39–40
    checklist, 196–98
    company description in, 44
    as competition aid, 40
    creation of, 155, 160
    daily action list for, 57–58
    defining, 43
    demo recordings, sample, 191
    e-commerce, sample, 192
    executive summary and, 159
    financial summary in, 44
    five-year window and, 58
    formatting, 159
    frequently asked questions on, 157–60
    fundamentals of, 156
    fundraising aided by, 40–41
    investors and, 157
    LAEDC aiding, 46
    length/detail of, 47, 158
    market overview/marketing strategy in, 44, 46, 184–85
    as measuring stick, 38
    "memory system" and, 43
    mission statement for, 51–52, 182
    necessity of, 17, 37
    operating plan in, 56, 156–57, 187–88
    as opportunity management tool, 38–39
    organizational overview in, 44
    percentage breakdown of, 45–46
    planning flow for, 51
    problem prevention with, 37
    product description in, 44
    product plan and, 55–56, 185
    revenue planning in, 157
    revising, 58
    as road map, 38
    sample of, 179, 181–94

showcase performances, sample, 192
    as stress management tool, 39
    for team-building, 42
    team organization and, 186–87
    updating, 159, 172
business registrations, 156
business services, 15
    product strategy and, 72
buyer characteristics, 212
buyer profiles, 68
buying habits, 115

capacity
    elements of, 107
    of salesforce, 108
capital purchase schedule, 57, 199
Cardwell, Nancy, xi
career(s), 212
    hobby v., 4
    in music industry, xvii–xviii
cash, 157
CD Baby, 63
channel of distribution, 100–101
checklists, 195–210
chemistry
    elements of, 107
    of salesforce, 109
collateral materials, 90, 212
commerce, 212
    art v., 6, 165
commodity, 212
common sense lessons, 147–53, 163–67
company description, 44
competence
    elements of, 107
    in salesforce, 108
competition
    assumptions/mistakes with, 166
    for audience attention, 176
    business lessons for, 152–53
    business plan as weapon for, 40
    competitive intelligence system helping understanding of, 125–26
    customer profiles and, 121–22
    goals and, 144
    identifying, 122
    marketing strategy, profile exercise for, 127–28
    market segment of, 126
    market trends and, 127
    music industry types of, 23
    profiling, 126
    SWOT analysis for, 125
    understanding, 122–23
competitive environment
    defining, 121–22
    describing, 23
    purpose of, 68
    sample, 185
competitive intelligence system, 212
    competition understood with, 125–26
    database basics for, 126–27
    public/private sources for, 126

using, 153
composer
    role of, 15
    workspace considerations for, 102
concert production companies, 22
conferences, 91–92, 207
    optimizing, 210
corporate music business, 20
    myths v. realities of, 21–22
corporations, 20–21, 212, 216. *See also* public
        corporations
creative goals, 212
    examples of, 135
    features of, 134
    three year goal exercise for, 136–37
    worksheet for, 201
creative objectives, 138
    worksheet for, 201
credit cards
    advances from, 157
    debt and, 29
culture. *See* world culture
customer profiles
    buying habits/preferences for, 115
    competition and, 121–22
    "deal-breakers" and, 116–17
    demographic information for, 113
    economic information for, 113–14
    exercise for, 118–19
    geographic information for, 114
    individual v. institutional, 116
    market segmentation for, 117–18
    psychographic information for, 114
customers, 213
    business lessons on, 151–52
    expectations of, 151
    genre considerations for, 114–15
    identifying, 15–16
    marketing and, 66
    of music industry identified, 22–23
    understanding, 113–14

daily action list, 57–58
day job, 213
    goals and, 149
    risk analysis for quitting, 32–33
"deal-breakers"
    customer profiles and, 116–17
    marketing considerations for, 119
debt, 29
demographic information, 113, 213
demo recordings, 90
    business plan sample for, 191
differentiation strategy, 82, 213
digital downloads, 170
digital v. analog, 170
direct competition, 23, 40, 213
    exercise for, 123–24
    identifying, 122
    indirect competition v., 121–22, 124
    sample, 192
direct mail, 91

direct marketing, 213
    promotional tool of, 90–91
    sample, 191
dream fulfillment, 3

eager rationalizations, 33
EBITDA, 213
e-commerce, 213
    business plan sample, 192
    as promotional tool, 94–95
economic information, 113–14, 213
"elevator test," 213
    brand positioning statement and, 54–55
end-user segments, 68
    sample, 192
entertainment, 213
    self-expression v., 6
executive summary, 159, 213
"external environment," 125

"Falling Slowly," 171–72
feasibility study. *See* risk analysis
financial goals, 213
    examples of, 135
    three year goal exercise for, 136–37
    worksheet for, 202
financial objectives, 138
    worksheet for, 202
financial schedules, 157–58
    sample, 194
financial summary, 44
Fitzgerald, Ella, 76
five-year window, 58
    using, 200
flexibility, 172
Foo Fighters, 171
401k, 29
full-time, 214
    part-time v., 4
fundraising. *See also* working capital
    advice for, 206
    business plan aiding, 40–41
    unviable sources, 30–31
    viable sources, 29–30

genre, 114–15, 117
geographic information, 114, 214
geographic territory
    place strategy and, 99–100
    sample, 192
Getz, Stan, 171
Gilberto, Joao, 171
Gill, Vince, 171
goals, 214. *See also* creative goals; financial goals;
        personal goals
    competition and, 144
    day job and, 149
    importance of, 133
    music industry and reality of, 143
    objectives created by quantifying, 138
    objectives v., 5, 133–34
    sharing, 143–44

taking stock of, 172
three year goal exercise for, 136–37
types of, 134–36
writing, 13
Grammy Awards, 171
gut feeling decisions, 147, 163–64

Hancock, Herbie, 171
Hansard, Glen, 171–72
hobby, 214
career v., 4
home offices, 102–3
hybrid, 214
hybrid jobs, xviii
hybrid strategy, 82–83

identity items, 214
as promotional tools, 93
sample, 191
illegal activities, 31
income statement, 214
independent (indie), 214
independent music business, 20
myths v. realities of, 21–22
indirect competition, 40
assumptions/mistakes with, 166
direct competition v., 121–22, 124
exercise for, 123–24
features of, 23
threat of, 23–24
understanding, 122–23
individual customers, 116, 214
influencers, 92–93, 214
infrastructure, 156
institutional customers, 116, 214
integrity
music industry and, xviii, 7
salesforce strategy and, 106–7
success and, 165
"Internal environment," 125
investors. *See also* angel investor; private investors
angel, 211
approaching, 205–6
business plan and, 157
mistakes in preparing for, 163
private, 29
IRA, 29
Irglova, Marketa, 171–72
iTunes, 63, 80, 170
The Beatles and, 169

James, Etta, 76
JC Penny, 172
Joel, Billy, 76
John, Elton, 76

key influencer relations, 92–93
sample, 191
King, B. B., xvii, 76
Knowles, Beyoncé, xvii
Krauss, Alison, 172

LAEDC. *See* Los Angeles Development Council
lawyers, 21, 151, 165
Led Zeppelin, 80
legacy, 3
licenses, 156
limited liability company (LLC), 20, 215
limited liability partnership (LLP), 20, 215
links in marketing chain, 214
Live Nation, 22
Madonna and, 169–71
live performances. *See also* auditions
product strategy and, 72
questions for, 15
LLC. *See* limited liability company
LLP. *See* limited liability partnership
loans, 30
Los Angeles Development Council (LAEDC), 46
low-cost producer, 215
pricing strategy with, 81–82

Madonna, 22, 76, 80
Live Nation and, 169–71
major label, 215
management, 215. *See also* attention management
growth of, 171
necessity of, 176
responsibilities of, 31
of territory for sales, 67
managers
buying habits, considerations for, 115
channel of distribution for, 101
commissions for, 16
friends/family as, xvi
influence of, 93
products of, 72
rates of, 80
role of, xvii, 15
sales of, 105
workspace considerations for, 102
wrong assumptions about, 165
market
competition, segment of, 126
customer profiles, segmenting, 117–18
risk analysis, considerations for, 28–29
marketing, 23, 31, 215. *See also* direct marketing; telemarketing
advertising/promotion in, 66
communicating with target market in, 66
customer relations and, 66
"deal breakers," considerations for, 119
method sample, 190
pricing strategy and ability of, 81
product planning/positioning in, 65–66
sales compared to, 65
marketing functions, 215
marketing plan, 56, 199
importance of, 64
salesforce attracted by, 110
sample, 188–93
seven links for, 68–69

marketing strategy. *See also* place strategy; pricing strategy; product strategy; promotional strategy; salesforce strategy
  business plan and, 44, 46
  competition profiles exercise for, 127–28
  sample, 189
market overview, 17
  business plan and, 44, 46, 184–85
  sample, 184–85
market segmentation, 215
  of competition, 126
  for customer profiles, 117–18
market trends, 127
Marley, Bob, xvii
media, xvi–xvii, 21, 149. *See also* advertising
"memory system," 43
missionary selling, 88
  examples of, 91
mission statement, 215
  business plan and, 51–52, 182
  excerpts from, 8
  guidelines for, 7–8
  purpose of, 7
  sample, 182
  worksheet for, 196
  writing, 9–10
mistakes
  assumption of audience, 164
  with competition, 166
  with indirect competition, 166
  of performers, 148
  in preparing for investors, 163
  in promotion, 149
  record producer, xvi
  in sales of products, 164–65
  time, 166
money, 14
Monroe, Bill, 76
Motown Records, 22
  revenue streams of, 171
music companies, 22
  record labels v., 171
music industry
  amateur v. professional in, 4–5
  art v. commerce in, 6
  business books for, 218–19
  business models changing in, 22
  business's key elements in, 31–32
  business trends in, 171
  careers in, xvii–xviii
  challenges in, 64
  common sense lessons for, 147–53, 163–67
  competition types in, 23
  corporate music business v. independent music business in, 20
  customers of, 22–23
  decline phase in, 75
  early growth phase in, 74
  entertainment v. self-expression in, 6
  full-time v. part-time in, 4
  future of, 172–73

  goals and reality in, 143
  goals v. objectives in, 5
  goods and services of, 71
  hobby v. career in, 4
  integrity and, xviii, 7
  introduction phase in, 74
  key elements in, 15–17
  maturity/saturation phase in, 74–75
  media and, xvi–xvii, 21, 149
  motivations for entering, 3
  myths v. realities of, 21–22
  overview/scope of, 19
  preparation for entering, 17
  pricing strategy in, 80–81
  product and industry role in, 55
  products in, 71–72
  profit for jobs in, 16
  risk and, 166–67
  sales' necessity in, 106
  schoolteacher paradigm and, 139–40
  shake-out in, 74
  song value in, 170
  statistics of, 19–20, 63–64
  strategy v. tactics in, 5–6
  stress and, 39
music publishers, xviii
  buying habits, considerations for, 115
music publishing
  advances for, 85
  product strategy and, 72
  royalties and, 80
music teachers, xviii

networking, 210

objectives, 215. *See also* creative objectives; financial objectives; personal objectives
  exercise for planning, 142–43
  goals quantified for creating, 138
  goals v., 5, 133–34
  importance of, 133
  key questions for creating, 138–39
  sales, achieving, 67
  sample, 190
  taking stock of, 172
  writing, 13
Once, 171–72
"one-hit wonder," 76
operating plan
  accounting and, 157
  in business plan, 56, 156–57, 187–88
  detailed plan for, 198–99
  elements of, 56–57, 156–57
  revising, 58
  sample, 187–88
  worksheet for, 198
opportunities, 125, 215
opportunity management, 38–39
organization plan, 56, 199
Oscars. *See* Academy Awards
"Our Band," 52–53

partnership, 20, 215
part-time, 215
    full-time v., 4
Pavoratti, Luciano, xvi
performers. *See also* live performances
    buying habits, considerations for, 115
    channel of distribution for, 100
    early growth of, 74
    influence of, 92
    mistakes of, 148
    products of, 72
    role of, 15
    sales of, 105
    workspace considerations for, 102
Performing Rights Organizations (PRO's), 220
personal goals, 215
    examples of, 136
    three year goal exercise for, 136–37
    worksheet for, 203
personal objectives, 138
    worksheet for, 203–4
place strategy, 215
    dimensions of, 99
    evolution of, 103
    geographic territory and, 99–100
    role of, 68
    venue type and, 100–101
    workspace and, 101–2
planning
    importance of, 41, 147
    of products in marketing, 65–66
    risks of not, 163–64
    for trade events, 208
planning flow, 216
    business plan and, 51
Plant, Robert, 172
pricing strategy
    avoiding problems with, 85
    booking agents and, 79
    consequences of being unrealistic with, 84–85
    conventions, traditions of, 80–81
    differentiation strategy for, 82
    factors of, 79–81
    hybrid strategy for, 82–83
    low-cost producer strategy in, 81–82
    of music industry, 80–81
    revenue planning and, 83–84
    role of, 68
    sales, marketing ability and, 81
    sample, 191
    supply and demand and, 80
private corporations, 21
private investors, 29
producer. *See* record producer
product concepts/rationale, 188
product delivery, 31
product development, 31, 216
product life cycle, 216
    duration and, 76
    product strategy and phases of, 74–76

product mix, 73
    sample, 190–91
product plan
    business plan and, 55–56, 185
    revising, 58
    sample, 185, 188–89
    worksheet for, 198
products, 216
    of booking agents, 72
    business plan and description of, 44
    defining, 55
    of managers, 72
    marketing, planning/positioning of, 65–66
    mistakes in sales of, 164–65
    in music industry, 71–72
    music industry, industry role and, 55
    of performers, 72
    of promoters, 72
    salesforce views on, 109–10
    of songwriters, 72
product strategy
    business services for, 72
    goods and services for, 71
    live performances in, 72
    music publishing in, 72
    product life cycle phases and, 74–76
    record sales in, 72
    role of, 68
    technical services and, 72
    worksheet for, 73
professional, 216
    amateur v., 4–5
profit, 216. *See also* reinvested profits
    art and, 7
    music industry jobs and, 16
promoter
    buying habits, considerations for, 115
    channel of distribution decisions for, 101
    influence of, 93
    products of, 72
    role of, 15
    sales of, 106
    workspace considerations for, 102
promotion
    cutting corners and, 152
    definition of, 87
    marketing and, 66
    mistakes in, 149
promotional strategy
    elements of, 87
    questions for, 95–96
    role of, 68
    sample, 191–92
promotional tools, 216
    advertising and, 88–89
    collateral materials as, 90
    demo recordings as, 90
    direct marketing as, 90–91
    e-commerce as, 94–95
    identity items as, 93

key influencer relations as, 92–93
missionary selling as, 88
publicity as, 89–90
sales literature as, 90
showcase performances as, 94
trade events as, 91–92
PRO's. *See* Performing Rights Organizations
psychographic information, 114, 216
public corporations, 21, 216
publicity, 216
    promotional tool of, 89–90
    sample, 191
publishers. *See* music publishers

Rasing Sand, 172
record label executives
    influence of, 93
    wrong assumptions about, 165
record labels, xviii
    models changing for, 22
    music companies v., 171
    releases per year, 63
record producer
    business mistakes of, xvi
    commissions for, 16
record sales
    amazon.com and, 63
    product strategy and, 72
    statistics and, 19
records v. music, 169
reference section. *See* appendix
reinvested profits, 30
reputation, 14
research and development, 74
revenue, 216
revenue forecast, 56, 199
    five-year window for, 141–42
    sales and, 140–41
    sample, 188
revenue planning, 83–84
    business plan and, 157
revenue stream, 16–17, 216
    of Motown Records, 171
    multiple, 170–71
reward, 14–15, 41, 175
ringtones, 169
"rip-off artists," 149
risk, 216
    assessing, 14, 167, 175
    conceptual importance of, 15
    defining, 13
    music industry and, 166–67
    of not planning, 163–64
    perspectives on, 27
    reward v., 14–15, 41, 175
    time and, 14
risk analysis, 216
    checklist, 195
    exercise for, 28

importance of, 17
    key questions for, 31–32
    market considerations for, 28–29
    for quitting day job, 32–33
River: The Joni Letters, 171
Rolling Stone Magazine, xvi
The Rolling Stones, xvi, 76, 80
royalties, 80–81, 188

sale of assets, 29
sales, 31, 217. *See also* record sales
    achieving objectives for, 67
    administrative tasks and, 68
    of agents, 105
    business lessons for, 149–50
    event participation for, 67
    follow-through for, 164
    management of territory for, 67
    of manager, 105
    marketing compared to, 65
    mistakes in products and, 164–65
    music industry, necessity of, 106
    of performers, 105
    pricing strategy and, 81
    of promoters, 106
    revenue forecast for, 140–41
    of songwriter, 105
sales channel strategy, 101, 155
    role of, 68
salesforce
    capacity of, 108
    characteristics for success of, 107
    chemistry of, 109
    competence and, 108
    marketing plan attracting, 110
    products, views of, 109–10
salesforce strategy
    integrity and, 106–7
    responsibilities in, 105–6
    role of, 68
    sample, 192
    success characteristics for, 107
sales functions, 217
sales literature, 217
    promotional tool of, 90
savings, 29
schoolteacher paradigm, 139–40
second mortgage, 29
Seeger, Pete, 76
self-esteem, 14
self-expression, 217
    entertainment v., 6
seminars, 92, 207
SESAC, 19, 63
shake-out, 74
showcase performances, 94, 217
    business plan sample, 192
singles, 169–70
sole proprietorship, 20, 217

song value, 170
songwriters
    associations for, 20
    channel of distribution for, 100–101
    introduction phase of, 74
    products of, 72
    role of, 15
    royalties and, 80–81
    sales of, 105
    similarity problems for, 152
    workspace considerations for, 102
SoundScan, 63, 170
Springsteen, Bruce, 76
staff organization, 156
statistics, 19–20, 63–64
Stern, Isaac, 76
Stills, Stephen, 172
strategy, 217. *See also* differentiation strategy; hybrid
       strategy; marketing strategy; place strategy;
       pricing strategy; product strategy; promotional
       strategy; sales channel strategy; salesforce
       strategy
    tactics v., 5–6, 134
Streisand, Barbra, 80
strengths, 125, 217
    business lessons on, 150–51
stress management, 39
"suffering for the music," 165
supply and demand, 80, 217
SWOT analysis, 217
    competition and, 125
    preparation for, 150–51

tactics, 217
    strategy v., 5–6, 134
target audience, 117, 151–52
teachers. *See* music teachers
team-building, 42
team organization, 186–87
technical services, 72
technicians, 80
telemarketing, 91
threats, 125, 217
360 Deal, 211
time
    assumptions/mistakes with, 166
    managing, 175
    risk and, 14
trade associations, 220

trade events, 217
    follow-up for, 209–10
    importance of, 207–8
    opportunities at, 92
    planning for, 208
    presentation for, 208–9
    as promotional tool, 91–92
    sample, 191
    success and, 208–10
trade shows, 91
treatment, 218

U2, xvii, 80
USA Today, xvi

value. *See* song value
values statement, 218
    excerpts from, 9
    purpose of, 8
    sample, 182–83
    worksheet for, 196
venue types, 100–101
VH1, xvi
vision statement, 218
    excerpts from, 8–9
    purpose of, 8
    sample, 181–82
    worksheet for, 196

weaknesses, 125, 218
    business plan and, 148–51
web resources, 219–20
websites, 192
    types of, 94–95
West, Kanye, 171
Winehouse, Amy, 171
working capital, 218
    sources of, 29–30, 157
    worksheet for, 205–6
working musicians, xvii
worksheets, 179, 195–210
workshops, 92
workspace
    home office pros/cons as, 102–3
    place strategy and, 101–2
world culture
    business, impact of, 181–82
    music's place in, xv